LANGUAGES FOR INTERCULTURAL COMMUNICATION AND EDUCATION
Series Editors: Michael Byram, *University of Durham, UK* and Alison Phipps, *University of Glasgow, UK*

Language and Learning in the International University
From English Uniformity to Diversity and Hybridity

Edited by
Bent Preisler, Ida Klitgård and
Anne H. Fabricius

MULTILINGUAL MATTERS
Bristol • Buffalo • Toronto

Library of Congress Cataloging in Publication Data
A catalog record for this book is available from the Library of Congress.
Language and Learning in the International University: From English Uniformity to Diversity and Hybridity/Edited by Bent Preisler, Ida Klitgård and Anne H. Fabricius.
Languages for Intercultural Communication and Education: 21
Includes bibliographical references.
1. English language--Study and teaching--Foreign speakers. 2. Second language acquisition. 3. Language and culture. I. Preisler, Bent, 1945- II. Klitgård, Ida. III. Fabricius, Anne H.
PE1128.A2L29424 2011
428.0071'1–dc222011015601

British Library Cataloguing in Publication Data
A catalogue entry for this book is available from the British Library.

ISBN-13: 978-1-84769-414-0 (hbk)
ISBN-13: 978-1-84769-413-3 (pbk)

Multilingual Matters
UK: St Nicholas House, 31–34 High Street, Bristol, BS1 2AW, UK.
USA: UTP, 2250 Military Road, Tonawanda, NY 14150, USA.
Canada: UTP, 5201 Dufferin Street, North York, Ontario, M3H 5T8, Canada.

The policy of Multilingual Matters/Channel View Publications is to use papers that are natural, renewable and recyclable products, made from wood grown in sustainable forests. In the manufacturing process of our books, and to further support our policy, preference is given to printers that have FSC and PEFC Chain of Custody certification. The FSC and/or PEFC logos will appear on those books where full certification has been granted to the printer concerned.

Typeset by Techset Composition Ltd, Salisbury, UK.
Printed and bound in Great Britain by Short Run Press Ltd.

Contents

Contributors

John Airey is a Senior Lecturer in English for Specific Purposes at the School of Language and Literature, Linnaeus University, Kalmar, Sweden. He is currently seconded to the Department of Language Education, Stockholm University, Stockholm, Sweden, where he is doing post-doctoral work. John's research interests concern disciplinary learning and its relationship to language and other semiotic resources.

Juhyun Back, PhD in Educational Studies from the University of York (thesis on the expectations and perceived difficulties of Korean students at UK universities), is currently a Lecturer in Kyungpook National University, Korea. Back's research interests include English for Academic Purposes (EAP), and Sociolinguistic Aspects of Second Language Acquisition.

Dennis Day is Associate Professor in the Department of Language and Communication, University of Southern Denmark. His research interests include ethnomethodologically inspired ethnographies of workplaces, membership categorization, interaction and communication technology.

Louise Denver is Associate Professor, Copenhagen Business School (CBS), has published in the fields of functional linguistics and translation process studies and is currently involved in a research project on the use of English as the medium of instruction at Danish Universities.

Anne H. Fabricius is Associate Professor of English at Roskilde University, Denmark, and has been a visiting scholar at the Universities of York (2002), Copenhagen (2005) and Cambridge (2008). Her main research area is variation and change in Received Pronunciation, with wider interests in quantitative sociolinguistics, sociolinguistic methodology, the analysis of spoken language, and qualitative issues such as those which are the focus of the CALPIU research network and centre, of which she is a founding member.

Christian Jensen is an Assistant Professor at the University of Copenhagen. He has a background in English and Phonetics. His primary research interests include speech prosody and contrastive studies of English and Danish pronunciation, usually through experimental designs. He is currently involved in several projects investigating the use of English as the medium of instruction at Danish universities.

David Killick is a Principal Lecturer at Leeds Metropolitan University. He has been active in the process of curriculum internationalisation in his own institution and across the sector for several years, and is known for his pioneering work on cross-cultural capability and global perspectives. He is currently researching global citizenship in the lived experience of UK students during international mobility activities.

Susanne Kjærbeck is Associate Professor in the Department of Culture and Identity, Roskilde University, Denmark. Her research interests are mainly in Conversation Analysis and Ethnomethodology, especially as relating to institutional talk, identities and storytelling in interaction, and business communication.

Ida Klitgård is Associate Professor in EAP at the Centre for Language and Intercultural Communication Services, Department of Culture and Identity, Roskilde University. She works in EAP, written communication, Stylistics and Rhetoric, currently focusing on the concept of written plagiarism in student assignments with special attention to unintentional plagiarism, foreign language learning and 'patch-writing' by non-native speakers of English in the international university where English is the working language.

Custódio Cavaco Martins is currently Assistant Professor in Linguistics at the Department of Portuguese of the University of Macau. His research interests are in Applied Linguistics and also in Second Language Acquisition from a psycholinguistic perspective. The author has been teaching English and Portuguese both in Europe and Asia, as second and foreign languages, for the past 16 years.

Inger M. Mees is Associate Professor at CBS, studied English at Leiden and Edinburgh and obtained her doctorate and first university appointment at Leiden University. In 1985, she held the post of Associate Professor at CBS specialising in English Phonetics. She has written books and articles on Contrastive Phonetics and pronunciation training for Danish and

Dutch students and has also published in the fields of Dialectology, Sociolinguistics and Historiography of Linguistics.

Catherine Montgomery is Associate Director for Research in the Centre for Excellence in Teaching and Learning at Northumbria University, UK. She has taught in higher education for 20 years, most recently in the fields of Sociolinguistics and Intercultural Communication and her research interests centre on sociocultural contexts of learning.

Bent Preisler (introduction author and general editor) is Professor of English Language and Sociolinguistics, Roskilde University. He received his DrPhil (Habilitation) from Aarhus University in 1987. He was a Visiting Professor in the United States during 1984 at State University of New York, Binghamton, and a 'Visiting Scholar' at University of California, Santa Barbara in 2000. His research interests include works on the structure and functions of English, including English as an international language, and the influence of English on other languages. He is the initiator and director of the international research centre, 'Cultural and Linguistic Practices in the International University' (CALPIU).

Carole Sedgwick is a Senior Lecturer at Roehampton University. She is interested in language assessment issues associated with the Bologna Process, particularly in relation to the aim to establish common standards and a system of quality assurance. She developed and coordinated the EAP provision and the Applied Linguistics and TESOL undergraduate programmes at Roehampton University.

Peter Sercombe is Lecturer in Applied Linguistics at Newcastle University. He has previously worked in Brunei, Malaysia, Turkey and the United Kingdom. Following work as Head of English in a rural secondary school in Borneo (under the auspices of Voluntary Services Overseas), he was appointed as a teacher-trainer with the Malaysian Ministry of Education, during the transition from English to Malay-medium education during the early 1980s. He has also worked in the Applied Linguistics Department at the University in Brunei, working on Sociolinguistics, and Austronesian Languages and Cultures, particularly Iban and Penan.

Roberval Teixeira e Silva is Assistant Professor at the Department of Portuguese of the University of Macau. His research interests are in socio-interactional approach to Discourse; Gender Studies; Identity; Cross-cultural Interactions; Learning, Teaching and Description of Portuguese as a Foreign and Second Language.

Charlotte Werther is Associate Professor, CBS, has held positions at the Royal School of Library and Information Studies and CBS, and her research interests include British Studies, Critical Discourse Analysis and the information literacy of university students. She is currently involved in a research project on the use of English as the medium of instruction at Danish universities.

Betsy Hu Xiaoqiong is Professor of Linguistics. Her special interests are in Applied Linguistics, Second Language Acquisition and Cross-Cultural Communication.

Marina Chen Yuehong is Associate Professor of Linguistics and Translation Studies. Her special interests are in Language Teaching and Translation Theories.

Preface

This book has come about within the context of the CALPIU Research Centre (Cultural And Linguistic Practices in the International University), funded by Roskilde University and the Danish Research Council for Culture and Communication.

It is the aim of CALPIU to coordinate international research into a new theoretical understanding of internationalisation processes currently underway in universities and other institutions of higher education. It focuses on the function of language in social and cultural practice, especially the significance of *language proficiency* and *language choice* within a context marked by power relations and hierarchies of influence, as well as the impact of such power relations and hierarchies upon the organisation, didactics, learning processes and academic content of educational programmes in the humanities and social and natural sciences. Thus, CALPIU works to support the professionalisation of university pedagogy within an international context.

CALPIU was initiated by an Applied Linguistics group of researchers within the fields of Sociolinguistics, Conversation Analysis and Discourse and Communication Analysis at Roskilde University. The Centre's research associates now comprise about 50 senior and junior researchers from 27 universities in Denmark, the other Nordic countries and countries across the globe (cf. http://calpiu.dk).

The particular focus of the present anthology is, as the title says, *Language and Learning in the International University*. It is often assumed that 'internationalisation' in this context means *use of English*. However, this book – as indeed is the case of CALPIU as such – is based on the assumption that internationalisation is about the relationship between many cultures and languages within the same educational institution, and about the possibility of practising *diversity* as a resource in education.

Very little is known about the significance of this kind of diversity vis-à-vis teaching and learning processes. Is language not just a neutral tool? Or, on the contrary, does teaching in a second language not affect teacher roles? What difference does it make whether students use English or their

L1 in student group work? Who is to supply, define or develop standards of 'Academic English' in an ELF (English as lingua franca) context? How do students construct 'internationalism' through language use? How do culturally different perceptions of teacher and student roles affect interaction in the multinational classroom?

The 12 chapters of this book, investigating some of these questions, are based on case studies from different parts of the world, organised into five parts each of which deals with a separate set of issues.

The local editors owe a debt of gratitude to Hartmut Haberland and Janus Mortensen for their kindness in helping us with bibliographies and providing technical assistance, respectively.

The CALPIU editors
Roskilde University
1 June, 2011

Introduction

B. PREISLER

The authors and editors of this book view the international university as a microcosm of a world where internationalization does not equate with the uniformity of across-the-board use of the *English* language and cultural heritage, but rather with the practice and utilization of cultural and linguistic *diversity*, even in the face of Anglophone dominance. The globalization–localization continuum thus manifests itself in every university trying to adopt internationalization strategies, regardless of its location on the map. The many cases of language/learning issues presented in this book, from universities representing different parts of the world, are all – basically – examples of various manifestations of a multidimensional space encompassing local vs. global and diversification vs. Anglicization.

To complicate matters further – although the Anglicization of higher education in EFL (English as a foreign language) countries is, as such, a globalization phenomenon – local diversity is greatly influenced by local *uses* of English affecting education as well as communicative and cultural practices generally. Conversely, in ENL (English as a native language) countries, we would expect local practices (e.g. the use of English in the United Kingdom) to be affected in various ways by the incoming forces of globalization, including – at the university – the cultural and sociolinguistic impact of transnational students and teachers.

The idea that cultural and linguistic diversity could actually be an *asset* in cross-national tertiary education lies at the heart of several chapters. Such diversity may help students identify with international issues and themes in the context of their field of study, and enable them to conceive of themselves as global citizens, although problems and conflicts often also arise.

The clash between English-based norms and deviating local practices is seen nowhere more clearly than in the teaching of academic (English) literacy standards. By definition, a standard or norm seeks to minimize diversity, and diversity is usually discouraged in the teaching of a written standard. In fact, there are obvious advantages to be gained in *harmonizing* academic literacy standards, and, to serve this purpose, there is a definite need for transnational research projects, as well as a new awareness of the writing of academic EFL as a process of transcultural translation and hybridity.

East–West encounters in tertiary educational environments are often said to constitute a serious challenge to any notion that diversity may be a strength and not a weakness in internationalization. That the East–West dichotomy in internationalized education may in fact be more complex than this is borne out by the three case studies concluding this volume, representing Western students at a Chinese university, Korean students in a British academic context and Macau students in the Portuguese L2 classroom.

The investigative methods represented by this book constitute a wide range of mainly sociolinguistic, conversation-analytical, ethnographic and culture-analytical methods, the majority of which are of a qualitative nature, although some are also quantitative. The qualitative methods and methodological schools listed below are instantiated in the book: *Conversation Analysis:* Day and Kjærbeck (Chapter 5); *Cultural Analysis:* Killick (Chapter 6), Klitgård (Chapter 9); *Ethnographical Analysis:* Fabricius (Chapter 7); *Interactional Sociolinguistics:* Silva and Martins (Chapter 12); *Interview Studies:* Airey (Chapter 1), Montgomery (Chapter 4), Back (Chapter 11); *Linguistic Ethnography:* Sedgwick (Chapter 8). Moreover, quantitative studies in the form of questionnaires are employed by Jensen *et al.* in Chapter 2, and by Hu and Chen in Chapter 10. Finally, a quantitative/qualitative combination (in the form of questionnaires and semi-structured interviews) appears in Chapter 3 by Sercombe.

In sum – anticipating our introduction to individual chapters – we suggest that the internationalization of universities should not be dealt with in simplistic terms of traditional polarity between, *on the one hand*, local practices and use of the national language; and, *on the other hand*, the invasion (in EFL countries) of an international lingua franca, English, to accommodate the influx of transnationally mobile students and teachers of the postmodern era. Nor can the phenomena be approached in a methodologically simple way. Rather, the internationalization of universities represents a new cultural and linguistic *hybridity* based on cultural interdependence, with the potential to develop new forms of identities unfettered by traditional 'us-and-them' binary thinking, and a new open-mindedness about the roles of self and others, resulting in new patterns of communicative (educational and social) practices.

The well-known background for the theme of *English as a Lingua Franca for Higher Education Teaching and Learning* (Part 1 of this book) is the paradox that English has become the most important and pervasive language of instruction in international higher education, while – in countries where English is a foreign language – the lingua franca function of English gives rise to all sorts of problems and challenges for university teaching and learning. In Chapter 1, *The Relationship between Teaching Language and Student Learning in Swedish University Physics,* John Airey summarizes the results of a major contemporary Swedish study of the learning experiences of undergraduate physics students exposed to lectures in both English and Swedish. The study demonstrates among other things that the Swedish students think that teaching language is unimportant: according to the students, it has no influence on their perceptions of the subject whether the teaching language is Swedish or English. The students thereby show unawareness of a number of problems occurring when Swedish students were taught physics in English. In fact, they were less able to efficiently describe disciplinary concepts in English, to interact successfully in lectures and to simultaneously listen and take notes – problems that may impede learning.

In Chapter 2, *Students' and Teachers' Self-Assessment of English Language Proficiency in English-Medium Higher Education in Denmark: A Questionnaire Study,* a number of Danish scholars within the SPEAC project (Students' Perceptions of the English of Academics) investigate the relationship between teachers' English language proficiency (as assessed by expert raters) and students' perceptions of the same teachers' academic and linguistic competences. The findings are compared with teachers' and students' self-assessment of English language skills. Thus, expert opinion and self-assessment are juxtaposed. The study asks questions such as the following: How on the whole do students rate their English proficiency? Are there certain definable segments of students who perceive their English skills to be better than those of other students? How do teachers rate their English proficiency? And do teachers feel just as capable of conducting their classes in English as they would in their own language? If not, are there certain aspects of the language they feel less confident about? In any case – as in Airey's study regarding Swedish students' unawareness of the role that linguistic problems play in their learning processes – the conclusions of the Danish study seem to indicate that neither students nor teachers think that shortcomings in English proficiency are an obstacle to successful teaching.

The common thread of the chapters in Part 2 is their focus on the situation of students visiting the United Kingdom. Titled *When the Lingua*

Franca Happens to be the First Language of the Majority: The Case of the United Kingdom, this part presents two chapters grounded in surveys of international students working in the United Kingdom (Sercombe and Montgomery), and one theoretically grounded chapter on the concept of curriculum internationalization (Killick).

The part begins with a chapter by Peter Sercombe titled *Perceptions of Identity and Issues of Concern among International Students* (Chapter 3), which focuses on themes and concerns of personal significance to students from countries other than the United Kingdom, as well as ways in which they perceive themselves as having adapted, as a result of relocating to the United Kingdom. The chapter reports on differing perceptions of self in relation to a range of issues identified by these students. Higher education is for the majority not perceived as an end in itself, but as a particular phase and one that is critical to future stages in life being realized successfully. The interview data reveal the diversity of students' responses and the definitional challenges of considering the highly heterogeneous category 'international student'. Sercombe considers how students' cultural and linguistic affiliations are part of their expanding repertoire of identities and how these may be reconfigured in the shift to a new context in which there is an emphasis on functioning, academically at least, in another language, in this case English.

Chapter 4, *Developing Perceptions of Interculturality in Student Group Work at University: A Troublesome Space?* by Catherine Montgomery, considers student perceptions of working in intercultural groups in a diverse international academic environment. The focus here is on how students construct themselves and each other socially, culturally and linguistically through their experience of working together at university. The chapter aims to present the intercultural higher education landscape not as a binary of self and other (Pierce, 2003) but as a complex site of struggle, tension and conflict. However, this 'troublesome space' in which intercultural interaction occurs is not presented here as being problematic but as useful and transformative (Savin-Baden, 2008). The chapter also argues that catalysts for these transformative troublesome spaces can be found in particular teaching, learning and assessment environments.

Chapter 5, *Internationalising the University Curriculum: Enabling Selves-in-the-World*, by David Killick, takes up some of the central literature underlying current understandings of the multicultural space in which so many individuals find themselves. The turbulent flows and ethnoscapes (Appadurai, 1997; Bauman, 1998) of a multicultural world are seen as more significant than the single dimension of the multilingual. The author presents a model of curriculum internationalization based on the constructs of cross-cultural capability and global perspectives. With reference to transformative learning theory (Mezirow, 1991), and in the discussion of accommodative learning processes, he argues that as temporary 'homes' for their students, international universities are well placed to help them identify themselves as global citizens, locate themselves in a global place and develop attributes to enact those identities.

In this volume, internationalization is, however, not only seen as an alien force coming from the outside. In Part 3, titled *The Construction of International Perspectives in 'International' Student Group Work*, internationalization is explored as a constructed perspective established among students themselves as they attend an international Basic Studies program at Roskilde University, Denmark. Thus, in Chapter 6, *Educational Practices in the International University: Language as a Resource for Intercultural Distinction in a Project Group Meeting*, Dennis Day and Susanne Kjærbeck investigate how these students co-establish an 'international' project group meeting. That is, rather than presupposing that the meeting is 'international' due to the background of its participants, the authors perform an ethnomethodological and conversation analytic examination of the practicality of such a characterization for the interactants themselves. In particular, Day and Kjærbeck explore the role of language, both as a medium and as a topic of talk within the project meeting.

In Chapter 7, titled *International Basic Studies in the Humanities: Internationalization and Localization in Four Dimensions*, Anne H. Fabricius discusses the relationship between a formal international study program and its reality in the work of teachers and students at Roskilde University. Students are required to carry out undergraduate-level research-like work in the form of group-based projects within one or more of four humanities dimensions each semester. This study examines ethnographically the process of defining project work topics, reflecting on how *international themes and questions* are broached in the context of the humanities disciplines in which they predominate. These are contrasted with cases where students have chosen to negotiate and work with *national Danish topics*, resulting in the general conclusion that the interplay between internationalization and localization in undergraduate academic interests seems fruitfully balanced and flexible. Fabricius reckons that 'Students clearly see a role for this hybridity and exploit the multilateral perspectives in their educational choices.'

Together, these chapters emphasize that international education is not only a question of formal standards and measures made in, for instance, Bologna. International education is also what the interactants decide it to be; what resources they decide to operate with; and how they make the local and the international interact in new constellations of educational hybridity.

Part 4 of this volume titled *Academic Writing and Literacy in a Transnational Perspective* contains two chapters which investigate aspects of university writing practice which become more complex when transposed to a transnational context. With a background of interest in implementation of the Bologna Process, which is designed to enable student mobility across the entire European Union, Carole Sedgwick reports on a comparative qualitative study of literacy and assessment practices on postgraduate English language majors at two universities, each in a different cultural and linguistic context, Hungary and Italy. Thus, Chapter 8, *Crossing Borders: The Feasibility of Harmonising Academic Literacy Standards across Europe*, describes her ethnographic approach to data collection and analysis, employed to investigate practices in relation to production of MA theses in each university. Interviews were conducted with students, assessors and supervisors, and graded theses, feedback and contextual documentation were collected. Similarities as well as differences in practice emerge and effectively expose some of the issues and concerns with regard to the aims for transparency of Master's degree level qualifications across borders in Europe. Moreover, the analysis of the data has demonstrated the utility of the approach in providing valuable insights into writing and beliefs about writing that can contribute to the debate about harmonization of qualifications and standards across Europe.

Chapter 9, *Plagiarism in the International University: From Kidnapping and Theft to Translation and Hybridity*, by Ida Klitgård, discusses the challenges international universities face in understanding and handling plagiarism among international students. It is prompted by anecdotal concerns expressed in the Danish media that the increase in international student mobility entails an increase in plagiarism, and motivated by a wish to understand the reasons why such assumptions thrive in academia. Through a review of recent literature on the subject, with special focus on Chinese cases, the author suggests that the dilemmas international students face when writing in EFL are related to a continuum between (a) their cultural and educational backgrounds, and (b) their struggles with mastering both English linguistic proficiency and the accepted academic discourse style. 'Academic language ... is no one's mother tongue,' as Bourdieu and Passeron write. As a counterweight to conventional labeling practices surrounding plagiarism, Klitgård reframes 'learning to write academically' as a complex process of translation and hybridization. Teachers and policy-makers working with international students need to understand and accept that writing academic EFL is a process of transcultural translation where imitation is an inherent part of the students' learning strategies.

The final part (Part 5) is devoted to *East and West at the International University*, whereby we have 'saved for last' a dichotomous metaphor which seems, in this context, to stand for one of the most pervasive challenges of internationalized higher education. Chapter 10 by Hu Xiaoqiong and Chen Yuehong presents the case of *International Students at China Three Gorges University: A Survey*. Until 2000, CTGU had only a few international students each year. By 2009, international students totaled 431, including students from the United States, Denmark, Norway, Germany and Italy (also students from some non-'Western' countries such as India). The authors conducted a survey of about half of them, and a number of interviews, also including some teachers and administrators, to investigate their use of language and cultural interactions on the campus. The findings, in these terms, show that CTGU is now definitely a multilingual university, with Chinese and English as the dominant languages. Most of the international students show an interest in learning Chinese, making Chinese friends and learning about Chinese culture, and cultural differences seem to be as much a facilitator for, as a barrier to, the students' academic and campus life. Teaching styles and teacher–student relations differ between Chinese teachers and teachers from the students' own countries, and CTGU faces certain challenges in teaching and management involving international students. The findings lead to suggestions as to how such challenges may be overcome.

In the next chapter, 'the tables are turned', the case being one of Asian students visiting a European university: *How Far Can Face and Hierarchy Affect Developing Interaction between Korean University Students and Their Supervisors in the United Kingdom?* (Chapter 11 by Juhyun Back). Korean university students are often reported as having serious difficulties when studying overseas, but thus far there have been few detailed research studies. In order to investigate cultural and language issues by Korean university students in the United Kingdom, in-depth interviews were undertaken with six Korean Master's students in the University of York. The purpose of the qualitative approach was to observe the pace of the participants' academic progress, their language improvement and social integration into a new environment in their one-year courses. At a longitudinal level, the study thus involved six sessions of individual interviews with each participant, across the three terms and summer vacations. The interviews developed as 'structured conversations' as discussed by Conteh and Toyoshima (2005). The interview data presented several specific patterns of developing interaction between students and academic staff, including various problematic features.

The perspective changes yet again in the final chapter (Chapter 12), where Chinese students are learning a European language (Portuguese) within a Macau foreign language classroom. More specifically, the chapter is titled: *Intercultural Interaction: Teacher and Student Roles in the Classroom of Portuguese as a Foreign Language in Macau, China* (by Roberval Teixeira e Silva and Custódio Cavaco Martins). The background of this study was that tertiary Chinese students and their Brazilian teacher were felt to have different perceptions of their roles in the classroom, this factor provoking discomfort/conflict in the interaction. The objective of the study was to identify Chinese students' perceptions of teacher and student roles, for the purpose of reducing interactive conflict and helping Western teachers to become efficient cultural mediators in Eastern classrooms. Two groups of data were analyzed: written texts, revealing students' perceptions of teacher and student roles; and a class video recording, to facilitate comparison between what students say and what they do in classroom interaction. The results show that it is necessary for teachers to understand the cultural identities of their interactants if they are to construct an adequate interactional style (Tannen, 1984) for intercultural interaction in the classroom.

The overall findings of the East–West case studies are consistent with some of the main points of the book as a whole: cultural differences and intercultural identities may facilitate as well as impede students' academic and social interaction; culture, beliefs and motivation play an important role in the use of learning strategies, affecting the learning process; teachers need to take into account the cultural identities of their students before deciding on an interactional style for the intercultural classroom; and teachers need to be aware that students have different assumptions about teacher and student sociocultural roles depending on their own cultural background.

In summary, the setting of this book is the international university, and many aspects and themes relevant to this emerging phenomenon and revolving around processes entailed in the internationalization in higher education are taken up again and again from different perspectives, each time adding to its postmodern complexity (cf. Killick, Chapter 5). The book moves from, for example, perceptions of the international student (in the chapters by Sercombe, Klitgård and Hu and Chen), and the international university as the setting for students constructing internationalism and inter- or multiculturality, through the detailed and microlevel interactive processes and language in student group work (chapters by Montgomery and Day and Kjærbeck), which provides us with an empirical window on the processes involved in helping them to discover and transform their identities within a global context (discussed in the chapter by Killick). Moreover, 'Internationalization at home' (see e.g. Nilsson & Otten, 2003) – that is, internationalization in one's home country, helped along by foreign residents or returning compatriots who have lived and worked abroad – offers even students who are unable to go abroad a chance to gain the international competence expected of university graduates in today's global market. Several of the chapters in the first half of the book reflect on aspects of 'internationalization at home'. Another example is the notion of Cultural mismatch, which is introduced by Back (Chapter 11), by way of explaining interactional problems between South East Asian (Korean) students and their 'Western' (British) teacher, due to different expectations regarding the student–teacher role relationship. This phenomenon is then corroborated by exposition of a similar relationship between Chinese students and their Brazilian teacher in the chapter by Silva and Martins. Finally, academic practice as a whole features in chapters by Airey, Sedgwick and Klitgård, spanning from multilingual and multicultural institutions of higher education using English as a lingua franca (cf. Airey, Chapter 1), academic literacy (Sedgwick, Chapter 8) and originality as opposed to plagiarism (Klitgård, Chapter 9).

References

Appadurai, A. (1997) *Modernity at Large*. Minnesota, MN: University of Minnesota Press.

Bauman, Z. (1998) *Globalization. The Human Consequences*. Cambridge: Polity Press.

Bourdieu and Passeron, cited in Angélil-Carter, S. (2000) *Stolen Language? Plagiarism in Writing* (p. 9). Harlow: Pearson Education/Longman.

Conteh, J. and Toyoshima, S. (2005) Researching teaching and learning: Roles, identities and interview processes. *English Teaching: Practice and Critique* 4, 23–34.

Mezirow, J. (1991) *Transformative Dimensions of Adult Learning*. San Francisco: Jossey-Bass.

Nilsson, B. and Otten, M. (guest eds) (2003) Internationalization at home. Special Issue of *Journal of Studies in International Education* 7, 3–4.

Pierce, A. (2003) What does it mean to live in-between? Paper presented at the 4th Annual IALIC Conference. Lancaster University, December 16, 2003.

Savin-Baden, M. (2008) *Learning Spaces: Creating Opportunities for Knowledge Creation in Academic Life*. Maidenhead: Open University Press.

Tannen, D. (1984) *Conversational Style: Analyzing Talk among Friends*. Norwood, NJ: Ablex.

Part 1

English as a Lingua Franca for Higher Education Teaching and Learning

Chapter 1

The Relationship between Teaching Language and Student Learning in Swedish University Physics

J. AIREY

A mouse woke up one morning feeling hungry. Outside his hole he saw a small piece of cheese. 'What luck!' he said to himself. He was just about to run out and enjoy his breakfast when he remembered the cat – maybe it was a trap! Being a cautious mouse, he stopped and listened. In the distance he heard the cat's 'Miaow'. Reluctantly, he decided that it was not safe to go out, and so he went back to bed.

The next morning the mouse was feeling very, very hungry when he saw a much larger piece of cheese outside his hole. But he still had the self-control to stop and listen. Once again he heard the cat's 'Miaow', and once again he was forced to abandon his breakfast plans and go back to bed.

On the third day the mouse was absolutely starving. He dragged himself out of bed and saw a gigantic piece of cheese outside his hole. But he still had just enough self-control to stop and listen. This time he heard 'Woof, Woof'.

Thinking that he was safe with the cat's natural enemy around, the mouse ran happily out to eat the cheese, at which point he was jumped upon and eaten.

Later that day, the cat was heard to boast, 'You see! That's the benefit of learning a second language!'

Background

There are many benefits of learning a second language – particularly if this second language happens to be widely understood by others and can function as a *lingua franca*. Recently, the notion of *English as a lingua franca* (ELF) has received a great deal of attention in research circles (e.g. Ammon, 2000; Björkman, 2008a, 2008b; Firth, 1996; Jenkins, 2007; Mauranen & Ranta, 2008; Seidlhofer, 2004; Shaw, 2008; Smit, 2007) (see also Chapters 3, 4, 5, 9 and 10 on English as a *lingua franca*). The interest is justified. As Graddol (2006) points out, non-native speakers of English now account for the vast majority of communication in English. The ELF approach is also gaining ground in higher education, with more and more courses being taught through the medium of English – often as a response to an increase in international exchange students (e.g. Maiworm & Wächter, 2002; Wächter & Maiworm, 2008). This trend towards increasing mobility of the student population and the corresponding increase in courses taught through the medium of English seems set to continue (see also Chapter 3 on mobility). For example, the goal of the 46 countries implementing the *Bologna Process* is that by 2020 at least 20% of their graduates will have spent some time studying abroad (Bologna Process, 2010) (see also Chapter 8 on the Bologna Agreement).

There are many advantages of using English as the teaching language in higher education. I have previously listed some of them for the Swedish context as follows:

- In a number of disciplines, the publication of academic papers takes place almost exclusively in English. Teaching in English is therefore seen as necessary in order to prepare students for an academic career (see also Chapter 2 on teaching in English).
- In many disciplines the majority of textbooks used are written in English. Teaching in English may then seem like a natural choice in order to have a match between lectures and course literature.
- The use of English develops the language skills and confidence of Swedish lecturers and can be seen as promoting movement/exchange of ideas in the academic world.
- Using English as the language of instruction allows the use of visiting researchers in undergraduate and postgraduate teaching.
- Teaching in English allows exchange students to follow courses at Swedish universities.
- Swedish students can be prepared for their own studies abroad.
- A sound knowledge of English has become a strong asset in the job market. (Adapted from Airey, 2003: 11)

Of course this list is by no means exhaustive, but it is sufficient to underline the fact that there are many potentially positive effects of teaching university courses in English. But might there also be the potential for negative effects associated with this type of teaching? What, for example, are the effects on disciplinary learning when the medium of instruction changes to English?

In this chapter, I present some of the findings from my PhD thesis (Airey, 2009b) where I examined the differences that occur when Swedish undergraduate physics students are taught in English rather than in Swedish (see also Chapters 2, 6 and 7 on the Scandinavian perspective). I have organized the chapter as follows. After a short presentation of earlier research findings, I go on to describe my study, and report the main results. I then discuss these results and make suggestions for teaching. Finally, I discuss the issue of language choice and parallel language use in higher education, making recommendations for how decisions about the teaching language might be taken (see also Chapter 7 on language choice).

Earlier Research

Even without the introduction of a second language, the relationship between disciplinary language and disciplinary learning is known to be complex. Halliday and Martin (1993), for example, claim that language does not simply *represent* disciplinary knowledge – it is actively engaged in bringing such knowledge into being. Moreover, Geisler observes that disciplinary language can '[...] afford and sustain both expert and naïve representations: the expert representation available to insiders to the academic professions and the naïve representation available to those outside' (Geisler, 1994: xi–xii). Thus, it has long been known that students studying in their first language often do not appropriately understand the disciplinary language that they meet in lectures, even though they may use such language themselves (Bourdieu *et al.*, 1965/1994). Bakhtin (1953/1986), calls this phenomenon *ventriloquation*, while diSessa (1993: 153) describes it as 'learning slogans' Elsewhere, I have termed this use of disciplinary language without the associated understanding, *discourse imitation* (Airey, 2009b; Airey & Linder, 2009a). If such problems exist in first language teaching then we should perhaps not be surprised if the introduction of a second language complicates matters still further. Both Met and Lorenz (1997) and Duff (1997) have suggested that limitations in L2 may inhibit students' ability to explore abstract concepts in non-language subjects, with Marsh *et al.* (2000, 2002) predicting that this problem will become more pronounced at higher levels of schooling.

Empirically, there are only a small number of international studies that claim to have found measurable effects of teaching in a second language on disciplinary learning at a tertiary level. Researchers in New Zealand, for example, report negative correlations between second-language learning and performance in undergraduate mathematics, with students disadvantaged by 10% when taught in a second language (Barton & Neville-Barton, 2003, 2004; Neville-Barton & Barton, 2005). These negative effects were found to be at their worst in the final undergraduate year – seemingly confirming the prediction of Marsh, Hau and Kong. Similar relationships have been found to some extent by Gerber *et al.* (2005) in their study of speakers of Afrikaans learning undergraduate mathematics in English in South Africa. Research in the Netherlands has also identified negative effects for Dutch engineering students' learning when they are taught in English (Klaassen, 2001; Vinke, 1995). However, the longitudinal nature of Klaassen's work led to an interesting result. After one year of study, there were no longer any measurable differences in engineering grades between research and control groups. At first glance, this result seems at odds with the other studies reported above. However, this may not be the case. In New Zealand and South Africa one can imagine that students had been *required* to learn in English, and that this may have affected their motivation and performance. However, the students in Klaassen's study were, in fact, very different – they were elite students who had *explicitly chosen* an English-medium programme. Elsewhere, I have suggested that the students in Klaassen's study may have adapted in some way to being taught in a second language (Airey & Linder, 2006, 2007).

If we accept that there may be negative effects associated with teaching in a second language, but students may be able to compensate through their own strategies, then a number of questions remain:

- What is it that students find specifically problematic when they are taught in a second language?
- By what means can students compensate for the language shift?
- Do all students have this strategic ability, or are certain language-groups or types of students disadvantaged by second-language teaching?
- And, can lecturers do anything to help their students cope with the language shift?

Klaassen (2001) suggested following up her work with stimulated recall sessions to find out what students are actually *doing* in lectures and this is precisely what I did in my own study.

The Study

So, it was from this background that I started my research into teaching in English in Swedish university physics courses. At the outset, I decided to focus on lectures given in English. I reasoned that listening to lectures would be potentially the most difficult situation for students to deal with. A student reading a book can stop, look up a word and then re-read the text, but a lecture just goes on and on – unless someone is brave enough to ask a question that is! I also wanted to carry out a comparative, naturalistic study, where the *same students* were taught in both English and Swedish as part of their regular degree program. This entailed searching the country for instances where the same students were reading two physics courses in parallel – one in English, and one in Swedish – as part of their regular degree programme. Eventually I managed to find and negotiate access to three such situations at two Swedish universities. I videotaped a total of six physics lectures with different lecturers. Each student in the study was present at two of these lectures – one in English and one in Swedish. Prior to filming, I interviewed the lecturers about their aims for the lecture and how it fitted into the 'whole', and their experiences of the group as learners and any areas where they expected students to have problems with the material to be covered (see also Chapters 3, 4, 8, 10 and 11 on interviews as method).

Since at this stage I did not know what aspects of a lecture might be important, I decided to focus on as many different types of activity as possible. Guided by my interviews with the lecturers, my field notes taken during the lecture and an interest in sampling as many of the types of activity as possible, I edited down the video footage to four to five segments for each lecture. The total running time of these segments was between seven and ten minutes for each lecture. I then arranged individual semi-structured interviews with each of the 22 students in the study (approximately 90 minutes per student).

In the first half of the interviews I asked students directly about their experiences of being taught in English and in Swedish. Here, I invited students to talk about their experiences of learning in the two courses they had attended, their working patterns for each course and their thoughts about learning in English rather than in Swedish. In the second half of the interviews I used *stimulated recall* (Calderhead, 1981; Haglund, 2003). Put simply, since each student had been present at one lecture in English and one in Swedish, I used my edited video footage from these two lectures to help the students remember the situation and talk about their experiences. For both lectures, I also asked students to describe and explain *in both English and Swedish* one of the concepts presented in that lecture.

Results

So what did I find in this study? Well, the bad news is that there do indeed appear to be some problems experienced by students when they are taught in English. On the other hand, the good news is that I also identified a number of strategies that successful students use to mitigate these problems.

Student descriptions of disciplinary content

One of the things I asked students to do in the interviews was to describe in both English and Swedish one of the disciplinary concepts presented in each of the two lectures they attended. This resulted in a total of 60 transcripts where students discussed the same concept in English and in Swedish. Somewhat surprisingly, for the majority of students, there was little difference between these two descriptions of the same concept from a disciplinary point of view. Note that this is not the same as saying that it does not matter in which language students are taught, but rather saying that from the point of view of a subject specialist, students' descriptions were just as good (or bad!) in both languages – regardless of the language that was used to teach the concept. Note too that I say *the majority of students*. Three of the students in the study had major problems describing concepts in English – with two of them effectively unable to say anything at all about disciplinary concepts in English. These three students were first years and this was the first time they had been taught in English. Interestingly, these three students encountered few problems when talking about their background in English at the start of the interviews, and thus I conclude that it is precisely disciplinary fluency in English that is lacking. Below is an excerpt from the interview transcript with the better of the three students:

Student: I didn't understand why it wasn't a real ... *er vad ska jag saga? Tal* – er only when you *har det upphöjd till två.* But she said it was an *imeg ... imag ett sånt där tal.*

Here, the student does not have access to the disciplinary words: number, squared, and imaginary. Such code-switching was not unusual when first-year students described physics concepts in English, and it was noticeable that their lexical gaps in disciplinary English were sometimes likely to cause a breakdown in communication. For example, the student in the interview excerpt below uses the false friend *feather* instead of the word *spring*:

Student: Yeah, yeah. I think it's a *feather*, that's ... it's going from potential energy to kinetic energy and if you combine, yeah, that with the *feather* constant you get this [...]

My analysis of the 60 transcripts also showed that the only situation where code-switching was uniformly absent was when students described in Swedish concepts that had *only* been taught in Swedish. The final observation I can make is that there was a major difference in the speed of the descriptions. Students spoke on average 45% slower when describing disciplinary concepts in English (see Airey, 2009a, 2009b for descriptions of the methods used to assess speaking rate).

The language does not matter

However, perhaps the most surprising finding in my study was that, in the first half of the interviews, students suggested that the teaching language was unimportant. They reported experiencing no real differ- ence between being taught physics in English or Swedish. Here is a typical student response:

Student: Language is not very important I think. It doesn't matter.
Interviewer: Why's that?
Student: Well, I think ... Like I said, understanding English is not a problem for me.

Had the interviews stopped here, I would now be presenting some quite puzzling results! Fortunately, I had two parts to the interviews – students reported their unreflected experiences in the first half before looking at specific situations that had occurred in the lectures in the stim- ulated recall section. It turned out that even though the students claimed that language was not an important factor in their learning in the first sec- tion, the *same students*, during stimulated recall, could point out a number of important differences in their learning when the teaching language changed to English. I will now present these differences.

Reduced interaction

It quickly became apparent to me as a researcher that students were less willing to ask and answer questions when the lectures were in English. In the stimulated recall parts of the interviews students confirmed this observation.

Student: If you want to ask a question, you have something you
                  want to ask, then I don't speak English so well as I speak
                  Swedish, so its easier for me to ask ... to talk in Swedish
                  and ask things.

Interviewer: I noticed in [the Swedish lecture] there were a lot more
                  questions than in [the English lecture] is that common or is
                  that just ...?

Student: No ... It's common, um actually [laughs]. Yes, that for sure
                  has to do with the language, that people don't er ... they're
                  a little shy to speak English because they cannot speak
                  English so well. Erm ... For me it is like that.

I believe that this is an important finding. Interaction between teacher
and students in lectures is limited at the best of times, and so any reduc-
tion in this interaction is a serious issue. In the worst case, lectures in
English might turn into a monologue and the shared space of learning
(Tsui, 2004) will be correspondingly reduced.

Paying too much attention to notetaking

The second important problem that students pointed out during stimulated recall was to do with taking notes in lectures. The first issue students
are faced with when they have lectures in English is whether to take notes,
or not. Then, if they choose to take notes, *which* language should they use?
The answers to these questions appeared to be different for different students. However, when lectures were in English, those students who did
take notes described how a large portion of their attention was focused on
the *process of writing*. These students had problems following the content
of the lecture.

Student   You're not as used to listening to someone speak English as
                  Swedish. ... You know speaking Swedish you can just er.
                  You can listen and you can write what he's saying and you
                  don't have to, you know, make such a big effort out of it.
                  But if it's in English you've maybe got to focus a bit more
                  on what he's saying and maybe the general message of the
                  physics or maths gets lost a bit more ...

Put simply students could either take notes or understand the content –
but not both. In the study, the success of students who did take notes
seemed to depend on work they did *outside* the lecture to make sense of
the lecture content.

Interviewer:	To what extent do you think that you can follow what's going on in the lectures? Do you follow then or do you follow when you work through afterwards?
Student:	For me it's more, I, in the lectures I write down what the teacher says and do[es] and don't reflect on it under the lecture. But then when I come home I go through the notes and try to understand what the teacher has done! [laughs].

So those are the differences that I found – reduced interaction and problems taking notes. However, my study also highlighted some important ways in which students can adapt to the challenges of English-medium lectures.

Student coping strategies

The students in the study used a range of successful strategies in order to cope with the shift from Swedish to English. These are to do with *asking questions, reading and taking notes*. In many cases students who had said nothing during the lecture came forward at the end to ask questions. Some of these questions were in English, but often students took the chance to ask questions in Swedish.

A number of students reported that they had started reading sections of work *before* the lecture, and without exception these students showed a better understanding of the lecture content.

Student:	I talked to the students that are in the third year. So they said you should read through everything before [the English lecture] so I've tried to do that – and I think it works really well.

Some students had changed their study habits so that they no longer took notes in class.

Student:	I read myself and I take notes, but I don't take any notes at the class because I think it's better just to listen then I can follow.

Others used the textbook to minimize their notetaking

Interviewer:	Do you have [the textbook] with you in class?
Student:	Er, *now* I have it because I don't have the time to listen to [the lecturer] and try to understand what he's saying and

taking notes at the same time. So now I have this book with me and do some notes in the text.

Students also reported finding second language lectures easier to follow when the lecturer followed a book closely, used overheads or wrote on the whiteboard a lot. I think that here students seem to be making use of the redundancy and extra affordances available from these multiple representations in order to better make sense of the disciplinary content.

Student: I think it's easier – actually I think it's *always* easier when the teacher writes a lot on the board …

Interviewer: So the lecturer has to, if it's taught in English, has to write down a lot otherwise it becomes very difficult?

Student: Yep.

Discussion and Recommendations

The first conclusion that can be drawn from the results of my interview study is that some students do in fact have severe problems describing disciplinary concepts in English. In the study these students were all first years who had not been taught in English before. It is tempting to believe that these students eventually do adapt, but since my study was not longitudinal and since there is an internationally recognized problem with student attrition in the natural science, we cannot be certain that they do not simply drop out. In any event, we can no longer assume that students will take a change of language 'in their stride'.

I now turn to my recommendations for minimizing the potentially negative effects of teaching in English. These are based partly on the research I did and partly on my own experience of teaching in tertiary settings.

Question your pedagogy

My first recommendation is that teachers should re-examine the way in which their courses are delivered. Perhaps there is a better way of teaching the course than through lectures. And, if lectures are needed, then you might consider recording them and putting them on the web – that way students could listen and re-listen; or perhaps the lack of interaction I found could be mitigated by adding an online discussion forum to the course

If you do decide that lectures are the way to go, then I have a number of recommendations.

Discuss language differences

The most surprising finding of my study was that students thought that there were no differences in their learning when they were taught English – even though they later pointed out a number of important differences. This suggests that students are often unaware of the changes that occur when they are taught in English. I therefore believe it is important to discuss these language differences. Students will have a better chance of coping with courses in English if they understand that (a) problems can occur in second language lectures, and (b) there are strategies that other students have used to counter these problems.

Stimulate discussion

To get around the lack of interaction I recommend using short, small-group discussions within a lecture. These *buzz groups* allow students to check their understanding, to come up with answers to questions and to generate new questions for the lecturer. Those students who dislike speaking English during lectures will still avoid speaking in class, but at least they participate in vicarious interaction with the lecturer through the group (Bligh, 1998).

Allow time for student questions

Allow time after the lecture for students to ask questions. Here, it may be useful to finish lectures early so that people do not need to be somewhere else. If possible, students should be allowed to ask questions in their first language.

Ask students to read material before the lecture

It is a good idea to ask students to read sections of work before the lecture. The lecture can then be used for clarification and confirmation of what students have already seen.

Follow a book or lecture notes

The problem of note taking can also be minimized by choosing a book or producing your own lecture notes that are followed closely in the lecture. Students can then follow this text and annotate it rather than making their own notes from scratch.

Use complementary representations

Oral explanations should be supported by other representations such as writing on the whiteboard, diagrams, pictures, overhead slides, handouts, demonstrations, computer simulations and so on. However, it is important that this extra input reinforces the message of the lecture. Using multiple representations in an unreflective way will only confuse students!

Language Choice and Parallel Language Use

Finally, I would like to finish this chapter by making some recommendations about achieving the desired 'language matrix' in undergraduate degree programmes. By way of illustration, in my particular area of interest (Swedish undergraduate science) the usual division between languages is to have lectures in Swedish with course texts in English. However, the presence of a single exchange student on a course can change the lecture language to English (Airey, 2004). I believe that treating language in this way, that is, as a simple bearer of disciplinary knowledge, underestimates the complex interrelationship between discipline and language. Here I agree with Postman and Wiengartner who claim that 'almost all of what we customarily call "knowledge" is language, which means the key to understanding a subject is to understand its language' (Postman & Wiengartner, 1971: 103). From this perspective, university lecturers are, in fact, teachers of disciplinary language. The question then becomes *which* language(s) we should teach?

In the Swedish debate there has been some argumentation in favour of an English-only approach (important for Sweden's standing in international research) while others have propagated for a Swedish-only approach (fighting against domain loss, promoting democratic values and rejecting the Anglo-Saxon research monopoly). However, there now seems to be a general agreement that *both* English and Swedish are needed in Swedish higher education, with the term *parallel language use* (Josephson, 2005) being adopted to describe the desired situation (see also Jensen *et al.*, 2009 for a discussion of the situation in Denmark). To date, questions about *what* the term parallel language use actually means and *how* it might be implemented remain largely unanswered. I have previously pointed out that the term parallel language use is unfortunate since it directs our focus towards the educational system, that is, the language *used* when educating students rather than the language *competencies* that graduates should attain with respect to their subject of study. I have therefore pressed for implementation of the parallel language requirement, suggesting that '[...] each degree course should be analyzed in terms of the *desired combination of language-specific disciplinary skills that we would like to be attained within that course*' (Airey & Linder, 2008: 150). But how might this be achieved?

Here I have suggested that the concept of *bilingual disciplinary literacy* might be helpful (Airey & Linder, 2009b). My assumption is that the goal of undergraduate education is the production of disciplinary literate graduates. The question is then what constitutes disciplinary literacy when two languages are used in the education of undergraduates? Drawing on Roberts (2007), I suggest that disciplinary literacy is in fact achieved through control of disciplinary language for two complementary domains: the academy and society. Further, I point out that this control can take two distinct forms – an interpretive form (reading and listening) and a generative form (writing and speaking). From this perspective, the decision about which language skills to develop in any given situation depends on three factors: the domain (within the discipline, within society or both), the language (local language, English or both) and the type of skill required (interpretive, generative or both). I suggest that the only people competent to make decisions about this language matrix are faculty themselves. Once a decision has been taken about the skills that a given course should develop, these skills will need to be written into the curriculum as learning outcomes. I believe that this is the only way of ensuring that the development of disciplinary language skills becomes both visible and valued.

References

Airey, J. (2003) Teaching university courses through the medium of English: The current state of the art. In G. Fransson, Å. Morberg, R. Nilsson and B. Schüllerqvist (eds) *Didaktikens Mångfald* (Vol. 1, pp. 11–18). Gävle, Sweden: Högskolan i Gävle.

Airey, J. (2004) Can you teach it in English? Aspects of the language choice debate in Swedish higher education. In R. Wilkinson (ed.) *Integrating Content and Language: Meeting the Challenge of a Multilingual Higher Education* (pp. 97–108). Maastricht, Netherlands: Maastricht University Press.

Airey, J. (2009a) Estimating bilingual scientific literacy in Sweden. *International Journal of Content and Language Integrated Learning* 1, 26–35.

Airey, J. (2009b) Science, language and literacy. Case studies of learning in Swedish University Physics. Acta Universitatis Upsaliensis. Uppsala Dissertations from the Faculty of Science and Technology 81. On WWW at http://publications.uu.se/theses/abstract.xsql?dbid=9547. Accessed 27.4.09.

Airey, J. and Linder, C. (2006) Language and the experience of learning university physics in Sweden. *European Journal of Physics* 27, 553–560.

Airey, J. and Linder, C. (2007) Disciplinary learning in a second language: A case study from university physics. In R. Wilkinson and V. Zegers (eds.) *Researching Content and Language Integration in Higher Education* (pp. 161–171). Maastricht: Maastricht University Language Centre.

Airey, J. and Linder, C. (2008) Bilingual scientific literacy? The use of English in Swedish university science programmes. *Nordic Journal of English Studies* 7, 145–161.

Airey, J. and Linder, C. (2009a) A disciplinary discourse perspective on university science learning: Achieving fluency in a critical constellation of modes. *Journal of Research in Science Teaching* 46, 27–49.

Airey, J. and Linder, C. (2009b) Tvåspråkig ämneskompetens? En studie av naturvetenskaplig parallellspråkighet i svensk högre utbildning. [Bilingual disciplinary literacy? A study of parallel language use in Swedish undergraduate science.] In L.G. Andersson, O. Josephson, I. Lindberg and M. Thelander (eds) *Språkvård och språkpolitik Svenska språknämndens forskningskonferens i Saltsjöbaden 2008. [Language Planning and Language Policy Proceedings of the Swedish Language Council Research Conference in Saltsjöbaden 2008.]* (pp. 195–212). Stockholm: Norstedts.

Ammon, U. (2000) Towards more fairness in international English: Linguistic rights of non-native speakers? In R. Phillipson (ed.) *Rights in Language* (pp. 111–116). London: Lawrence Erlbaum.

Bakhtin, M.M. (1953/1986) The problem of speech genres. In C. Emerson and M. Holquist (eds) *Speech Genres and Other Late Essays*. Austin, TX: University of Texas Press.

Barton, B. and Neville-Barton, P. (2003) Language issues in undergraduate mathematics: A report of two studies. *New Zealand Journal of Mathematics* 32 (Suppl), 19–28.

Barton, B. and Neville-Barton, P. (2004) Undergraduate mathematics learning in English by speakers of other languages. Paper presented to *Topic Study Group 25 at the 10th International Congress on Mathematics Education*, July 2004.

Björkman, B. (2008a) English as the lingua franca of engineering: The morphosyntax of academic speech events. *Nordic Journal of English Studies* 7, 103–122.

Björkman, B. (2008b) So where we are? Spoken lingua franca English at a technical university in Sweden. *English Today* 24, 35–41.

Bligh, D. (1998) *What's the Use of Lectures?* (5th ed.). Exeter: Intellect.

Bologna Process (2010) Bologna Process. Towards the European higher education area. On WWW at http://www.ond.vlaanderen.be/hogeronderwijs/bologna. Accessed 5.1.10.

Bourdieu, P., Passeron, J-C. and De Saint Martin, M. (1965/1994) *Academic Discourse* (R. Teese, trans.). Stanford, CA: Stanford University Press.

Calderhead, J. (1981) Stimulated recall: A method for research on teaching. *British Journal of Educational Psychology* 51, 211–217.

diSessa, A. (1993) Toward an epistemology of physics. *Cognition and Instruction* 10, 105–226.

Duff, P.A. (1997) Immersion in Hungary: An ELF experiment. In R.K. Johnson and M. Swain (eds) *Immersion Education: International Perspectives* (pp. 19–43). Cambridge: Cambridge University Press.

Firth, A. (1996) The discursive accomplishment of normality: On 'lingua franca' English and conversation analysis. *Journal of Pragmatics* 26, 237–259.

Geisler, C. (1994) *Academic Literacy and the Nature of Expertise: Reading, Writing, and Knowing in Academic Philosophy.* Hillsdale, NJ: Erlbaum.

Gerber, A., Engelbrecht, J. and Harding, A. (2005) The influence of second language teaching on undergraduate mathematics performance. *Mathematics Education Research Journal* 17, 3–21.

Graddol, D. (2006) *English Next.* On WWW at http://www.britishcouncil.org/learning-research-englishnext.htm. Accessed 12.6.08.

Haglund, B. (2003) Stimulated recall. Några anteckningar om en metod att generera data. [Stimulated recall. Notes on a method of data generation.] *Pedagogisk forskning i Sverige* 8, 145–157.

Halliday, M.A.K. and Martin, J.R. (1993) *Writing Science: Literacy and Discursive Power.* London: The Falmer Press.

Jenkins, J. (2007) *English as a Lingua Franca.* Oxford: Oxford University Press.

Jensen, C., Stæhr, L.S. and Thøgersen, J. (2009) *Underviseres holdninger til engelsk som undervisningssprog – en spørgeskemaundersøgelse på Københavns Universitet. [Teacher Attitudes to English as a Teaching Language – a Questionnaire Administered at Copenhagen University.]* Copenhagen: Centre for Internationalisation and Parallel Language Use, Copenhagen University.

Josephson, O. (2005) Parallellspråkighet. [Parallel language use.] *Språkvård* 1, 3.

Klaassen, R. (2001) The international university curriculum: Challenges in English-medium engineering education. PhD thesis, Department of Communication and Education, Delft University of Technology, Delft, The Netherlands.

Maiworm, F. and Wächter, B. (eds) (2002) *English-Language-Taught Degree Programmes in European Higher Education, Trends and Success Factors.* Bonn: Lemmens Verlags & Mediengesellschaft.

Marsh, H.W., Hau, K-T. and Kong, C-K. (2000) Late immersion and language of instruction (English vs. Chinese) in Hong Kong high schools: Achievement growth in language and non-language subjects. *Harvard Educational Review* 70, 302–346.

Marsh, H.W., Hau, K-T. and Kong, C-K. (2002) Multilevel causal ordering of academic self-concept and achievement: Influence of language of instruction (English compared with Chinese) for Hong Kong students. *American Educational Research Journal* 39, 727–763.

Mauranen, A. and Ranta, E. (2008) English as an academic lingua franca – The ELFA project. *Nordic Journal of English Studies* 7, 199–202.

Met, M. and Lorenz, E.B. (1997) Lessons from U.S. immersion programs: Two decades of experience. In R.K. Johnson and M. Swain (eds) *Immersion Education: International Perspectives* (pp. 243–264). Cambridge: Cambridge University Press.

Neville-Barton, P. and Barton, B. (2005) The relationship between English language and mathematics learning for non-native speakers. On WWW at http://www.tlri.org.nz/pdfs/9211_finalreport.pdf. Accessed 21.9.05.

Postman, N. and Wiengartner, C. (1971) *Teaching as a Subversive Activity.* Harmondsworth: Penguin Education.

Roberts, D. (2007) Scientific literacy/science literacy: Threats and opportunities. In S.K. Abell and N.G. Lederman (eds) *Handbook of Research on Science Education* (pp. 729–780). Mahwah, NJ: Lawrence Erlbaum Associates.

Seidlhofer, B. (2004) Research perspectives on teaching English as a lingua franca. *Annual Review of Applied Linguistics* 24, 209–239.

Shaw, P. (2008) Engelska som lingua franca och som internationellt veten-skapsspråk. [English as a lingua franca and as an international disciplinary language.] In E. Jansson (ed.) *Vetenskapsengelska – med Svensk Kvalitet?* (pp. 21–34). Stockholm: Språkrådet.

Smit, U. (2007) ELF (English as a lingua franca) as medium of instruction – Interactional repair in international hotel management education. In C. Dalton-Puffer and U. Smit (eds) *Empirical Perspectives on CLIL Classroom Discourse* (pp. 227–252). Frankfurt: Peter Lang.

Tsui, A.B.M. (2004) The shared space of learning. In F. Marton and A.B.M. Tsui (eds) *Classroom Discourse and the Space of Learning* (pp. 165–186). Mahwah, NJ: Lawrence Erlbaum Associates.

Vinke, A.A. (1995) *English as the Medium of Instruction in Dutch Engineering Education.* Delft: Department of Communication and Education, Delft University of Technology.

Wächter, B. and Maiworm, F. (2008) *English-Taught Programmes in European Higher Education. The Picture in 2007.* Bonn: Lemmens.

Chapter 2

Students' and Teachers' Self-Assessment of English Language Proficiency in English-Medium Higher Education in Denmark: A Questionnaire Study

C. JENSEN, L. DENVER, I.M. MEES and C. WERTHER

Introduction

Higher education in Denmark is currently undergoing a fast-moving process of internationalisation. An increasing number of degree programmes and courses are offered in English, especially at the Master's level. This situation is very similar to what can be observed in the Netherlands, Finland, Sweden, Norway and many other European countries (Wächter & Maiworm, 2008). In Wächter and Maiworm's survey, which was conducted in 2006–2007, Denmark had the third highest proportion of programmes offered in English, behind only the Netherlands and Finland (Wächter & Maiworm, 2008: 26). The increase in English-medium instruction has led to considerable interest from language researchers. Some of the topics that have been addressed are students' learning experiences (Airey & Linder, 2006), the effect on students' learning results (Klaassen, 2001) and lecturers' experiences and teaching behaviour (Vinke *et al.*, 1998). This chapter focuses on lecturers' experiences of using English as the medium of instruction in 12 programmes at a Danish institution of higher education and on the self-assessed English competences of both the lecturers and students in those programmes (see also Chapters 1, 5, 6 and 7 on internationalisation 'at home').

The SPEAC project (*Students' Perceptions of the English of Academics*) explores university students' perceptions of their teachers' linguistic competences and how this may influence their perceptions of the same teachers' academic and pedagogical competences. The data that form the basis of the study described below were collected at the Copenhagen Business School (CBS), the largest business school in Denmark. The students' perceptions are compared with evaluations of the teachers' English skills by a group of expert raters in addition to the lecturers' own assessments of their proficiency in English. The lecturers' self-assessments are used primarily as an indication of whether they feel that their English is adequate to the task of teaching courses in English, and these are therefore supplemented by questions about how the lecturers experience teaching in English compared with teaching in their mother tongue (see also Chapter 1 on teaching in English). The students in our study were also asked to rate their own competence in English to enable us to examine the extent to which (self-perceived) proficiency in English (along with a number of other background variables) can influence their perceptions of the teachers' English.

Students' self-assessment of language proficiency has in a number of studies been shown to correlate positively with more objective measures. Blanche summarises the research on self-assessment of foreign language skills up to the late 1980s and concludes that 'the emerging pattern is one of consistent overall agreement between self-assessment and ratings based on a variety of external criteria' and states that '[correlation coefficients] ranging from .50 to .60 are common, and higher ones not uncommon' (Blanche, 1988: 81). In other words, although the correlation is not perfect, self-assessments can be seen as a useful approximation to a more objective measure. Some of the variance in the analyses of the correlation between self-assessment and more objective measures stems from non-random factors such as cultural or linguistic background (Alderson, 2005). Since the student population in the international degree programmes, also at CBS, is extremely diverse, it is of significant interest to explore the differences in self-assessment scores in such programmes. In addition, self-assessment is interesting in its own right, as an expression of the students' perception of their own skills. In fact, some research has indicated that self-assessment of language proficiency can be a better predictor of academic success (or difficulties) than objective measures such as the TOEFL test (Xu, 1991).

Research Questions

In this multi-stage project it was decided as a first step to carry out an attitude study inspired by the results obtained in social psychological research on native speaker perceptions of varieties of their own language (e.g. Giles, 1970). As stated earlier, we wished to measure students' perceptions of their own and their teachers' English skills, as well as probe into the teachers' self-assessments of their English proficiency. Obviously, self-report questionnaires of this type may suffer from the drawbacks which are well known in fields such as psychology, sociology and criminology, namely that the subjects may not always provide truthful or reliable answers (whether this is intentional or not), and that the results therefore have to be treated with caution (see also Chapter 3 on the questionnaire as a method; and Chapters 3 and 10 on self-reporting). Nevertheless, although perception studies may not reflect reality in a more objective sense, they will give us an indication of how students and teachers themselves feel about the level of English employed in the courses. At a later stage, the data obtained in this manner will be measured against the backdrop of expert evaluations of the same teachers.

When planning international degree programmes, it is obviously important that the language skills of both lecturers and students are adequate to ensure successful communication. At CBS there are currently English language requirements that students have to meet to be admitted to an international programme (roughly equivalent to a B2 on the Common European Framework of Reference), but no formal requirements for the lecturers have as yet been established. If dissatisfaction with the lecturer's English is evident from the student evaluations of a course, such problems are tackled only after they have actually occurred. One aim of this study was to examine whether such problems could be predicted reliably at an earlier stage, either from the lecturers' self-reported proficiency in English or from expert assessments of sample lectures.

The questions we asked ourselves were:

(1) How do students on the whole rate their English proficiency?
   (a) Do students differentiate between their various linguistic skills? Notably, is there a difference between the way they rate their global English skills and a range of academic English skills?
(2) Are there certain clearly definable segments of students who perceive their English skills as being better than those of other students?
   (a) Are there differences in the perceptions of male and female students?
   (b) Are there differences between students at different levels/years of study?
   (c) Are there differences between students with different language backgrounds?

(3) How do teachers rate their English proficiency?
  (a) Do teachers differentiate between their global English skills and
       their academic English skills?
(4) Do teachers feel just as capable of conducting their classes in English
     as they would in their own language? If not, are there certain aspects
     of the language they feel less confident about?

Method

A combination of questionnaires and audio recordings, all collected at
CBS, was used to attempt to answer the issues outlined above. Audio
recordings were made of a 45-minute lecture, in which the teacher gave a
20–30 minute presentation, usually followed by a brief discussion or questions from the students. At the end of the lecture, separate questionnaires
were distributed to students and teachers who filled them in on the spot.
The analyses of the audio recordings will not be discussed in this article.

The student questionnaire contained 38 items about attitudes towards
the lecture, the teacher and the teacher's command of English. The first
three items serve to gauge the students' global and immediate perception
of each of these three aspects: they were asked to rate, on a scale from 1 to
5, (1) *this lecture*, (2) *the teacher* and (3) *the teacher's English skills*. The remaining 35 attitude items were phrased as statements to which the students
were required to respond on a four-point Likert scale ranging from
'strongly agree' to 'strongly disagree' (with an additional option of 'don't
know'). The statements were divided into sections in the following way:

- The *content* and *structure* of the lecture.
- The teacher's *interaction* with the students.
- The teacher's *competence* and *teaching style*.
- Different aspects of the teacher's *English skills*.

The responses to these six sections were subsequently subjected to
Rasch analysis (Rasch, 1960), and a single scale was constructed for each
section. One item was excluded from the *content* scale as a result of this
process, and the *interaction* section was excluded in its entirety, since
several lectures contained very little interaction. Also excluded was a
single statement about the academic level of the lecture. This left 32 items
for further analysis, in addition to the Rasch scales that will be used in the
statistical analyses wherever applicable.

The attitude statements were followed by a large section with questions
concerning the students' biodata, including age, gender, nationality, native
language, exposure to English and self-assessment of English skills (both
general proficiency and proficiency in connection with specific academic

activities). The teachers' questionnaire was similar to the student version but included sections on the teachers' own presentations and their perceptions of the students' motivation and interest in the specific class. They were also asked to provide information about special preparation for giving the lecture in English, for example checking terminology, pronunciation and grammar. In addition, questions were included on whether they thought they would have been able to perform better (on a number of parameters) in their native language. Finally, there were questions on biodata very similar to the ones asked of the students.

The sample is drawn from 12 international (i.e. English-medium) degree programmes at CBS – six BA/BSc programmes and six MA/MSc programmes within the fields of economics, politics, management and business administration. In total, 33 lectures were included in the study, 22 of which were at undergraduate level and 11 at the postgraduate level. The 33 teachers comprised seven women and 26 men. In terms of nationality, 24 were Danes and nine were non-Danes, including two native speakers of English.

Altogether, 1794 student questionnaires were collected, but the actual number of individual respondents is smaller than this, since some students attended two sessions. All student responses were completely anonymous, and the response rate was close to 100%. This high rate was achieved because we opted for handing out the questionnaires in class rather than conducting the study over the Internet. The number of responses per session varied between 20 and 183, with a mean of 55. Approximately 60% of the respondents were Danes, while the remaining students had a variety of other nationalities (see below).

Results

In addition to the scales mentioned above a Rasch scale was also constructed from the self-assessment questions, after excluding one of the five items in this section. This scale is referred to below as the Rasch *self-assessment* scale. In the sections below, results are generally summarised and exemplified using the original scale labels or mean values of the numeric coding, but wherever applicable the statistical analyses are performed on the more reliable Rasch scores.

Students' self-assessments

Both students and teachers rated their English on a labelled six-point scale. They were asked to assess both their overall proficiency and skills in performing certain academic tasks. The student responses are summarised in Table 2.1. Native speakers have been excluded from all counts in this section since for obvious reasons they were instructed to skip this part of the questionnaire. Note that the number of observations (*N*) varies slightly across the different tables because of missing answers in the data set. Only students who have provided answers to all relevant items in a particular analysis are included, and so, for example, in Table 2.2 only students who indicated their gender, overall rating of English proficiency and responded to all items included in the 'Ac. Eng.' scale are included (in this case, 1659 of the 1794 respondents).

Table 2.1 shows the distribution of students' self-assessments of their proficiency in English, both in terms of the overall question 'How good is your English' (the category *Overall proficiency*) and in relation to certain specific academic activities (*writing essays and reports; reading course material; understanding lectures; interacting in groups; making presentations*); the mean percentages of ratings of these academic activities have been calculated and shown as *Average, academic activities*. It came as no surprise that very few students placed themselves at the lower end of the scale – most rated

Table 2.1 Distribution of students' ratings (%) of their proficiency in English (overall and specific academic activities)

Rating	*Excel-lent*	*Very good*	*Good*	*Satisfac-tory*	*Sufficient*	*Poor*	*N*
Overall proficiency	18.4	43.8	30.8	6.3	0.5	0.1	1674
Academic English skills							
Writing essays and reports	14.1	37.8	34.4	11.5	1.7	0.5	1676
Reading course material	18.2	46.7	28.2	6.1	0.6	0.2	1676
Understanding lectures	29.4	48.4	18.9	2.7	0.5	0.1	1676
Interacting in groups	23.0	40.2	28.3	6.7	1.1	0.5	1676
Making presentations	14.4	35.7	34.6	11.9	2.5	0.9	1676
Average, academic activities	19.8	41.8	28.9	7.8	1.3	0.4	

themselves as *excellent* (nearly one in five) or *very good* (more than two out of five). Students rated their overall proficiency and their English for academic purposes at more or less the same level (see also Chapter 9 on English for academic purposes). If the rating categories are assigned numeric values from 1 (*poor*) to 6 (*excellent*), the average scores for overall proficiency and for academic English are 4.73 and 4.70, respectively. There was some variation across the different items, however. As might be predicted, students seem to feel better equipped to understand a lecture in English than to make a presentation themselves.

Self-assessment and gender

As pointed out in the Introduction, some studies have found a difference between men and women with regard to self-assessment of various skills (Lanyon and Hubball, 2008; Pallier, 2003), to the effect that men tend to be more confident and give higher self-ratings than women. However, Alderson (2005) reports no statistically significant difference between the self-assessment of language proficiency of males and females in the DIALANG piloting project (Alderson, 2005: 109). The average self-assessments of men and women in our study are shown in Table 2.2.

It would appear from Table 2.2 that the men in our study assessed their English language proficiency slightly higher than the women did. However, the difference is very small and not statistically significant ($p = 0.51$, two-sided Mann–Whitney U-test on Rasch *self-assessment* scale). Gender differences were also examined across nationalities, but no clear interaction between gender, nationality and self-assessment could be established (Table 2.3). The only moderately sizeable differences are found for Italian and Icelandic students, but the number of observations is too small to allow for any firm conclusions. Overall, our group of respondents is more homogeneous than might have been expected on this particular point.

Table 2.2 Gender differences between students' self-assessment of proficiency in English. The labelled scale has been converted into numeric values from 1 (poor) to 6 (excellent)

Gender	Overall Eng.	Ac. Eng.	N
Women	4.66	4.65	939
Men	4.82	4.76	720

Table 2.3 Nationality and gender differences across students' self-assessment of proficiency in English. Labelled scale has been converted into numeric values from 1 (poor) to 6 (excellent)

Nationality	Gender	Overall Eng.	Ac. Eng.	N
Danish	Women	4.71	4.65	582
Danish	Men	4.88	4.78	482
Swedish	Women	4.73	4.83	56
Swedish	Men	4.88	4.92	43
German	Women	4.62	4.63	45
German	Men	4.50	4.56	42
Norwegian	Women	4.73	4.76	49
Norwegian	Men	4.61	4.76	18
Icelandic	Women	4.80	4.81	15
Icelandic	Men	5.35	5.28	17
Italian	Women	4.00	4.28	15
Italian	Men	4.86	4.81	14

Self-assessment and length of study

Some studies have found that students' attitudes towards non-native teachers become more positive with increased 'length of study' (Ling & Braine, 2007: 269) or contact with non-native teachers (Plakans, 1997: 99). It might be expected that students' self-assessments would also become more positive as they progress through their English-medium programme, on the assumption that their proficiency in English improves simply by the amount of exposure to English when following such a programme. The courses that were included in our investigation span four years of study and, since our data were collected in the autumn semester, the respondents were at that point in their first, third, fifth and seventh semesters of study, respectively. If attending an English-medium programme improves a student's English, it is to be expected that self-assessment scores will increase with each successive year of study. The results from our questionnaire are presented in Table 2.4.

Table 2.4 Students' self-assessment of language proficiency as a function of length of study

Year of study	Overall Eng.	Ac. Eng.	N
First (BA/BSc)	4.75	4.64	522
Second (BA/BSc)	4.78	4.75	471
Third (BA/BSc)	4.61	4.61	153
Fourth (MA/MSc)	4.70	4.73	520

It appears from Table 2.4 that no difference can be discerned between students in their first, second, third and fourth years of study. This is perhaps surprising. However, since the students were not asked to take a language test, it cannot be determined whether this finding reflects a real lack of difference in proficiency. A possible explanation for the lack of any clear progress in self-ratings might be that students judge their proficiency relative to that of their fellow students, that is, that they expect more of themselves at later stages, but this is an issue that deserves further study.

Self-assessment and language background

As mentioned above, a wide range of nationalities were represented. Even though more than 60% of the responses came from Danish students, there were also fairly large groups of Swedish, German, Norwegian, Icelandic, Italian, American, French and Chinese students. The range of native languages largely overlaps with the range of nationalities, but we also found relatively large groups of speakers of English, Danish–English bilinguals and multilingual students, who often had Danish and/or English as one of their three or four languages.

In the DIALANG piloting project mentioned above, Alderson (2005) found significant effects of language background on self-assessment scores, even after adjusting for actual ability in reading, writing and listening, as measured by the DIALANG tests (Alderson, 2005: 103–115). Similar adjustments for ability cannot be made in this study, but the 'raw' self-assessment scores for all languages with 10 or more respondents are listed in Table 2.5. Although we collected information about both nationality and native language, the table is based only on the latter due to the significant overlap between the two.

Table 2.5 Students' self-assessment by language background

Language	Overall	N
Icelandic	5.06	31
Russian	5.00	13
Bulgarian	4.92	12
Swedish	4.80	84
Danish	4.76	936
Romanian	4.76	17
Polish	4.71	14
Norwegian	4.68	65
German	4.51	83
Italian	4.43	28
Dutch	4.33	12
Lithuanian	4.33	15
Spanish	4.18	17
Chinese	3.94	16
French	3.62	26

The results are strikingly similar to those in Alderson (2005). In our study, the highest ratings are given by Icelandic speakers; speakers of Scandinavian languages have also given high ratings, while Spanish and French speakers give the lowest ratings of the European languages and much lower than Italian and Romanian speakers despite the shared Romance background. German speakers give slightly more modest ratings in our study than in the DIALANG study, where they rated themselves higher than Norwegian and Swedish speakers, while self-ratings from Dutch speakers are fairly low in both studies.

Alderson (2005) also reports on actual test scores from the DIALANG project in three different skills – reading, listening and writing. The resulting rankings are similar to, though not identical with, the self-assessment scores (Alderson, 2005: 131, 147, 163), which is an indirect confirmation that the differences in self-assessment scores are not (just) related to different cultural practices, but do in fact reflect a certain difference in actual proficiency. Alderson makes the observation that 'those who spoke a language more closely related to English achiev[ed] significantly higher Reading test scores' (Alderson, 2005: 137), suggesting that differences in language typology is an important factor. To follow up on this observation, it was hypothesised that the self-assessments of students with a Romance background[1] would deviate from those with a Germanic background. The assumption was mainly based on certain typological differences between those languages, Romance languages being exocentric (the lexicon contains highly informative nouns), and Germanic languages endocentric (the lexicon contains highly informative verbs), which leads to systematic differences in the sentence (and text) structures (Korzen & Lundquist, 2005). Although a great part of the English vocabulary is derived from French, English is fundamentally a Germanic language. Furthermore, the educational systems of Romance countries have historically given English a rather low priority and generally the exposure to English is low. As a consequence, their English competence might actually be lower and/or they might be less familiar with English, and it was expected that these students would rate themselves lower than would students with a Germanic language background. Table 2.6 shows self-assessments of English by language background for the groups 'Danish (only)', 'Danish multilingual', 'Germanic' and 'Romance' students. Students with English as one of their native languages have been excluded from the analysis.

The average self-assessment scores for students with Danish monolingual or multilingual background and other Germanic language backgrounds are very similar, at around 4.7 on the scale from 1 to 6. The small differences that do exist are not statistically significant ($p = 0.381$,

Table 2.6 Students' self-assessment by language background

L1	Overall	Ac. Eng.	N
Danish (only)	4.76	4.67	917
Danish multilingual	4.66	4.72	95
Germanic	4.70	4.76	286
Romance	4.21	4.27	92

Kruskal–Wallis rank-sum test on Rasch *self-assessment* scale). When the Romance students are included in the analysis, there is a significant effect of language background ($p < 0.001$, Kruskal–Wallis), which is evidence that the Romance students in our study did in fact rate their English language proficiency lower than did students with Danish or other Germanic backgrounds. It is not possible to determine from our data whether this result reflects a difference in actual language proficiency or a difference in self-assessment of proficiency based on cultural background. However, both possibilities may have consequences for the integration of students with culturally and linguistically diverse backgrounds into the same programme.

Teachers' Self-Assessments

The teachers were asked to rate their proficiency in English on (largely) the same scale as the students, and they too were given questions about overall proficiency and proficiency with respect to specific academic activities. As can be seen in Table 2.7, the formulations in the teacher questionnaire were slightly different from those in the students' questionnaire. Two different averages are included – one for all academic skills (*Average academic English*, which is the mean of rows 2–8), and a mean value for the items we believe are not only the most relevant for teaching purposes, but also the skills on which students are most likely to base their ratings of the teachers' proficiency (*Teach. rel. ac. Eng.*), namely, *Speaking English, Participating in dialogue, Making presentations* and *Responding to questions*.

The teachers' ratings of their *Overall proficiency* is on average slightly lower compared to that of the students, but their assessment of their academic English skills is about the same on average, though if we look at the individual English skills, both the higher (*excellent*) and lower (*satisfactory, sufficient*) ends of the scale are used more frequently by the teachers than the students. The most noticeable difference between the students' and the teachers' self-assessment of their English for academic purposes is that the teachers rate their ability to read and understand academic English (i.e. their receptive skills) much higher than their productive skills. It is not surprising that this should be the case since, being employed in a university and engaged in various types of research, the teachers would be used to reading books and articles in English, and also habitually going to conferences, where their subject would be discussed in English – whether this is the English of native or non-native speakers.

Some caution should be exercised in the interpretation of this result in a more absolute sense, that is, whether the lecturers have indicated that their

Table 2.7 Distribution of teachers' ratings (%) of their proficiency in English (overall and for specific academic activities). $N = 31$ (the two NS teachers have been excluded)

Rating	Excellent	Very good	Good	Satis-factory	Sufficient	Barely sufficient
Overall proficiency	16.1	35.5	29.0	12.9	6.5	0.0
Academic English skills						
Understanding spoken English	45.2	25.8	22.6	6.5	0.0	0.0
Reading English	51.6	38.7	9.7	0.0	0.0	0.0
Writing English	22.6	19.4	48.4	6.5	3.2	0.0
Speaking English	19.4	35.5	19.4	16.1	9.7	0.0
Participating in dialogue	22.6	35.5	22.6	16.1	3.2	0.0
Making presentations	19.4	29.0	25.8	19.4	6.5	0.0
Responding to questions	19.4	32.3	25.8	19.4	3.2	0.0
Average, academic Eng.	28.6	30.9	24.9	12.0	3.7	0.0
Average, teach. rel. acad. Eng.	20.2	33.1	23.4	17.7	5.6	0.0

English is good *enough*. Just over half of them rate their English as *excellent* or *very good*, with another 25% rating their English as *good*, and only one or two of the non-native lecturers rated their English as merely *sufficient*. However, while it seems reasonable to take a self-rating of *excellent* and perhaps *very good* as an indication that the lecturers feel that their English is up to the task, it cannot perhaps be assumed that a rating of *good* carries such implications. Choosing the third-level category on a six-level scale could also be interpreted as an acknowledgement that there is 'room for improvement'. To gain further insight into lecturers' experience with teaching in English, a number of items were included in the questionnaire about how the lecturers experienced teaching in English compared to teaching in their L1. The results are presented in the following section.

Teaching in English versus Teaching in L1

The central part of the teacher questionnaire consisted of two groups of items where the teachers were asked to speculate whether (a) they would have performed better if they had given the lecture in their mother tongue (referred to below as *Group F*), and (b) the lecture that day was as successful as it would have been if they had used their mother tongue (referred to below as *Group G*). All statements are listed here for reference.

Group F:

- *q25*: 'I would have been more fluent'
- *q26*: 'I would have managed to explain difficult issues more precisely'
- *q27*: 'I would have found it easier to find the appropriate words'
- *q28*: 'I would have found it easier to re-phrase the meaning of key concepts and terms'
- *q29*: 'I would have found it easier to include issues/examples that occurred to me during the lecture'
- *q30*: 'I would have had fewer hesitations'
- *q31*: 'I would have found it easier to produce grammatically correct sentences'
- *q32*: 'I would have had fewer unfinished sentences'
- *q33*: 'I would have been more certain of the pronunciation of words'
- *q34*: 'I would have relied less on a manuscript/notes'[2]

Group G:

- *q36*: 'I was just as spontaneous'
- *q37*: 'I was just as pedagogically successful'
- *q38*: 'I found it just as easy to find appropriate examples'
- *q39*: 'I was just as successful at keeping the students' interest'
- *q41*: 'I was just as successful at involving the students'

The responses to the first group are illustrated in Figure 2.1 which shows that, overall, teachers disagreed more than they agreed with statements that they would have performed better in their L1. In other words, although there are individual differences, most teachers feel that they are linguistically well equipped to teach in English. There are some differences between the items, though, which follow a fairly clear pattern.

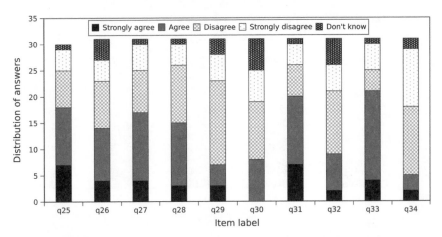

Figure 2.1 Distribution of teacher responses to statements that they would have performed better in their L1 on a range of language-related issues

The four items where the teachers are most inclined to agree that they would have done better in their mother tongue, namely *q25, q27, q31* and *q33*, deal with specific linguistic skills, such as fluency and correctness. However, the teachers seem to disagree that such difficulties would have any major negative influence on their teaching or planning of the lecture (and, in fact, it turned out that very few consulted reference works of any kind). This perceived lack of difficulties is apparent from the fact that most teachers indicated disagreement with statements *q29* and *q34* about teaching activities that we believe to rely very much on language skills. In other words, responses to these statements indicate that the teachers do not recognise any particular restriction just because they have to teach in English. Stronger confirmation of this is provided by the responses to statements in *Group G*, where the teachers were asked to imagine a scenario in which they had given the same lecture in their mother tongue. All items except for one (*q40*, which has not been included in the analysis) had formulations to the effect that the teacher was just as successful in English. The distribution of responses is illustrated in Figure 2.2.

Most of the teachers indicated agreement that they were not only as spontaneous in English as they would have been in their L1, but also that they were as successful pedagogically, or in finding appropriate examples, in involving the students and in keeping their interest.

If we generalise from responses to the statements reported in this section, it would appear that the majority of teachers are aware that they may have some problems with fluency and certain formal linguistic skills, such

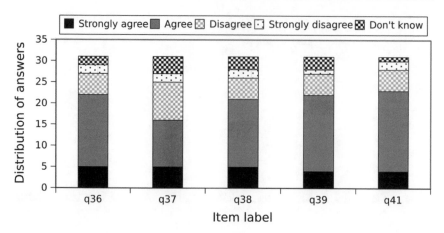

Figure 2.2 Distribution of teacher responses to statements about how they would have performed if they had given the lecture in their mother tongue

as grammar and pronunciation, but the teachers do not feel that communication is impaired to the extent that they need to consult reference works in order to check pronunciation, grammar and so on.

It is perhaps unsurprising that teachers who rate their English skills to be at the high end of the scale also experience fewer difficulties when teaching in English. This connection is illustrated in Figure 2.3, which shows the relationship between the teachers' attitudes towards and experiences with teaching in English (as expressed in Figures 2.1 and 2.2) and their self-assessment scores. The responses to the two groups of attitude questions have been converted into numeric values on 'agreement scales' from 1 (*strongly disagree*) to 4 (*strongly agree*) and mean values calculated across each group for each of the lecturers in the study. Note that *agree* (higher numbers) for *Group F* indicates more problems with teaching in English while *agree* in *Group G* indicates that teaching in English was not perceived as a problem.

The plot on the left-hand side of Figure 2.3 (*Group F*) shows that there is a negative correlation between the teachers' self-assessment of their English and the extent to which they felt that they would have performed better in their L1. The correlation is significant ($rho = 0.80$, $p < 0.001$). And similarly, the plot to the right shows a positive correlation between self-assessment scores and the extent to which teachers felt they were as successful in English as they would have been in their L1 (on a different set of items). The trend is not as clear with these questions, although the correlation is still (modestly) significant ($rho = 0.47$, $p < 0.05$).

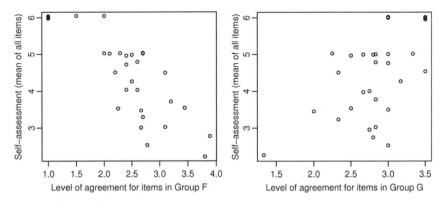

Figure 2.3 Teachers' self-assessment in relation to responses to questions about teaching in English versus teaching in their L1

Analyses were also carried out to see whether *age, teaching experience in L1* and *teaching experience in English* were connected with either self-assessment of English or with responses to *Group F* and *Group G* (about difficulties experienced with teaching in English), but no significant correlations were found (Spearman rank correlation, two-sided, $p > 0.05$ in all cases). Although the present sample is fairly small, it is interesting to note that the assumption which is often voiced, that older teachers will have more problems with English, is not supported by our findings, as far as the self-reported proficiency and experiences with teaching in English are concerned.

Discussion

Below we shall address the results for each of the research questions (RQ) we asked in the first section. The students in our study generally assessed their English to be of a high standard; more than 60% rated their English as either *excellent* or *very good* (RQ1). There were no significant differences in self-assessment scores between female and male students (RQ2a), and the scores were not affected by the number of years the students had attended an English-medium programme (RQ2b). Students with a Romance language background were found to give lower ratings to their own English (RQ3c), which may reflect a true difference in proficiency. This could result from the greater typological distance between English and Romance languages than between English and (other) Germanic languages as well as the difference in exposure to English at school and from the media. If the different self-ratings among students with Romance vs. Germanic language backgrounds turn out to be an accurate reflection of actual differences in proficiency, it might prove worthwhile to examine whether students with a Romance background experience more academic difficulties than students with a Germanic language background. Xu (1991) found a strong correlation between self-assessment of English language skills and perceived difficulties in performing a wide range of academic tasks in a study of international graduate students. Interestingly, self-assessment of English skills was by far the strongest predictor of academic difficulty in this study, whereas 'TOEFL scores, the most commonly used measure of English proficiency and readiness for international students to begin their academic programs in U.S. higher education institutions, were not found to be significantly associated with the level of academic difficulty.' (Xu, 1991: 567). The TOEFL test and similar European equivalents are also used in the formal language requirements at CBS, but if the results from Xu (1991) generalise beyond their particular setting, TOEFL (and IELTS etc.) may turn out to be poor screening mechanisms. Xu does not suggest how one can reliably use the self-assessments in a screening process – all data were collected from students already enrolled in graduate programs.

The teachers in our study were also, on the face of it, generally positive about their proficiency in English (RQ3); more than 50% responded that their English was *excellent* or *very good* and around 30% felt that it was *good*. Neither students nor teachers showed significant differences between the assessment of their global English skills and their English for academic purposes (RQ1, RQ3a). Teachers did, however, rate their receptive skills higher than the students did. It also appeared that the majority of the teachers indicated that they were just as capable of conducting classes in English as they would be in their first language (RQ4), not only in terms of pedagogical success but also with regard to most of the general communicative activities included in our questionnaire. This is very similar to the results for Dutch lecturers in Vinke *et al.* (1998: 387). Only when it came to more specific issues of linguistic correctness or accuracy (fluency, grammar and pronunciation) did a small majority state that they would have performed better in their L1. Part of the explanation for this might be that it is less 'face-threatening' to admit to less-than-perfect command of linguistic subtleties than to admit to not being able to perform one's teaching obligations perfectly, but it appears that many teachers in our study do not consider any shortcoming in terms of linguistic accuracy as an obstacle to successful teaching; they state that they can teach in English just as well as in their mother tongue (see also Chapter 11 on 'face').

However, although the conclusions above summarise the overall impression, as expressed by the *majority* of the teachers, it is worth noting that there was some variation within our sample of about 30 teachers: around 20% stated that their English was only *sufficient* or *satisfactory*, and these teachers also tended to be the ones who themselves experienced most problems with teaching in English. Approximately 25% of the teachers agreed with statements to the effect that they would have done better if they had taught the class in their L1 and disagreed with statements that they were just as successful pedagogically as they would have been in their L1. This can be interpreted as an indirect acknowledgement that the quality of the teaching suffers as a result of using English as the medium of instruction and, consequently, the quality of the students' learning will suffer as well.

Notes

1. This includes speakers of French, Italian, Portuguese, Spanish and Romanian in our study.
2. One statement (q35), 'My presentation material (PowerPoint, overheads) would have been more elaborate,' was excluded since the interpretation of this result was subsequently found to be ambiguous.

References

Airey, J. and Linder, C. (2006) Language and the experience of learning university physics in Sweden. *European Journal of Physics* 27, 553–560.

Alderson, C. (2005) *Diagnosing Foreign Language Proficiency. The Interface between Learning and Assessment*. London: Continuum.

Blanche, P. (1988) Self-assessment of foreign language skills: Implications for teachers and researchers. *RELC Journal* 19, 75–93.

Giles, H. (1970) Evaluative reactions to accents. *Educational Review* 22, 211–227.

Klaassen, R. G. (2001) The international university curriculum: Challenges in English-medium engineering education. Doctoral thesis, Department of Communication and Education, Delft University of Technology, Delft, The Netherlands.

Korzen, I. and Lundquist, L. (eds) (2005) *Sprogtypologi og oversættelse [Language Typology and Translation]*. Copenhagen: Samfundslitteratur.

Lanyon, L. and Hubball, H. (2008) Gender considerations and innovative learning-centred assessment practices. *Transformative Dialogues: Teaching & Learning Journal* 2. On WWW at http://kwantlen.ca/TD/TD.2.1/TD.2.1_Lanyon&Hubball_Gender_Considerations.pdf. Accessed 29.6.09.

Ling, C.Y. and Braine, G. (2007). The attitudes of university students towards non-native speakers English Teachers in Hong Kong. *RELC Journal* 38, 257–277.

Pallier, G. (2003) Gender differences in the self-assessment of accuracy on cognitive tasks. *Sex Roles* 48, 265–276.

Plakans, B.S. (1997) Undergraduates' experiences with and attitudes toward international teaching assistants. *TESOL Quarterly* 31, 95–119.

Rasch, G. (1960) *Probabilistic Models for Some Intelligence and Attainment Tests.* Danish Institute for Educational Research, Copenhagen.

Vinke, A.A., Snippe, J. and Jochems, W. (1998) English-medium content courses in non-English higher education: A study of lecturer experiences and teaching behaviours. *Teaching in Higher Education* 3, 383–394.

Wächter, B. and Maiworm, F. (2008) *English-Taught Programmes in European Higher Education. The Picture in 2007.* Bonn: Lemmens.

Xu, M. (1991) The impact of English-language proficiency on international graduate students' perceived academic difficulty. *Research in Higher Education* 32, 557–570.

Part 2

When the Official Lingua Franca Happens to be the First Language of the Majority: The Case of the United Kingdom

Chapter 3

Perceptions of Identity and Issues of Concern among International Students in the United Kingdom

P. SERCOMBE

Introduction

This chapter reports on a study into perceptions of self- and personal adjustment among international students, in Newcastle upon Tyne. The research for this chapter focused on ways in which students perceive themselves as having adapted, or changed, as a result of having relocated (albeit temporarily) to the United Kingdom and, more often than not, social, cultural and linguistic milieus that are different from those with which they inhabited. Also, how these students support themselves (emotionally) in their goal to attain a higher education qualification from a 'foreign' university. The chapter discusses perceptions of self, affiliation and identification that highlight, in particular, the salience of family, personal goals, religion, language and the need to adapt to a new geographical social context. The study used a questionnaire survey and semi-structured interviews; these two methods, although different, complement each other (questionnaires appear further in Chapters 2 and 10; interview methods are also employed in Chapters 1, 4, 8, 10 and 11 of this volume).

The number of people who now leave their home country and transfer overseas for further study (Bailey & Sercombe, 2008; Byram & Feng, 2006; Jackson, 2008; Montgomery, 2010; see also Chapters 1 and 4 of this volume), as well as for purposes of work, is larger than ever before, and is part of an increasing trend of international mobility (see also Chapter 1). Just as the population of British students in higher education has become considerably more diverse in recent decades (with widening participation), so have the varying profiles of international students (also with widening participation); and, concomitantly, ways in which they relate to host contexts. As a result of experiences international students undergo, through studying in the United Kingdom (in this instance), and elsewhere, students' sense of themselves may undergo reconfiguration in ways separate from, or at least additional to, an evolving process of maturation or internal growth and change; and this adjustment has qualities shaped by undergoing 'new' contexts of experience, as Strathern (cited in Dilley, 2002: 153) points out: 'when people shift contexts they make knowledge for themselves.' It should be noted, however, that a student does not need to relocate in order to face an unfamiliar context and learning experience. Pyvis and Chapman (2005) argue, for example, that a student can be international when studying 'offshore', by enrolling in a programme offered and administered in an overseas institution located in their home country and can suffer culture shock (see also Chapter 10 of this volume) in ways similar to students moving 'onshore', that is, by relocating overseas (cf. Zhou *et al.*, 2008).

Background

Identity is largely concerned with how an individual relates to others within society. The term is often used to refer to clusters of overlapping behavioural (and sometimes conflicting) traits that are concerned with social roles (see also Chapters 7 and 11, this volume). This chapter reports on a study into perceptions of identity adaptation and issues of personal concern, among international students in Newcastle, in the process of studying in a new context.

Identity has emerged as a theme widespread across both social and behavioural sciences, particularly following the development of Tajfel and Turner's (1979) and Tajfel's (1982) theory of social identity. Every individual constitutes a convergence point for different allegiances (cf. Maalouf, 2000); and as Maalouf suggests: there 'is always a certain hierarchy among the elements that go to make up individual identities. Also, that hierarchy is not unalterable; and can change over time and, by doing so, can bring about essential changes in behaviour' (Maalouf, 2000: 12). (On *hierarchy*, see also Chapter 11.) As DeVos *et al.* suggest,

> the self is not a static concept, a reified entity, but that selfhood is something that is continuously defined in one's experience in interaction with others, and that it is this interactional process that contains the meaning of social experience. (DeVos *et al.*, 1985: 10)

What resolves an individual's affiliations is largely the effect of others (Maalouf, 2000). Individuals' responses to others in interaction affect and are affected by their identities and behaviours that form part of an individual's experience of the social environment (cf. Cast, 2003: 44). And, as Cast proposes: 'one of the main ways that social structures reproduce themselves is by producing selves that reflect those social structures' (Cast, 2003: 50).

By the term 'identity', I am referring to an individual's psychological self-conception within society, rather than that of a social group[1] (Joseph, 2004: 760; cf. also Lemke, 2007: 21 on 'agency'), for the purposes of this chapter. A sense of identity, or identities, gives us all a particular place in the world and reflects the kinds of links we have with the society we inhabit (Tajfel, 1982; Tajfel & Turner, 1979; also cf. Woolard, 1997) at a particular time. As Lemke suggests:

> Our identities are the product of life in a community, and we learn how to interact with many sorts people very different from ourselves, in the process building up a cumulative repertoire of roles we can play, and with them of identities we can assume. (Lemke, 2007: 20)

A person's behaviour expresses meanings attuned to the identities that they hold, and these are real to the degree to which individuals partake in ordered social relationships (cf. Burke, 2003). From this it can be seen, as Lemke (2007: 18 – 19) stresses, that identity is inherently multiplex and, quite probably, plural (rather than unitary).

Research into the experience of studying 'abroad' is not new and Jackson (2008), in particular, articulately summarises some of the main issues that have been considered in this area. This chapter is a further contribution to an expanding field in a period of greater mobility for those who have the resources to relocate for purposes of higher education.

International students arriving in the United Kingdom are likely to experience more contact with members of a range of previously unfamiliar social and cultural communities (cf. Zhou *et al.*, 2008). And the quality and quantity of contact differs greatly for these students. For many international students relocation is also likely to involve being in a second or foreign language context. The category 'international student' may seem somewhat vague; and it is accepted here that 'international' students do not constitute an absolute classification nor by any means, of course, a homogeneous set. However, it is proposed that international students can share some or all of the following features (although Pyvis & Chapman

(2005) suggest there has been a tendency for research to focus too much on students coming 'onshore'):

(1) Citizenship of a country other than that with which their chosen institution of higher learning is associated.
(2) A home country different to that with which the institution is associated.
(3) A different first language to (in this case) English or, at least, knowledge and use of another or other languages (in addition to English) from that which is the primary language medium of the university.
(4) Temporary residence in the country in which the university is located.
(5) A probable intention to return to the home country following study abroad.[2]

(Note that the concept of *international student* appears repeatedly in this volume: see also Chapters 4, 5, 6, 9, 10.)

Methods

The study of subjective experience has gradually re-emerged as a legitimate means of considering human behaviour. DeVos *et al.* (1985: 2) suggest that there is, in fact, a necessity to include 'subjectivity as an essential ingredient in the social sciences' (cf. also Denzin & Lincoln, 2002; Sökefeld, 1999).

The main purpose of the study was to obtain insights about how international students relate to the host society and deal with their transition, in terms of resources and their significance. The setting of this study was Newcastle upon Tyne, UK and the sample comprised international students who participated voluntarily, from both Northumbria and Newcastle Universities. As mentioned, the purpose was to elicit the extent to which, since moving overseas, international students perceive certain aspects of their lives as having become more or less significant, and the extent to which they see themselves as having undergone shifts or alterations in their sense(s) of self and what is or are important to them in this process.

Initially, a questionnaire was distributed which was adapted from Cheek *et al.*'s (1994) instrument for investigating personal, social and collective identity orientations administered to (those referred to as) Asian-American and European-American college students (questions for which are in Appendix A). Data from this survey have been presented previously (Sercombe, 2005). In the questionnaire, issues of potential interest were selected, relating to personal, social and collective identity. Statements were framed and survey forms were distributed for completion by students. Responses were given on a four-point scale: 'not relevant', 'more important', 'about the same' and 'less important'. The data were collected between October and November 2004 and totalled 126 responses. The sample comprised international students originating from 24 countries, of whom over 44% came from China, Hong Kong and Taiwan, a common pattern in postgraduate higher education in the United Kingdom.

Subsequently, semi-structured interviews were conducted with 12 students, all of whom had been part of the survey. In this chapter, a synopsis of salient questionnaire findings is reported, along with results from the interviews, and the degree to which these separate sets of data resonate with each other.

Findings and Discussion

Discussion remains preliminary, partial and exploratory, given the sample size and the synchronic nature of the study.[3] While the questionnaire responses may have statistical significance, correlations cannot necessarily be seen as causal. Thus, a perceived increase or decrease in the value of an item, for example, is not necessarily seen as a direct result of coming to the United Kingdom as an international student. A general point worth noting however, is regarding the questionnaire data – there was only a moderate level of perceived change in salience for the issues raised. The topics were divided into three clusters: 'personal', 'collective' and 'social' identity with the following impressions emerging.

Taken as a whole, there was only a moderate level of perceived change in salience for the issues raised. In just over half the returns, 50% or more of the respondents deemed that issues had no greater importance since they had arrived in the United Kingdom. Two of these, [8] 'physical appearance' and [13] 'sex', can be seen as givens or fixed attributes[4], and one might not expect a shift in their level of importance.

Personal Identity

Personal identity is seen as an idiocentric dimension of self and relates to aspects of a person that can be seen as relatively autonomous, separating a person from others, as well as including some degree of agency in relation to other identity dimensions. The areas perceived to have become more important, since coming to the United Kingdom, relate largely to personal identity and the student-centred experience, constructed as self-oriented aspirations and ambitions (Table 3.1).

Table 3.1 Personal identity ratings (%)

Item	Personal identity issues	Not relevant	More important	About the same importance	Less important
7	Personal goals	2.4	64.3	29.4	8
20	*Academic performance*	0.8	65.9	29.4	4

This category of responses indicates the extent to which international students are focused on what surely constitutes their primary purpose of coming to the United Kingdom, that of a formal educational experience and gaining a recognised qualification, with [20] 'academic performance' being the area that is listed highest overall, as 'more important since coming to the UK', alongside [7] 'personal goals'. The general level of salience for these topics is corroborated by work undertaken by Montgomery and Shipton (2005) in which they found that, understandably, international students tend to share a common goal of academic success, and both a strong social and emotional determination to achieve. Not only academic but also social lives appear to revolve around university and their courses of study. This sense of determination is also seen by international students as differentiating them from UK students in that, among UK students, it has been found that the university experience appears to be partly a quest to find a more robust sense of self, and is less concerned with realisation of academic goals (Montgomery & Shipton, 2005).

Interestingly, Reddy and Gibbons (1995), in a study of personal identity among a sample of Indian teenage students, found that those who attached more importance to matters of personal identity tended to come from higher socio-economic backgrounds. One might assume that this is the case here (although I have not considered socio-economic background), given the increasing numbers of international students who are self-funding or, rather, financially supported by their families at UK universities.

Social Identity

Social identity, vis-à-vis personal identity, can be understood as the various ways in which people see themselves in relation to others within various social groupings (cf. Peirce, 1995) and how people relate to others along social lines (Table 3.2).

Table 3.2 Social identity ratings (%)

Item	Social identity issues	Not relevant	More important	About the same importance	Less important
22	*My role as a student*	0	68.3	25.4	5.6

'Role as a student' [22] scored highest of all the responses in terms of increased importance. It seems central to the international student-centred experience and is related to a person's position in the academic community. It ties in with a drive to achieve the required results, also identified by Montgomery and Shipton (2005). Sercombe (2003) also found, in a survey of learning styles among postgraduate mainland Chinese students at Newcastle University, that many professed to be in the United Kingdom not so much to integrate, locally, but more to learn what is necessary to obtain their degree. Interestingly, however, females were found to differ in some degree from males, appearing willing to learn what was demanded (by academic staff) and immerse themselves in recommended supplementary reading, and not just what was perceived as relevant to ensure attainment of academic goals. Also Lapsley *et al.* (1990), in a study of adjustment to college life, found that female students were likely to be less alienated from their peers and to score higher on both personal identity and social identity than their male counterparts.

Collective Identity

Collective identity, in counterpoint to personal and social identity, is here associated with the different ways in which people see themselves in relation to others within cultural groups, in this case those with similar interests (Table 3.3).

Regarding the same or reduced importance of 'own language', for some students, this is probably an indication of the increased salience of English

Table 3.3 Collective identity ratings (%)

Item	Collective identity issues	Not relevant	More important	About the same importance	Less important
21	My own language	9.5	20.6	46	23.8

(vis-à-vis own language) in a new context, an issue raised by students in their interviews as outlined below. Proficiency in and use of English can help mediate where there is stress felt in contact with (previously) unfamiliar people, the language acting as a conduit for greater psychosocial adjustment to being in the United Kingdom. In connection, Noels *et al.* (1996) suggest, from their own study regarding language identity and adjustment among Chinese students in Canada, that the higher the level of English language proficiency, the lower the level of importance of the first language. This finding has been corroborated in other research on adjustment and adaptation to new contexts of learning (e.g. Gao, 2000). Writing about international students enrolled on a pre-sessional English language programme, Hewitt notes that, in spite of high levels of English, international students had seen a pre-sessional English language course 'as an opportunity for cultural adjustment, and for settling in to university and city life' (Hewitt, 2002: 2). However, as Kramsch notes 'the ability to "behave like someone else" is no guarantee that one will be more accepted by the group who speaks the language, nor that mutual understanding will emerge' (Kramsch, 1993: 181). It is here that matters of power and dominance, following the role of English as both first language and lingua franca (see also Chapters 1, 4, 5, 9, 10 on lingua franca) in UK educational settings and possible perceptions of lower status in connection with these may well be pertinent.

Relocating to another country to study for a year or more carries considerable implications both in the present and for the future. Montgomery and Shipton (2005) suggest that, for both local and international students, a sense of identity is worked out in the university context following, for many, what is the first experience of living away from home. As one Chinese student said to me: 'When I was in China I didn't have an identity – it only happened when I came to Britain,' in connection with which one might note Geertz's point regarding the Western concept of self:

> a bounded, unique, more or less integrated motivational and cognitive universe, a dynamic center of awareness, emotion, judgement and action organized into a distinctive whole and set contrastively against other such wholes and against its social and natural background. (Geertz, 1973: 34)

Interview Data

Interviews were conducted, based on themes that emerged as significant in the questionnaire. These were undertaken with students having also completed the questionnaires. Interviews were semi-structured, allowing respondents to foreground issues that were of personal significance (also employed in Chapter 8 of this volume). The range of responses seems testament to the variation in concerns and issues across the international student population, in contrast to the easy option of grouping them as if they had uniform sets of attributes (cf. Lemke, 2007). A number of issues arose as a result of the application of this method. The sample was relatively small, at 12 students; nonetheless, what stands out is the diversity of responses and concerns, both within and across nationalities, ethnic groups and genders. This raises a question about both the value and validity of categorising students on the basis of being 'international', as referred to above, and brings to mind Lemke's discussion of the characteristics of identity: 'What culture announces as one natural kind is in fact a distribution of dissociable traits which do combine in many different ways in individuals' (Lemke, 2007: 19).

Regarding issues that were raised by students themselves, there were four main themes that appeared to predominate for respondents, in that they were raised without students being prompted. These issues are listed on the basis of how often they were raised and the level of significance that appears to be attributed to them by students in their responses: 'family', 'language use', 'religion' and, what is loosely referred to here as, 'adaptation'. In some form or another, nearly all respondents raised the topic of 'family' and its importance.

Family

Poland,[5] male, 25, Polish 'I miss family a lot; keep in touch by phone and internet.'

Libya, male, 36, Arabic 'I feel homesick and keep in touch with my family.'

Japan, male, 24, Japanese 'I miss my family. Sometimes they would call me. Or we would write email each other.'

Taiwan, female, 29, Taiwanese 'I contact my family 3–5 times a week.'

Taiwan, male, 29, Mandarin 'Family are always the most important thing on my mind. By phone once a week and by internet.'

Taiwan, male, 31, Chinese 'My family is always important.'

Mainland Chinese, (Han ethnic group), male, 23, Chinese 'Family are always important for me no matter where I am. I keep in touch by telephoning and emails twice a week.'

Family is, thus, not a marked topic by any means, and one would expect respondents to value such fundamental links, especially when physically removed from them. Comments made indicate the importance of physical dislocation from family and ways in which respondents maintain these links, telephone being the most common. However, Philo (n.d.: 26) reports, from a study of 'Cultural Transfer: The Impact of Direct Experience on Evaluations of British and Chinese Societies', that among his sample of Chinese students: 'Those who did meet British people were able to form close relationships, which affected them deeply. Living in Britain was described by some as a life-changing experience' (n.p.); and, this kind of deep personal interaction, which can enrich the overseas experience, stresses the importance of these relationships, even if they were reported as exceptional rather than the norm in Philo's study. Furthermore, relationships and ways in which respondents relate to people seem significant, and it appears to shape people's impressions of other aspects of their lives at Newcastle, as well as perceptions of the wider local and national population. Thus, positive views of the kinds of relationships people are able to develop in the new setting appear to impact on impressions of the overseas or international experience, overall, and vice versa.

Language Use

Understandably, language is also a salient issue on a number of levels, and the need for a certain minimum level of proficiency in English, in terms of academic discourse, is critical in order to catalyse the quality of the formal educational experience for students. However, this should be distinguished from proficiency to deal with contexts that require more informal types of interaction, since this notional split appears to impose different kinds of demands on speakers (cf. Jackson, 2008). In both areas, there is also an issue of power that can be implicitly linked to non-first-language speakers and the extent to which non-first-language speakers of English can claim ownership of English and be considered, as well as considering themselves, legitimate speakers (Norton, 1997). Increased proficiency and self-confidence in using English can be related to both linguistic and cultural acculturation (cf. Gao, 2000; Noels *et al.*, 1996). Research by Gao (2000), based on a questionnaire survey among Chinese international students in Australia, indicated that first language and first culture had significant effects on students' levels of success in intercultural communication with Australian nationals. Gao nonetheless found it difficult to distinguish explicitly between the effects of first language and aspects of first culture on actual intercultural communication. It was concluded, perhaps predictably, that the more a Chinese student has higher levels of proficiency in English, the more likely she/he can function with less difficulty in Australian society.

Poland, male, 25, Polish 'I try not to speak Polish so I can improve my English by speaking it more; and I try to think in English.'

Libya, female, 31, Arabic 'English has become more important for study and socialising.'

Taiwan, female, 27, Taiwanese 'Learning English well. That can benefit my personal career for the future.'

France, Algerian ethnicity, female, 20, French, Arabic (understands but does not speak) 'I try to speak more English. But if someone can speak French, I would talk with him or her in French.'

Japan, male, 24, Japanese 'I try to speak English more than Japanese because I live here and want to improve my English skill. Actually, I do not like English.'

Taiwan, female, 29, Taiwanese 'Less Taiwanese spoken now usually just to show my feelings. English is more important. I have to read and speak with classmates, watch tv in English.'

Taiwan, male, 29, Mandarin 'I think Mandarin is going to become the most important language in the world. I still speak Mandarin so often even though I live in Britain now.'

Taiwan, male, 31, Chinese 'English is important for communication.'

Mainland Chinese, Han, male, 23, Chinese 'I have a little anxiety about language. I speak Chinese all day like I am in China. I hardly speak English. So, it's a big problem for me now.'

Responses foreground functional roles of English, over attachment to the language. Interestingly, self-rating in English language (Young & Sercombe, 2009) also appears to correlate positively and significantly with overall final degree grade, in ways that no other issues do (cf. Arthur, 2004; Poyrazli *et al.*, 2004). Students who profess relatively high levels of proficiency and whose IELTS results tally with these self-assessments (as appears to be the case) are more likely to achieve a merit grade (i.e. 60–69%) than students who perceive themselves as having lower or inadequate levels of English. In fact, language proficiency seems, so far, to be the sole factor that positively correlates and can predict degree results, in ways that no other factors can (cf. Block, 2007).

Religion

In the questionnaire survey responses, religion did not appear statistically significant, yet comments were made that showed the salience of religious beliefs in interviews, specifically for Muslim students in this sample where no other kinds of religious affiliation were raised.

> **Sudan, female, 30, Arabic** 'Religion is most important ideals in my life.'

> **Libya, female, 31, Arabic** 'This has the same level of importance as before.'

> **Libya, male, 36, Arabic** 'My religion has become more important because I feel lonely sometimes and I can meet new Muslim friends when I go to the mosque.'

> **France, Algerian ethnicity, female, 20, French, Arabic** 'Islam is my life central because I believe our God.' 'I believe I can do everything well because of my religion.'

While for students from non-Muslim backgrounds, religion does not arise as a significant variable, even if this does not mean that respondents have no religious affiliations.

> **Poland, male, 25, Polish** 'Before I had my pc I had more time for my religion – Catholicism.'

> **Japan, male, 24, Japanese** 'I never think about religion in my daily life.'

> **Taiwan, male, 31, Chinese** 'I don't care about religion.'

> **Hong Kong, male, 19, Cantonese** 'Religion I don't think about since I came here. But I believe in Buddhist theory.'

> **Mainland Chinese, Han, male, 23, Chinese** 'I don't have a religion.'

Integration

The final theme raised, seen to have some significance for respondents, is termed here 'integration', i.e. the extent to which international students feel some sense of belonging and meaningful participation in their new environment, while also 'high in ... home culture identifications' (Zhou *et al.*, 2008: 67; cf. also Byram & Feng, 2006: 2); and this can be seen to link with the notion of adaptation.

> **Poland, male, 25, Polish** 'I try to lose my roots in Sunderland. It is not good to be a foreigner here. I try to be an individual – I am an artist – and match this identity and blend in.'

> **Taiwan, female, 29, Taiwanese** 'It is important to change your lifestyle in a new country, otherwise it would be the same as at home.'

> **Taiwan, male, 29, Mandarin** 'If you want to live here for a long time then you have to love it.'

However, Young and Sercombe (2009) found that neither degree of social support nor psychological well-being is necessarily associated with academic achievement, with the conclusion that, while students may not feel as if they have gained some degree of social and cultural foothold in the new setting, this need not adversely affect their final academic result. Furthermore, as referred to above, it seems that the extent to which international students can show flexibility in the face of difference is closely allied to language level in the host language, in this case English. It is common for international students to have feelings of uncertainty, as well as concerns about how to adapt to the host society, and one way of coping with this is to develop friendships with students from nations nearby their own, 'to create a conational subculture to support themselves emotionally and socially in the host country' (Zhao & Wildemeersch, 2008: 57). However, Zhou *et al.* (2008) suggest that organised peer-pairing programmes with local students can help catalyse social adjustment. These are initiatives that universities, wishing to be proactive in attempts to be more 'internationalised', can engage in, given the benefits that can appear to accrue for all concerned.

Conclusions

This chapter has presented results from a sample of international students regarding self-perceptions and issues of personal significance.

Despite the intended integrity of the investigative procedures, various limitations can be noted, including the variations in meaning of identity which make up a multi-faceted construct, a veritable 'Pandora's box' to unpack with any common level of agreement (Edwards, 1995: 125). People maintain multiple identities since, as Cast suggests, 'individuals occupy a variety of different positions in society and, thus, there may be more than one identity that is relevant to a particular behaviour or context' (Cast, 2003: 51). The notion of 'international student' (as mentioned earlier) might reasonably be argued to be too broad a classification, that needs unpacking in ways that go beyond simplified social categories such as gender, age, nationality and ethnicity (cf. Lemke, 2007: 20, who notes the contradictions 'between our subjective identities and, who we are to ourselves, and our projected identities, who we wish to seem to be to others'). Also, shifts in identity patterns are inevitable and part of the continually evolving person, although one might argue that the experiences of international students can lead to changes in perceptions that are additional to and distinct from the phenomenon of the continually developing person, and that these can be identified and categorised. In addition this study has sought to explore issues that are essentially diachronic in nature, but has undertaken investigation in a synchronic way.

From the previously presented questionnaire data (Sercombe, 2005), it has emerged that, (in this sample, at least) many international students did not see themselves as having undergone marked shifts in self-perceptions since moving to a new context. This might be seen as a testament to the resilience and self-determination of many international students. Second, and perhaps unsurprisingly, the samples are preoccupied with ways in which the academic experience in Newcastle can help them meet their (professional) aspirations in the future. Higher education is not perceived as an end in itself, but a particular phase and one that is critical to future stages being successfully realised. What the interview data reveal is the diversity of students' responses and the challenges when considering the highly heterogeneous category 'international student'. However, what seems to unify the students in this sample, at least, is the fundamental importance of family. Religion, for Muslims in this sample, certainly seems to be a significant personal mainstay and provides support in ways that other factors may do for other international students, whether these include, for example, shared ethnicity, or common language. The matter of adapting to a new context has differing levels of significance, but some students here saw this as an integral experiential dimension of being in a new environment.

Notes

1. Within the social sciences, there has been a tendency for the term identity to be extended to include social, cultural and ethnic identity (cf. Seymour-Smith, 1986).
2. Pyvis and Chapman (2005) conducted research on culture shock among students at an overseas institution based in their home country. Thus, there are counter-examples for what constitutes an international student, although these features can still offer a useful starting point when considering what can be meant by 'international students'.
3. Overall results are contained in Appendix A, at the end of this chapter.
4. It might also be argued that, for certain groups, [9] 'religion', too, is a fixed attribute.
5. Bold words prior to each quote relate, respectively, to: 'nationality', 'gender', 'age' and 'first language'.

References

Arthur, N. (2004) *Counselling International Students: Clients from Around the World.* New York: Kluwer.

Bailey, R. and Sercombe, P.G. (2008) Adjusting the paradigm: A theme-based approach to EAP. *The Buckingham Journal of Language and Linguistics* 1, 1–20.

Block, D. (2007) *Second Language Identities.* London: Continuum.

Burke, P.J. (2003) Introduction. In P.J. Burke, T.J. Owens, R.T. Serpe and P.A. Thoits (eds) *Advances in Identity Theory Research* (pp. 1–11). New York: Kluwer.

Byram, M. and Feng, A. (2006) Introduction. In M. Byram and A. Feng (eds) *Living and Studying Abroad: Research and Practice* (pp. 1–10). Clevedon: Multilingual Matters.

Cast, A.D. (2003) Identities and behavior. In P.J. Burke, T.J. Owens, R.T. Serpe and P.A. Thoits (eds) *Advances in Identity Theory Research* (pp. 41–55). New York: Kluwer.

Cheek, J.M., Tropp, L.R., Chen, L.C. and Underwood, M.K. (1994) Identity orientations: Personal, social, and collective aspects of identity. Paper presented at the *102nd Annual Convention of the American Psychological Association*, Los Angeles.

Denzin, N.K. and Lincoln, Y. (2002) *The Qualitative Inquiry Reader.* London: Sage.

DeVos, G., Marsella, A.J. and Hsu, F.L.K. (1985) Introduction: Approaches to culture and self. In A.J. Marsella, G. De Vos and F.L.K. Hsu (eds) *Culture and Self: Asian and Western Perspectives* (pp. 2–23). New York: Tavistock Publications.

Dilley, R.M. (2002) The problem of context in social and cultural anthropology. *Language and Communication* 22, 437–456.

Edwards, J. (1995) *Multilingualism.* Harmondsworth: Penguin.

Gao, M.C.F. (2000) Influence of native culture and language on intercultural communication: The case of PRC student immigrants in Australia. *Journal of Intercultural Communication* 4, n.p.

Geertz, C. (1973) *The Interpretation of Cultures: Selected Essays.* New York: Basic Books.

Hewitt, J. (2002) Toon and Gown: Perceptions of Chinese students in Newcastle. In W. Lancaster (ed.) *Northern Review* II, 1–7.

Jackson, J. (2008) *Language, Identity and Study Abroad*. London: Equinox.
Joseph, J.E. (2004) *Language and Identity*. Basingstoke: Palgrave.
Kramsch, C. (1993) *Context and Culture in Language Teaching*. Oxford: Oxford University Press.
Lapsley, D.K., Rice, K.G. and FitzGerald, D.P. (1990) Adolescent attachment, identity, and adjustment to college: Implications for the continuity of adaptation hypothesis. *Journal of Counseling and Development* 68, 561–565.
Lemke, J.L. (2007) Identity, development, and desire: Critical questions. In C. Caldas-Coulthard and R. Iedema (eds) *Identity Trouble: Critical Discourse and Contestations of Identification* (pp. 17–42). London: Macmillan/Palgrave.
Maalouf, A. (2000) *On Identity*. London: The Harvill Press.
Montgomery, C. (2010) *Understanding the International Student Experience*. Basingstoke: Palgrave.
Montgomery, C. and Shipton, A. (2005) *Worlds Apart: A Comparison of International and UK Students at Northumbria University*. Northumbria University English Language Centre Seminar Paper, presented 15 June 2005.
Noels, K., Pon, G. and Clément, R. (1996) Language, identity and adjustment: The role of linguistic self-confidence in the acculturation process. *Journal of Language and Social Psychology* 15, 246–264.
Norton, B. (1997) Language, identity and the ownership of English. *TESOL Quarterly* 31, 409–430.
Peirce, B.N. (1995) Social identity, investment, and language learning. *TESOL Quarterly* 29, 9–31.
Philo, G. (n.d.) Cultural transfer: The impact of direct experience on evaluations of British and Chinese societies. On WWW at http://www.gla.ac.uk/centres/mediagroup/cultural%20transfer.pdf. Accessed 12.11.08.
Poyrazli, S., Kavanaugh, P.R., Baker, A. and Al-Timimi, N. (2004) Social support and demographic correlates of acculturative stress in international students. *Journal of College Counseling* 7, 73–82.
Pyvis, D. and Chapman, A. (2005) Culture shock and the international student 'offshore'. *Journal of Research in International Education* 4, 23–42.
Reddy, R. and Gibbons, J.L. (1995) Socioeconomic contexts and adolescent identity development in India. Paper presented at the annual meeting of the Society for Cross-Cultural Research, Savannah, Georgia.
Sercombe, P.G. (2003) A preliminary survey of learning styles among postgraduate Mainland Chinese students. Unpublished Research Paper.
Sercombe, P.G. (2005) Perceptions of identity among international students in Newcastle. Paper presented at conference, *Interrogating Third Spaces in Language Teaching*, University of Leicester, UK, 27–28 June 2005.
Seymour-Smith, C. (1986) *Macmillan Dictionary of Anthropology*. London: Macmillan.
Sökefeld, M. (1999) Debating self, identity and culture in anthropology. *Current Anthropology* 40, 417–447.
Tajfel, H. (1982) *Social Identity and Intergroup Relations*. Cambridge: Cambridge University Press.
Tajfel, H. and Turner, J.C. (1979) An integrative theory of intergroup conflict. In W.G. Austin and S. Worschel (eds) *The Social Psychology of Intergroup Relations* (pp. 285–293). Monterey, CA: Brooks/Cole.
Woolard, K. (ed.) (1997) *Identity and Difference*. London: Sage & Open University.

Young, T.J. and Sercombe, P.G. (2009) International postgraduate students' transitions: Linguistic, academic and intercultural. Unpublished Research Paper.

Zhao, M. and Wildemeersch, D. (2008) Hosting foreign students in European universities. *European Education* 40, 51–62.

Zhou, Y., Jindal-Snape, D., Topping, K. and Todman, J. (2008).Theoretical models of culture shock and adaptation in international students in higher education. *Studies in Higher Education* 33, 63–75.

Appendix A

The aspects of identity are shown in Table A.1.

Table A.1 Statement results on aspects of identity, (%) ($n = 126$)

	Please read each item carefully and decide if it applies to you. If it does, please indicate whether its importance for you has changed since you arrived in the United Kingdom. (In other words, is it more important, equally important or less important than when you were in your home country?) When you have decided, please tick the appropriate box.	*Not relevant to me*	*More important since I came to the United Kingdom*	*About the same importance as before*	*Less important since I came to the United Kingdom*
1	My possessions	7.9	38.1	46	7.9
2	My personal values	3.2	44.4	50	2.4
3	My popularity with people	11.2	27.2	44	17.6
4	The way I get on with people	7.9	50	30.2	10.3
5	My friends in my home country	5.6	42.1	45.2	7.1
6	My ethnic background	15.9	35.7	38.1	10.3
7	My personal goals	2.4	64.3	29.4	8
8	My physical appearance	8.7	19	59.5	12.7
9	My religion	26.2	25.4	33.3	11.9
10	The food of my home country	8.7	52.4	24.6	13.5
11	My age group	1.6	57.9	34.9	3.2
12	My anxieties	2.4	46.8	46	4.8
13	My sex	23	11.9	52.4	10.3
14	My feeling of being a unique person	11.9	29.4	50.8	7.1
15	My social group or economic group	19.8	18.3	45.2	14.3
16	Knowing I continue to be the same person inside	32	42.9	40.5	13.5

Table A.1   (continued)

		Not relevant to me	*More important since I came to the United Kingdom*	*About the same importance as before*	*Less important since I came to the United Kingdom*
	Please read each item carefully and decide if it applies to you. If it does, please indicate whether its importance for you has changed since you arrived in the United Kingdom. (In other words, is it more important, equally important or less important than when you were in your home country?) When you have decided, please tick the appropriate box.				
17	My pride in my country	5.6	41.3	34.9	16.7
18	My career plans	4	59.5	34.1	2.4
19	My political attitudes	25.4	18.3	43.7	12.7
20	My academic performance	0.8	65.9	29.4	4
21	My own language	9.5	20.6	46	23.8
22	My role as a student	0	68.3	25.4	5.6

Chapter 4

Developing Perceptions of Interculturality: A Troublesome Space?

C. MONTGOMERY

Introduction

This chapter considers student perceptions of working in intercultural groups in a diverse international academic environment. The focus here is on how students construct themselves and each other socially, culturally and linguistically through their experience of working together at university. The study is set in traditions of intercultural communication (Gumperz, 1982; see also Chapters 6 and 12 in this volume) and social network analysis (Milroy, 1987). It is an empirical study that interrogates a particular educational context where the complex interaction of language, social groups and social identities is evident in the learning process (Coupland, 2001). The chapter aims to present the intercultural higher education landscape not as a binary of self and other (Pierce, 2003) but as a complex site of struggle, tension and conflict. However, this 'troublesome space' in which intercultural interaction occurs is not presented here as being problematic but as useful and transformative (Meyer & Land, 2005; Savin-Baden, 2008; again, see also Chapters 6 and 12 on intercultural interaction). The chapter also argues that catalysts for these transformative yet troublesome spaces can be found in particular teaching, learning and assessment environments where students are given extended opportunities to interact through authentic and collaborative learning and assessment tasks.

This chapter reports on a study that was carried out in 2008 that aimed to reconstruct a research project carried out in 1998 investigating students' views of working in international groups. The research of Volet and Ang

59

(1998) in Australia considered factors that students believed to be affecting the formation of mixed nationality groups in the completion of academic group work. The 2008 study in the United Kingdom followed the same methodology, collecting qualitative data from group interviews (a method also employed in various chapters in this book) and focusing upon how student perceptions of working in diverse groups, particularly for assessment purposes, may have developed over the decade. The 2008 study concentrated on data sites where Assessment for Learning (McDowell *et al.*, 2005) approaches had been introduced and these particularly focused on authentic and challenging assessment tasks.

This chapter reports on one aspect of the data collected in the 2008 study and is the second part of an iterative process of data analysis. The first analysis that looked at the whole data set is reported in Montgomery (2009). This chapter concentrates on a case study from the discipline of Design in order to show how students' perceptions of working with other cultures may illuminate the complexity and tensions of the developing intercultural learning environment in higher education.

Methodology: The Case Study

The study as a whole looked at two studies that are separated by 10 years. The intention was not to draw a direct comparison between these studies as they were carried out on two different continents in different educational contexts and with different student samples. The idea of putting these two projects together was to give a historical context to the research carried out in 2008, to revisit the data of the earlier project and to present the contemporary study in the light of earlier data (Montgomery, 2009). For the purposes of this chapter, however, the 1998 study will be referred to only briefly as a means of indicating the starting point for this research.

The data for the 2008 study were collected in a 'new' (post-1992) university in the United Kingdom within the context of a wider research programme being carried out in a Centre for Excellence in Teaching and Learning that focuses on Assessment for Learning (AfL). AfL (McDowell *et al.*, 2005), or 'learning-oriented assessment', strongly emphasises the educational significance of authentic and challenging learning and assessment environments and cultures. It also champions peer support, peer assessment and the building of learning communities that include both students and staff. This approach encourages emphasis on the social and cultural contexts of learning and aims among other things to enable students to build their own informal learning communities, again stemming from a belief that competences and effectiveness learned in doing this at university will equip them to make personal, professional and academic judgements later in life (Boud & Falchikov, 2006).

The focus groups that were carried out for this project are part of an interpretive, qualitative approach that aimed to provide insights into a 'key site' where students were interacting across cultures. Students were asked about their experience of working in cross-cultural groups, particularly for assessment purposes, and they were invited to comment on how they felt before, during and after the experience of working in these groups. The focus groups themselves, being made up of mixed nationalities, replicated the students' experience of cross-cultural group work as they 'position[ed] themselves in relation to each other as they process[ed] questions, issues and topics in focused ways' (Kamberelis & Dimitriadis, 2005: 904; on cross-cultural group work, see also Chapter 6 of this volume). The data gathered from these focus groups were analysed using an emergent and interpretive framework, making use of qualitative data analysis software. 'Chunks' of data were allocated topics (or nodes), thus allowing themes to develop from the categorisation of the data. Table 4.1 gives details of the whole data set and the section of data that is being considered in detail here.

The sites of Design data presented in this chapter had introduced AfL approaches into both the undergraduate and postgraduate curricula, focusing in particular on authentic tasks that provided a complex and challenging learning environment and extended opportunities for interaction. In the undergraduate curriculum students were engaged in a 'live' project with industry where the assessment task was to design a 'hand-held device' for the mobile phone company 'Motorola'. The students were linked virtually in a 'global studio' with groups of Korean students in Korea and the UK-based and Korean-based group was asked to come up with a group Design brief by exchanging feedback in a virtual environment (Bohemia *et al.*, 2009). In the PG curriculum the students worked on a community-based project. Students, who were from a wide range of nationalities, were required to research a local building (the Guildhall), its history and its status in the local community. They worked with staff from the council and other stakeholders in the community to develop a design for the building and present it at a public exhibition. In both the undergraduate and postgraduate context, these authentic, enquiry-based activities formed the core of students' assessment task.

The significance of these curriculum designs to the data presented here will be discussed later in this chapter where I argue that the teaching, learning and assessment environment can exert a strong influence on perceptions of interculturality (for the latter concept, see also Chapter 6).

Table 4.1 Data

Study and Setting	Methodology	Discipline	Nationalities
Early study: 1998 Volet and Ang in Australian university	40 students interviewed in 11 focus groups with semi-structured interview	Single discipline -Business School	23 international (18 Chinese from Singapore and Malaysia, 5 'other SE Asia'); 17 Australian
Full data set: 2008 Montgomery in British university	70 students interviewed in 12 informal and situated focus groups with semi-structured schedule	3 different disciplines Business, Design and Engineering	37 British; 33 international (China, India, Taiwan, Indonesia, Thailand, Russia, Spain, Italy, Cyprus, France, USA, Sri Lanka, Germany)
Design case study for this paper: Two specific teaching projects: the Guidhall community project and Motorola 'live' projects with industry	47 students, interviewed in 5 informal focus groups using semi-structured schedule	Design: UG Design for Industry, Year 2 (mainly UK) MA Design (mainly international)	UG 19 UK; 7 International (Italy, China and Taiwan) MA 17 International (India, China, Taiwan, Indonesia, Thailand); UK 4

The Findings

The 1998 project

As mentioned above, the early project is described only briefly here to indicate the starting point for the research. The research project carried out by Volet and Ang (1998) in Australia considered student perceptions of mixed nationality academic group work. The study looked at the nature of the change in views after a 'successful' experience of working in intercultural groups. The article focused on both home (here Australian) and international students' views on the experience in an attempt to show that the responsibility for difficulties in 'cultural mixing' lay with both home and international students. Volet and Ang's article begins from a premise that one of the main purposes of internationalisation is to prepare students for life in an intercultural setting. They state:

> One of the major educational goals of the internationalisation of Higher Education is to prepare students to function in an international and inter-cultural context. (Volet & Ang, 1998: 5)

They note, however, that the resource provided by cultural diversity on campus is not being explored to the benefit of the student group as a whole and at the time of their study there was a lack of interactions between 'local' and international students. (For discussions of *diversity*, see also Chapters 5, 9, 10 and 12 of this volume; international exchange students are discussed in Chapters 1 and 3.)

A Desire to Stay with Your 'Own People'

Results showed that overall both Australian and international students preferred working in groups with their 'own people'. There was a perception by both international students and Australian students that common cultural backgrounds facilitated communication and made group management easier. One Indonesian student noted the following:

> I find it easier to work ... with people from my own country, we can work with our own language and I am more comfortable telling the others to work if they are not putting in effort. I am also more comfortable advising them.

In the Volet and Ang study only a few international students declared that mixed nationality groups were important during their study abroad. Overall, it was noted that both groups believed that working with students with a similar cultural background minimised conflicts and misunderstandings, preferring the company of peers from similar ethnic backgrounds. Language was perceived by students as an influencing factor with an Australian student stating:

> Sometimes we don't understand what they are saying and sometimes they don't understand what we are saying.

Volet and Ang questioned the nature of this perceived problem and asked about the extent to which communication problems were real or whether they were influenced by a lack of willingness to understand each other and 'tolerate a degree of broken English' (Volet & Ang, 1998: 13).

In the 1998 study, there was also evidence of negative stereotypes (on which, see also Chapters 8 and 12 in this volume) and ethnocentric views on the part of both international and Australian students and these were seen to be significant barriers to the effective formation of culturally mixed groups. Stereotypical views about other nationalities appeared to be at the centre of reasons given for not wanting to join a team of mixed nationalities. One Asian student noted:

> I prefer working with students from Indonesia or at least Asians rather than Australians ... I had a previous experience with a group of Australians where at the first meeting, there were lots of suggestions and ideas from the Australian students but they left all the work to the last minute. I believe they have great ideas but no motivation to work.

Volet and Ang also noted that none of the international student group made reference to the diversity inherent in Australian ethnic backgrounds. It appeared that they did not notice that many Australian students are from Asian and non-Anglo-Saxon origins (Volet & Ang, 1998: 14).

Developing Positive Attitudes to Culturally Mixed Group Experiences

The 1998 study found that once students had experience of working in mixed nationality groups, they developed a more positive attitude to working with students from a range of backgrounds but also found that some students still harboured stereotyped views of the other group, particularly in terms of their work-related attitudes. The study noted that this prejudice was operating from both the international and the Australian point of view.

Volet and Ang thus noted the two-way nature of the interaction between international and local students. The study noted the significance of gaining the opportunity to work in mixed groups in order to dispel those preconceived ideas. In the 1998 study, it was considered that there were not enough opportunities for 'spontaneous intercultural contact' (Volet & Ang, 1998: 17). Volet and Ang were concerned that should this situation continue higher education in Australia could fail in its major educational aim to prepare students for a global future.

The 2008 project

Interculturality as a 'troublesome space'

Martin and Nakayama constitute culture 'as a site of struggle, a place where multiple interpretations come together' (2000: 40). The second analysis of the 2008 project data of the students in the discipline of Design uncovered a great deal of contradictions and tensions that appeared to show the intercultural interaction in these learning contexts as a contested place, where struggles were evident and students' interpretation of the learning environment were contradictory. Because of this, the construct of the 'troublesome space' (Meyer & Land, 2005; Perkins, 2006; Savin-Baden, 2008) seemed to have resonances in the complex intercultural context from which students in this study were perceiving themselves and each other. Troublesome spaces are places where 'stuckness' or 'disjunction' occurs but which once experienced can lead to a transition or development in learning (Savin-Baden, 2008). Perkins' (1999) early use of the idea of troublesome learning was developed by Meyer and Land (2005) who linked this with threshold concepts, key concepts that, once grasped, allow learners to progress in their understandings. These mental and metaphorical spaces are highly complex and involve a learning process involving stages of confusion and fragmentation. For students and staff these difficult spaces are often seen as problematic but as Savin-Baden suggests, on the contrary, these difficult and contested places are 'useful and transformative' (2008: 95). Movement into such spaces may be caused by catalysts that include perceptions of difficulty, threats to learner identity, troublesome power and challenging dominant narratives.

Savin-Baden (2008) suggests that the transitional or transformative nature of learning spaces is dependent on how 'stuckness' (the realisation that particular knowledge is troublesome) is dealt with. She suggests that 'disjunction' is a troublesome learning space that emerges when forms of active learning such as problem-based learning are used as these prompt students to engage with procedural and personal knowledge. The key factor is how students respond to such troublesome spaces: whether they choose to engage with the challenging nature of disjunction or whether they retreat and are alienated by this. In the case of this research study, students' experience of intercultural interaction during group work appear to have resonances with the idea of troublesome space and this chapter considers students' reactions to the challenges presented therein. It is suggested here, then, that the context of the case study presented in this chapter resembled a troublesome space in that the students' perceptions of their experience of intercultural interaction held conflicting positions: the experience of intercultural contact was confusing and complex for students. Students also, however, strongly indicated that these difficulties were transformative learning experiences and significant despite not always being enjoyable. The following sections will show aspects of the data that suggest this.

Language and Communication: A Site of Tensions

Language is at the centre of the complexity of social interaction in a learning context, and when considering the data in this study it is crucial to note that language is not only a marker of social identity (as Vygotsky made very clear) but it is the most important mediation tool for learning (Perret-Clermont, 2009). Language is often viewed as a barrier to students interacting in an international university. However, previous research has indicated that language competence is often secondary to communicative competence in its influence on intercultural interaction at university (Montgomery, 2010). In this case study there appeared to be a dichotomy in students' perception of the role of language in their intercultural interaction. On the one hand students noted that the 'loose' nature of the tasks they were working on made working together and communication easy. Yet at the same time the interaction within intercultural groups was perceived to be difficult and problematic. Students noted that language was an issue but they also suggested that the issue was one of communication rather than language competence. Students did report language difficulties where levels of language competence impeded the ability to work together. However, in this case study extreme examples where language competence was low were presented as isolated incidents and students more commonly talked about the issue being one of communication. Students reported some anxiety being caused by 'difference in communication' but that this was common to all students, including those who spoke the same languages. This difference in communication was not predicated on the language spoken but on 'different ways of thinking'. One PG female Chinese student noted:

> In my team every member can speak Mandarin so it's easier for my team to communicate. But since we were still from different countries [Taiwan and Mainland China] so it's another different problem that we have different kinds of thinking and that makes a problem when we communicate.

Another international student reported that even where there was a second language in common in which all were competent there were still difficulties when students were communicating. So even where there was a *lingua franca* (see also Chapters 1, 3, 5, 9, 10) for the group there were more complex communication issues that affected their interaction. Indeed students reported experience of highly complicated translation processes on the path to communication and understanding the ideas of others. A PG female Chinese student explained:

> Half the time we were just trying to translate to the other person. The Japanese student in my group had the same problem. He wouldn't understand what the Taiwanese were trying to say. Then I would translate everything for him and it was another girl who would translate for me because they would start talking in Taiwanese.

The interesting aspect of these 'translations' was that they were not necessarily occurring in students' first languages but consisted of explanations in shared languages, sometimes but not exclusively English.

Despite the reported difficulties in communication there was also a strong sense of students' willingness to overcome communication difficulties by any means possible. Students talked about their creative ways of achieving understanding of each other. One PG female Taiwanese student talked about creativity in the discipline of Design and non-verbal communication as being vehicles for developing understandings.

> We can understand maybe by body language. Because we are Design students so you can understand in Design. Image is easier to understand.

Another student described her group's approach to coming to a consensus on a design as involving the drawing of mind-maps that enabled them to communicate. The PG female Indian student said:

> There were a million mind-maps and that's how we got to it because we decided the global communication wasn't the best way to get anywhere so we started drawing maps.

Students viewed the process of struggling to communicate as an authentic one and the experience of this struggle was something that would prepare them for the world of work and life beyond the university. A PG female Chinese student noted:

> It's all the way how we try to communicate but it's okay because in real life you go into a company and you work there as a Designer. You might also find that you cannot choose [who you work with] and you might face the same problem.

Despite the difficulties in communicating and the effort required to reach a consensus in discussion, students described the troublesome experience of intercultural academic group work as a transformative one. It came out very strongly in the data that it was the interaction of cultures and peoples that made the experience transformative. One PG female Taiwanese student said:

> We see that we are dealing with so many different cultures and different people. I think you also change your personality, I mean eventually you change yourself.

In support of that a PG male Indonesian student described the transformation in himself as follows:

> You interact with so many people. You know how they are working and how they are dealing with work so if you are not easy or if you are not comfortable with them, you have, I think, you have to change yourself. That's very important. If you want to fit in.

Thus, students emphasised that their experience of collaboration in diverse international groups was a problematic and difficult process but that they learned important and useful things about themselves and other people. This sort of learning was also seen as being highly relevant to the academic discipline and to their future.

Among the positive comments about the value of communicating across cultures, there also appeared to be some vestiges of prejudice. This seemed to manifest itself in what Harrison terms 'passive xenophobia'. Peacock and Harrison (2009: 24) describes the idea of passive xenophobia as belonging to a 'majority culture' who present a reluctance to interact voluntarily (beyond the most surface level) with those from 'minority' or international groups. Other cultural groups are in this way accorded the status of an 'invisible other'. In these data, language appeared to be a site where it was possible to express quite negative and normative views about other national groups. For example, some of the UK students expressed strong views about the requirement on international students' to adapt to the UK university 'way of doing things'. Language competence was presented as a responsibility of the international student and no personal responsibility was taken for communication by students expressing this view. One UG male UK student noted:

> If there's language difficulties then I don't think that's something we necessarily have to struggle against and make a conscious effort. Because you know, if they've come here that's on the understanding that they will be able to speak on the same level.

This reluctance to make an effort or take responsibility for interaction appears to fit with the idea of (passive xenophobia) and while there was very little evidence of this in this case study, the quote above shows vestiges of this view.

The complexity of student responses to language and communication issues in this case study remind us that language is not a neutral medium and that values and cultural meaning are carried by language. Voloshinov tells us that:

> Whenever a sign is present, ideology is present too. (Voloshinov, 1973: 10)

It appears from these data that it is often ideologies that cause the difficulties in communication and it may be conflicting ideologies that are the catalyst here for the movement into 'troublesome spaces'.

Disciplinary Cultures as a Source of Conflict

Academic disciplines can be framed as cultures, symbolic dimensions that embody traditions, myths, rituals, occupational beliefs and values that have grown up about universities and the life and work of academics (Harman, 1989). These academic cultures can be the bases for conflict as well as community. Becher and Trowler (2001) indicate that as well as demonstrating coherence, disciplinary communities may be seen as convergent in varying degrees. These cultures can show a sense of collectivity and mutual identity, or they can be divergent and ideologically fragmented (Becher & Trowler, 2001). In this case study, conflicts in group work appeared to centre for the most part upon disagreements over the direction of the subject and the differences in disciplines rather than over 'cultural' conflicts. For the students the emphasis seemed to be predominantly on difficulties that had arisen as a result of students having different disciplinary backgrounds within the School of Design. The struggles within the groups appeared to revolve around different opinions about ways of thinking and practising in the subject and also in 'how to get things done' in groups. This was particularly strong in the data collected from the area of Design where cultural misunderstandings seemed to occur because of Design cultures, not because of national cultures. A PG female Taiwanese Design student commented:

> There was a little bit of friction because ... everyone is professionally qualified in their field and everyone thinks that they are right so there is like a clash between opinions and things like that.

There were instances where different students' perceptions of Design concepts also caused conflicts. For example one group had chosen to produce a design that was based on the idea of 'Classical English style', but each student in the group from different national and disciplinary backgrounds had very different ideas about what constituted this. A PG female student said:

> I'll tell you what my experience of Classic English is, it's like a fireplace and those chandeliers and the long table … but the furniture designer, for example, the chair he came up with, I mean, that would go very well in a Star Trek spaceship. So we ended up changing that thing to 'Classic English with modern touches'!

The students perceived their particular discipline areas to be 'cultures' in their own right. One student identified the Design students as a 'culture' thus unifying the group with their discipline and pushing into the background the idea of national cultural differences. A PG female Indian student labelled her group mates by saying:

> I mean, because as Design students, that's one culture in itself isn't it?

In this disciplinary culture, diversity was perceived by the students to be an advantage. Students noted that the diversity in culture allowed them to see the concepts they were working on in Design in a different and new light. A PG female Indian student said:

> We have different approaches to how we tackle the same problems.

Indeed, because students appeared to perceive their disciplinary group as a culture in itself students reported feeling that they had experienced intercultural interaction in working with students in their group who were of the same nationality. Two Indian students who worked together had commented that they were 'culturally' very different from each other with one stating 'between Bombay and Delhi there's so much difference.' These students had noticed that sometimes working with other students from their own country represented a cross-cultural experience. Another Indian student noted:

> I worked with people from other cities in India and that itself is an experience because every city has something different about it and the people are different in every city in India.

From their description of their experiences, the students reported an improved understanding of each other as professionals and said that they had developed a respect for the knowledge and skill of others. A PG Indian Design student said:

> I mean after working with them [other nationalities in the group] I did find out that they are good designers … originally I didn't know whether she is a good designer or not, only after I worked with her.

The students in this case study felt that approaches to teaching and learning in their course had strongly influenced their ability to work effectively in intercultural groups. One UG male UK student noted:

> On this course it's easier maybe to talk to other people because of the way it works, sat around tables. It's more about group conversation.

Another UK student also noticed that the 'loose' and open-ended nature of the task they had been given made intercultural interaction easier. He said:

> It's been more about sharing ideas so it's going to be loose group work in a way. It's not going to be quite the same end so in that sense it's probably been dead easy.

Students' prior experience of working together in intercultural groups and extended opportunities to interact were also influential factors, with another UG female UK student saying:

> We've known each other for three years now so it's a continuation of a general conversation.

Students also framed their intercultural experience in the particular teaching and learning context as authentic with one student noting:

> It was the first time I had something 'real' to do at university.

People as a Source of Conflict and Transformation

'People are pretty argumentative …!'

Students talked about the conflicts between people who they worked with. Again these conflicts were not described as stemming from differences in culture but from the fact that people are simply difficult! One PG female Taiwanese student said:

> There was a difference of opinion about everything! People are pretty argumentative. It's not very easy to shake … that was a problem – to get people to be a little more flexible about things.

Students also described 'personality' as a perceived immovable object and there were reports of great personal variation from students in response to tasks set. However, it came through very strongly that this troublesome interaction with others was a crucial part of the transformative learning experience.

> Experience with others [is important] because we can get different experience from different areas ... so when we go back to our country we [have] more international information from each area.

Students noted the importance of experience particularly where it linked with the knowledge of the academic discipline. Experience with others was for the students 'what sticks in your mind' but it was not always perceived as enjoyable. However, students recognised the value of developing sensitivities to the way people are and the way they work.

> You can see personalities when you are working with a team. It's quite obvious when you look at people working with you. You can see the way that they are working with the team.

In the data there were many examples of students talking about what they had learned about themselves and others. There was reflection about how the experience of intercultural interaction had changed their sense of themselves. One UG male UK student noted:

> What do we learn? Patience for one thing!

International students were seen in some cases as holders of knowledge and the image of international students as de-skilled and dependent seemed to be absent. International students' knowledge was seen as an opportunity to get different perspectives on the subject. Particularly in Design the subject itself was again relevant as students believed that to a certain extent Design was 'about tastes' and so it is advantageous to your subject knowledge to know something about a wide range of tastes in different contexts.

Finally, students noted that it was the experience of conflict and tensions and the transition through troublesome spaces with others that began to engender respect and real friendships. A PG female Indian student said:

> We really got, like angry with each other. But it worked out fine in the end and we are very good friends now because we know, you know? Now we have gone through all the things ... if we hadn't done that then I don't think we would be good friends now.

Conclusions

Savin-Baden suggests that we live with 'provisional identities' and notes that

> our identities are constantly changing and ... do not always sit easily with one another, therefore collision and uncertainty result in disquietude and a sense of fragmentation. (Savin-Baden, 2008: 137)

Again, this uncertainty and collision is not to be framed as a negative thing. On the contrary it is these states where we embrace dilemma and its accompanying risk that lead us to 'greater self-understanding and a means of moving forward' (Savin-Baden, 2008: 138). Furthermore, the idea of the 'third space' encompasses the suggestion that there are 'particular discursive spaces ... in which alternative and competing discourses and positioning transform conflict and difference into rich zones of collaboration and learning' (Gutierrez *et al.*, 1999: 286–287; Savin-Baden, 2008: 139).

It is suggested here that these spaces of risk, conflict and uncertainty are present in intercultural interaction as indicated in this case study. The challenge and contestation in the troublesome space provided by intercultural group work is a good thing; it engages learners and gets them to understand themselves, each other and their subject. Teaching, learning and assessment approaches need to cultivate these sorts of space or students may remain in the 'easy' spaces. One UG male UK Design student in this case study notes:

> It's just to do with laziness. If you have an easier way why would you want to take the harder way?

It is important to note the potential influence of the teaching, learning and assessment context of this case study. The research sites in Design were developing Assessment for Learning approaches that emphasise authenticity, challenge, collaborative learning and peer review. Students were accustomed to assessed group work tasks and these factors may have exerted an influence on developing students' positive perceptions of intercultural group work. Carroll and Li (2008) found evidence of negative student attitudes to intercultural group work where assessment tasks involved high stakes. In their study the assessment task was not designed to value or draw upon the varied skills and experiences of the group and all marks were based on the final product. This is in contrast to AfL approaches where incremental tasks and low stakes assessment environments are emphasised. This suggests that the wider teaching, learning and assessment context could have an impact on the development of challenging learning spaces where intercultural learning can take place. Further research in this area would be interesting.

Meyer and Land (2005) suggest that in order for students to move on from 'stuckness' and disjunction beyond 'liminal' stages, higher education programmes, particularly at undergraduate levels, need to have 'fluid' spaces where students are allowed to visit and revisit new knowledge. The data presented in this chapter are taken from learning contexts where students were allowed extended opportunities to experience intercultural interaction within challenging learning and assessment tasks. Not all learning environments in higher education allow for this. Mann (2008) suggests that if HE is to continue to develop creative and transformative learning (as opposed to alienating learning experiences) we need to provide spaces and opportunities and may have to rethink curricula, letting go of the idea that acquisition of 'knowledge commodities' is the aim of university learning. It may be necessary to make space in curricula by disengaging with 'content'. Mann notes:

> Challenging the assumption that university learning is equivalent to the acquisition of knowledge commodities and credentials, and working with students to develop ways of thinking, being and acting that can productively engage with the crises that face modern society requires a different organisation of time and space within the curriculum. (Mann, 2008: 94)

These spaces and new curricula will allow for the development of students' perceptions of interculturality as a positive and transformative part of their university learning.

References

Becher, T. and Trowler, P.R. (2001) *Academic Tribes and Territories: Intellectual Enquiry and the Cultures of Disciplines* (2nd edn). Buckingham: Open University Press/ SRHE.

Bohemia, E., Harman, K. and Lauche, K. (2009) *The Global Studio*. Amsterdam: IOS Press BV.

Boud, D. and Falchikov, N. (2006) Aligning assessment with long-term learning. *Assessment and Evaluation in Higher Education* 31, 399–413.

Carroll, J. and Li, R. (2008) Assessed group work in culturally diverse groups: Is normative guidance useful in addressing students' worries about grades? Conference paper presented at Oxford Brookes University: Using informal and formal curricula to improve interaction between international and home students. June 2008.

Coupland, N. (2001) Introduction: Sociolinguistic theory and social theory. In N. Coupland, S. Sarangi and C.N. Candlin (eds) *Sociolinguistics and Social Theory* (pp. 1–26). Essex: Pearson Education.

Gumperz, J.J. (1982) *Discourse Strategies*. Cambridge: Cambridge University Press.

Gutierrez, K., Baquedano-Lopez, P. and Tejeda, C. (1999) Rethinking diversity: Hybridity and hybrid language practices in the third space. *Mind, Culture and Activity, an International Journal* 6, 286–303.

Harman, K.M. (1989) Culture and conflict in academic organisation: Symbolic aspects of university worlds. *Journal of Educational Administration* 27, 30–52.

Kamberelis, G. and Dimitriadis, G. (2005) Focus groups: Strategic articulations of pedagogy, politics and inquiry. In N. Denzin and Y.S. Lincoln (eds) *The Handbook of Qualitative Research* (3rd edn) (pp. 887–907). Thousand Oaks, CA: Sage.

Mann, S.J. (2008) *Study, Power and the University*. Maidenhead: Open University Press/SRHE.

Martin, J. and Nakayama, T. (2000) *Intercultural Communication in Contexts* (2nd edn). Mountain View, CA: Mayfield.

McDowell, L., Sambell, K., Bazin, V., Penlington, R., Wakelin, D., Wickes, H. and Smailes, J. (2005) Assessment for learning: Current practice exemplars from the Centre for Excellence in Teaching and Learning. *Northumbria University Red Guide*, Paper 22.

Meyer, E.F. and Land, R. (2005) Threshold concepts and troublesome knowledge: Epistemological considerations and a teaching and learning framework for teaching and learning. *Higher Education* 9, 373–388.

Milroy, L. (1987) *Language and Social Networks* (2nd edn). Oxford: Blackwell.

Montgomery, C. (2009) A decade of internationalisation: Has it influenced students' views of cross-cultural group work at university? *Journal of Studies in International Education* 13, 256–270.

Montgomery, C. (2010) *Understanding the International Student Experience*. Basingstoke: Palgrave MacMillan.

Peacock, N. and Harrison, N. (2009) It's so much easier to go with what's easy: Mindfulness and the discourse between home and international students in the United Kingdom. *Journal of Studies in International Education* 13, 487–508.

Perkins, D. (1999) The many faces of constructivism. *Educational Leadership* 57, 6–11.

Perkins, D. (2006) Constructivism and troublesome knowledge. In J.H.F. Meyer and R. Land (eds) *Overcoming Barriers to Student Understanding: Threshold Concepts and Troublesome Knowledge* (pp. 33–47). London: Routledge.

Perret-Clermont, A. (2009) Introduction. In M. Cesar and K. Kumpulainen (eds) *Social Interactions in Multicultural Settings* (pp. 1–12). Rotterdam: Sense Publishers.

Pierce, A. (2003) What does it mean to live in-between? Paper presented at the *4th Annual IALIC Conference*, Lancaster University, 16 December 2003.

Savin-Baden, M. (2008) *Learning Spaces: Creating Opportunities for Knowledge Creation in Academic Life*. Maidenhead: Open University Press.

Volet, S.E. and Ang, G. (1998) Culturally mixed groups on International Campuses: An opportunity for inter-cultural learning. *Higher Education Research and Development* 17, 5–23.

Voloshinov, V. (1973) *Marxism and the Philosophy of Language* (M. Ladislav and I.R. Titunik, trans). New York, NY: Seminar Press.

Chapter 5
Internationalising the University: Enabling Selves-in-the-World

D. KILLICK

Introduction

> The primary creators of the global world are people, their value systems, and the means they employ to achieve their goals. (Group of Lisbon, 1995: 14)

> Students today live in a global society – a society where they cannot ignore global interdependence and global inequalities. How are today's students going to understand and respond to the freedoms, problems and responsibilities they are inheriting? How are today's students going to find their individual roles in a global society? And where do they start? (Bourn, 2010: 18)

In a context in which universities are being increasingly driven into the business of competing within global markets and responding to the pressures to produce 'employable' graduates to feed the needs of industry, it is worth remembering that as the new generation, it is also these same graduates, their value systems and their capabilities, who will shape the future of our 'global world'. As individuals, they are at the 'crossroads' of their lives; as a generation, they are surrounded by breathtaking change, global-scale challenges and a lack of moral or ethical fixity. The fact that this volume speaks to the implications of multicultural universities dominated by the growing hegemony of the English language precisely situates higher education itself as similarly challenged. My concern here is to ask what role can and should the international university play in helping our students find their way in their world? Regardless of the language of instruction, this chapter presents a view of the contemporary, multinational and multi-cultural university as a temporary home for students on their journey of 'becoming', and suggests that it is the rightful responsibility of the university to offer a curriculum through which they may come to identify themselves as global citizens. This casts higher education as a force for individual agency, within a broad ethic of global social justice, rather than as a force for 'domestication' (Freire, 1970, 1972). Internationalisation, then, is not 'simply' a matter of presenting an English language curriculum, or of developing inclusive pedagogies. It is a process through which universities can take their own place as responsible institutions in a globalising world, realisable in part through the cultural diversity (see also Chapters 4, 9, 10 and 12) which inhabits them. To illustrate how a university might address such a responsibility, I include a short case study of a curriculum review process in one British university.

A Global Context

Zygmunt Bauman's concept of liquid modernity (Bauman, 1987, 2005) captures a sense of the turbulent flows (Bryant, 2007) that have replaced the more fixed and fixing certainties of contemporary life. The multilingual, 'international' university is an emerging site of global flow in which Appadurai's – *scapes* (Appadurai, 1997, 2006/1966), the 'imagined worlds' we inhabit and which mould our understanding of our selves, are given shape. The global economic turmoil which shook the world in 2008 highlighted in particular the impacts of financescapes (the movement of global capital – 'megamonies through national turnstiles at blinding speed' (Appadurai, 2006/1966: 183). However, in the context of this chapter I am concerned particularly with ethnoscapes (the people who inhabit our lifeworlds). Here the issue is not essentially that between our parents' and our children's generations the world population will have soared from two billion to nine billion, nor is it 'simply' that many more of those nine billion aspire to the standards of consumption that the 'Western' world has enjoyed for so long – with all the consequences of inequitable access to inadequate resources, diaspora flows, ideological conflict and further environmental degradation. What Appadurai alerts us to is that across those nine billion individuals, the lifeworld is experienced in radically different perspective. Perhaps that has always been the case, but the new global media and communications technologies, massive shifts in world political and economic power, and greater personal contact with the 'other' are leaving us with no choice but to hear the 'voices talking back to the West' (Featherstone, 1995: 10). Global inequalities may always have been stark, but hitherto they have been dim shadows to any in the West who chose to keep them so; today, global tourists and global vagabonds (Bauman, 1996, 1998) rub shoulders in their millions everyday – and personal identities are called into question at each encounter.

In such a context, the notion of the ethnoscape as a site of individual challenge can be contextualised through reflecting upon the cumulative impact upon the self of:

- Significantly greater direct contact with the 'other' – for example, through international tourism, multinational work teams, migrant workers – and student mobility.
- Significantly greater indirect contact with the 'other' – for example, through internationally based customer services (call centres), and multinational company HR policies and practices.
- Significantly greater virtual contact with the 'other' – for example, participation in virtual worlds and global social networks.
- Significantly greater intellectual and affective exposure to the 'other' – for example, through media focus on and exploitation of 'exotic' cultures, high-profile international aid appeals and events, and the growth in 'world-culture' industries.

And significantly for this volume, the international university is alive with the opportunities and threats created by all of these; a global space housing a temporary diaspora in search of identities, sureties and a location in the world.

As we rub real and virtual shoulders each day, and multiple socio-cultural existences jostle at the borders of our lifeworld, it becomes increasingly difficult to consider ourselves ethically as anything other than co-habitants of a single planet; but simultaneously it is increasingly difficult to anchor ourselves in such a way that we can make sense of what such a position might mean and of how we may make our way within it. Bauman argues that postmodern 'life strategies' are fragmentary forces, leaving human connection distant and vague, and leading us to 'cast the Other primarily as the object of aesthetic, not moral, evaluation; as a matter of taste, not responsibility' (Bauman, 1996: 33). But this cannot be an adequate human response. If the connectivities established across the scapes of liquid modernity are to bring anything to our own identity within humanity, the globalising world leaves us with no option but to situate ourselves *among* not *apart from* global others.

Framing this in terms of *being* and *becoming*, that essence of our humanity which is 'capable of wondering about its own existence and inquiring into its own being' (van Manen, 1990: 173) is captured in Heidegger's notion of *Dasein* (Heidegger, 1998/1962), within which, '[b]eing is not just there, but is *in* there' (Barnett, 2007: 27). Today, this must come to mean a self situated *in* a *global* 'there'. *Dasein* is 'determined by the world and the horizon in which we are placed' (Weber-Bosley, 2010: 58). The horizons pushing strongly at the lifeworld today are global, and we have no choice but to find ways to enable our selves to accommodate them. In the context of this chapter, this broad notion of being and becoming is framed specifically around the self-as-citizen, requiring us 'to expand our concept of citizen identity to include global identity' (Kubow *et al.*, 2000: 132). I suggest that this requires us to incorporate 'global citizen' identity within our self-identity, and universities as temporary homes are uniquely placed to enable students in this process.

A Global Citizen

There is significant contestation surrounding the term 'global citizen'. Some argue that the absence of an established set of international institutions mirroring those to be found within the nation-state, through which citizen responsibilities can be enacted and citizen rights protected, means there can be no such 'being' (Anker, 2002). One reason to question this view today is the very apparent diminishing ability of the nation-state itself to perform either of those primary functions (Delanty, 2000; Isin & Wood, 1999; Olssen, 2006/2004). At one level, this is a 'reality' deriving from the 'deterritorialisation' (Dower, 2003) of capital, of the means of production, of the movement of labour and so on. More relevant here, though, is Bourdieu's suggestion that a nation is only as real as the stories we tell and believe of it, 'Once [we] cease to believe in it … its identity melts into air' (Webb *et al.*, 2002: 90). At that moment, perhaps the moment we are in today, our own identities are in danger of also beginning to dissolve into the soup of the postmodernists. Alternatively, we may come to 'imagine' ourselves as *being* within a more global community; the horizons of our lifeworld expanded, and did not melt away. We have increasingly few options but to reject the notion that citizenship can only be enacted in contexts of nation-states, or that global citizenship cannot operate until we have in place global structures of law and governance, and embrace instead the *possibility* of reclaiming individual agency among the turbulence.

Dower proposes that global citizenship involves 'some kind of self-identification as a global citizen' (Dower, 2003: 11). Dower and Williams (2002) suggest it to be intrinsically dependent upon subscribing to a global ethic. Colby *et al.* propose that responsible global citizenship requires us to:

> ... consider questions of a greater or common good, consider the impor-
> tance of values or long-term goals beyond our narrow self-interest, and
> take personal responsibility for our commitments and actions. (Colby
> *et al.*, 2007: 23)

Taking these perspectives, we can propose global citizenship to be *principally* a matter of how I identify myself, rather than how I am identified through the institutions and systems of politics, law, economics and governance that make up the current, mutable configuration of nation states. Such self-identification is concerned with an ethical stance based on a recognition that we all occupy a shared planet and have a shared responsibility for its well-being and our 'own' – where 'own' encompasses both local and global 'others'. Nussbaum seems to suggest that humanity is at least half way capable of such a positioning:

> Despite the evident differences in the specific cultural shaping of the
> grounding experiences, we do recognize the experiences of other
> people in other cultures as similar to our own. We do converse with
> them about matters of deep importance, understand them, allow
> ourselves to be moved by them. (Nussbaum, 1993: 261)

But against this undoubted truth is also the more common reality of adversarial stances to differing ontologies at the macro level, and the simple fact that we each seem regularly capable of *not* recognizing or allowing ourselves to be moved by inhumanities which we would not tolerate against the 'local' when they are enacted upon the global 'other'. In terms of intercultural adaptation theory, what we are proposing finds echoes in the counter-intuitive shift from ethnocentricism to ethnorelativism (Bennett, 1993). To be an ethnorelativist is to be other than where most of us start from. And, crucially, it is an aspect of identity, a way of *being*, not just a way of seeing.

Developing and sustaining such an identity requires personal qualities such as self-confidence, curiosity, the ability to tolerate uncertainty and ambiguity, openness to change. Learning of this kind demands a strength 'to tolerate the vulnerability that openness brings' (Illeris, 2002: 113). Put differently, agency within an enlarged, 'global' lifeworld is dependent upon enhancing our attributes for engagement, some of which are not easily welcomed in our lifeworld. Such difficult learning requires, *from the first*, a will to become the person I am not yet. Only when we have situated ourselves among the global others who flow along the horizons of the lifeworld will we find the inclination to act. Therefore, I suggest a notion of global citizenship which encompasses two dimensions of *Dasein* – being and becoming in the context of a global place:

(1) How I view my relationship to the global other – my sense of *self-in-the-world*.
(2) How I behave within that relationship – the capabilities I have to *act-in-the-world*.

I shall return to these when we come to look at cross-cultural capability and global perspectives as aspirations for a global citizenship curriculum within the international university. As a site of global flow, the international, multicultural university has the opportunity to offer a temporary home in which self-identification as a global citizen (*self-in-the-world*) along with enabling attributes (*act-in-the-world*) can take form. This, though, requires something akin to Ron Barnett's (2007: 9) call for an 'ontological turn' in the current identification of the university itself.

An International University

In this volume, Montgomery speaks of the 'troublesome space' of 21st-century higher education as a site of struggle through which transformative learning can be enabled. The 'international' university can be conceptualised as one inhabited by multiple cultures and languages, where cross-cultural spaces, events, contestations and re-identifications are increasingly realised in *English as a lingua franca* (see also Chapter 1 of this volume, as well as discussions of lingua franca interaction in Chapters 3, 5, 9 and 10). There are significant differences in cultural norms and practices and in the related issues of power between those institutions where English is a foreign language for all and those where it is only foreign to a small percentage (as in the United Kingdom). However, *in either case*, 'university' is a time and a space in which students may be enabled to gain the confidence to recognise themselves in the world, to establish the curiosity to seek greater understanding of the others in that world and to build at least some of the capabilities that will help them to act therein. Baxter Magolda's (2001) study of young people passing through university and into lives as young adults identified this as a period of transition from the earlier stages of *following external formulas* through *the crossroads*, when we realise the need to look inwards for our own identification, and on into *becoming the author to one's own life*. From hearing the multiple stories of her participants over many years, she notes:

> the interviews revealed the central role internal self-definition plays in self-authorship. Internal self-definition is crucial to balancing

external and internal forces and relating to others. (Baxter Magolda, 2001: xvii)

While Sercombe's chapter in this volume illustrates the tenacity of personal and social identity, it also points out the role of environment and our interactions with others in the process of identity (re)formation. A university alive with multiple nationalities and a colourful spectrum of 'otherness' (cultures, ethnicities, genders, sexualities and ages), all able to communicate through the common language of English *and* the common language of their disciplines, offers a very rich site for the discovery of a more 'global' self. The university as a potential home for anchoring myself and exploring my discipline in the 'supercomplex' world of these others has more hope within it, I would suggest, than Barnett's 'constellation of fragility' (Barnett, 2000: 63), offering only *uncertainty, unpredictability, challengeability* and *contestability*. The capabilities to deal with these are necessary but insufficient for securing identities amidst turbulence and locating the self as one alongside global others.

As discussed in much of the literature on internationalisation at home (Crowther *et al.*, 2000; Nilsson, 2003; see also Chapters 1, 2, 6 and 7 in this volume), the international, multicultural university has the opportunity to foster environments and experiences in which *all* students might better recognise themselves in a global context, for example:

- As potential sites of intercultural and cross-cultural student encounter – notwithstanding the substantial amount of research to indicate that this barely happens (Volet & Ang, 1998).
- As organisers of international exchanges, placements and volunteering opportunities – though we know how lamentably few students participate globally in such opportunities, and how these percentages are even smaller in the United Kingdom than in most of Europe.
- As employers and temporary importers of academic staff – though exposure of students to such is highly differentiated, and typically a matter of happenstance within a particular department at a particular time.
- Through their own policies and practices relating to inclusive behaviour, ethical purchasing, sustainable business practices and so forth.

If committed to the process of internationalisation, institutions will attend to these and other opportunities with a view to becoming a model of a globally responsible and responsive institution. However, as our undergraduate students journey through their temporary homes, it is the curriculum that most significantly shapes their engagement with the university; and it is through our role as sites of learning that we should be most focused on helping students locate their 'selves' and develop their capabilities for *being* and *becoming* in the rapidly evolving worlds of the 21st century.

Bourn argues for curriculum with a 'strong values base of social justice' (Bourn, 2010: 27). In line with the proposals I am making in this chapter, I have elsewhere argued for the development of global citizenship 'values' which will incline students 'to globally responsible, informed and ethical actions in their personal and their professional lives' (Killick, 2008: 52). Rather than shy away from values education, universities of the 21st century have a responsibility of 'not simply sharing values with the rest of society but also helping to shape society' (Robinson & Katulushi, 2005: 256). As some may be feeling uncomfortable with a value-based higher education, it deserves a little further explication. Collins very usefully defends accusations that a global perspectives approach is uniquely 'values-laden' by setting it against its opposite:

> A global perspective approach is ... no more prescriptive than a 'traditional' approach which channels its students, like it or not, through a course that takes no account of these global realities. It refutes the notion that any academic activity is value free, and invites academics to explore the sometimes hidden values and exclusiveness that underpin their practice. (Collins, 2005: 224)

More broadly, Arthur notes:

> Higher education has ... a set of values and a 'hidden curriculum' that conveys moral messages to students and influences their character ... Universities through their mission statements, structure and cultural life exercise an influence on their students' character formation. (Arthur, 2005: 21)

As simple examples of values permeating our everyday academic practice, consider plagiarism and the protocols for evidencing research ethics. Plagiarism is a complex ethical issue related to intellectual rights on the one hand and what we see as scholarly 'honesty' on the other, while even rudimentary research ethics are tied to the 'rights' of a subject to be consulted and informed about how they are being used and interpreted by another. Of relevance to the international student body, Klitgård's chapter in this book discusses issues of plagiarism in the light of the processes of learning academic writing for non-native English students. A further example raised by Annette and McLaughlin (2005: 82) relates to the ethic of social justice which surrounds the current debates on equitable university access and funding; while institutions and individuals may publicly lament the pressures which widening participation policy places on both, we hear few voices objecting the *values* which underpin the principle of more equitable access. The same authors go on to summarise their perspective that, whatever our view on the contested notion of universities directly engaging in the 'making of citizens', such making 'is nevertheless taking place' through a range of what most would consider ordinary and expected activities and objectives (Annette & McLaughlin, 2005: 91). As they go on to discuss, those who deny the legitimacy of making such work explicit might want to consider the ethics of leaving it undisclosed. In all these examples, universities adopt a particular ethical standpoint, and in doing so promote one set of values over others.

Within the United Kingdom, Crick has argued for universities playing a more active role in the development of citizenship:

> Universities are part of society and … should be playing a major role in the wider objectives of creating a citizenship culture. (Crick, 2000: 145)

Internationally, UNESCO's World Declaration on Higher Education for the 21st century has several clauses that are clearly aimed at the promulgation of values. Directly related to the subject of this chapter are two extracted from Article Six (original bold):

> (b) Higher education should **reinforce its role of service to society**, especially its activities aimed at eliminating poverty, intolerance, violence, illiteracy, hunger, environmental degradation and disease, mainly through an **interdisciplinary and transdisciplinary approach** in the analysis of problems and issues.
>
> (d) Ultimately, higher education should aim at the creation of a new society – non-violent and non-exploitative – consisting of highly cultivated, motivated and integrated individuals, inspired by love for humanity and guided by wisdom.
>
> (UNESCO, 1998: 5 and 6)

In summary, values permeate our curriculum and our campuses; as such, they form part of the context that informs and influences those journeying through. The question, then, becomes not *whether* but *which* values we should seek to model and promote (Case, 1993: 320). And, perhaps, we do not have the luxury of time to debate this issue for too long before we act:

▷ In times of increased global interdependence, producing interculturally competent citizens who can engage in informed, ethical decision-making when confronted with problems that involve a diversity of perspectives is becoming an urgent educational priority. (King & Magolda, 2005: 571)

Learning

The affective cognitive dualism of much learning theory is problematic (Illeris, 2002; Jarvis, 2006). Nonetheless, it can be helpful in highlighting that there is more to the whole business of personal change than the acquisition of new *knowledge*. In the 'tension field' of Illeris' three-dimensional model of learning (Illeris, 2002: 17), the third dimension is the 'social' – echoing the constructivist site in which such capacity change is enabled. Lave and Wenger (1998) speak to 'communities of practice' as sites of learning, and I suggest that we have the opportunity and the responsibility to stimulate these as 'international' and 'multi-cultural' communities in the milieu of the international university.

Learning that can facilitate individual identity development from the parochial to the global, the ethnocentric to the ethnorelative, suggests quite fundamental personal change. Conceptualised in classical learning theory (Piaget, 1972, 1977) as an 'accommodative' shift rather than an 'assimilative' incorporation into existing mental schemes (on this, see also Chapter 12). Such shifts are suggested to be stimulated by disorientation or dilemmas, as developed schemes reveal themselves incapable of finding 'fit' with how the lifeworld presents itself. Accommodations of this kind are modelled on the cognitive level (particularly) in Jack Mezirow's construct of transformative learning (Mezirow, 1991, 2000; Mezirow & Associates, 2000), while within a more holistic paradigm, Carl Rogers (Rogers, 1961) offers a model of 'significant learning':

Transformative learning refers to the process by which we transform our taken-for-granted frames of reference (meaning perspectives, habits of mind, mind-sets) to make them more inclusive, discriminating, open, emotionally capable of change, and reflective.... (Mezirow, 2000: 7–8)

[Significant learning] is learning which makes a difference – in the individual's behaviour, in the course of action he chooses in the future, in his attitudes and in his personality. It is pervasive learning which is not just an accretion of knowledge, but which interpenetrates with every portion of his existence. (Rogers, 1961: 280)

[From these standpoints, university curriculum development, aiming for significant shifts to our sense of *self-in-the-world* to foster the willingness and the capabilities for global agency, needs to enable student engagement across cognitive, affective and social learning dimensions. To achieve 'accommodative' learning will require the international university to offer experiential, engaging and often disorienting encounters with the self and the other. This brings in the highly significant question of appropriate and effective pedagogy as much as curriculum content, but it is the curriculum itself that I wish to deal with here.

There can be many approaches to the way we adapt or transform our curricula to respond to the new demands of the globalising world. The next section of this chapter presents just one by way of a case study. It is not intended as a blueprint for others, and has not yet, by any means, achieved its ambitious aims.

Internationalisation: Cross-Cultural Capability and Global Perspectives in the Curriculum

With the notions of the global citizen, the international university and transformative learning presented so far, we can consider more concretely, what capabilities might contribute to the capacity to act upon the choices which the student-as-global citizen, might make. I will take just two examples from the substantial literature setting out features of both national citizenship and global citizenship by way of leading into the concepts of cross-cultural capability and global perspectives which have underpinned a curriculum review project at one British university.

Of the several abilities examined through the Delphe method employing a 'prestigious, multinational panel of experts' (Kurth-Scai *et al.*, 2000: 93) researched by Karsten *et al.*, the three most important for citizens of the 21st century in which there was agreement between both Eastern and Western panellists were the abilities to:

• Look at and approach problems as a member of a global society.
• Work with others in a cooperative way and to take responsibility for one's roles/duties within society.
• Understand, accept, appreciate and tolerate cultural differences.
(Adapted from Karsten *et al.*, 2000: 113)

The personal dimension within Kubow's model of multidimensional citizenship calls for us to enhance:

* Our capacity to think critically and systemically.
* Our understanding of and sensitivity to issues of cultural difference.
* Our repertoire of responsible, cooperative and non-violent conflict resolution and problem-solving.

(Adapted from Kubow *et al.*, 2000: 134)

A project was initiated in 2004 to review all curricula across Leeds Metropolitan University against a set of guidelines on cross-cultural capability and global perspectives (later revised, see Killick, 2006). In brief, following incorporation into the Corporate Plan and subsequently the Assessment, Learning and Teaching Strategy, course teams were given a four-year period in which to review their provision against the guidelines document. To facilitate the process, the guidelines included a set of key questions relating to both knowledge and experience gained through participation in a programme of study. The process and its rationale are documented in full elsewhere (Jones & Killick, 2007). Table 5.1 summarises key attributes of cross-cultural capability and global perspectives delineated as 'awareness and understanding' and 'abilities'. I am suggesting that collectively these may be considered as the attributes contributing to a global citizen's abilities to *act-in-the-world*. The underpinning sense of *self-in-the-world* is not amenable to being 'taught' and much less to being assessed. It is, though, envisaged that coming to *know* the other, to *experience* her or his presence in my lifeworld, to see my professional (disciplinary) home as a home shared with global others, to *critique* accepted knowledge and practice in the other's perspective, will establish the global other in my lifeworld, and so offer the global as a familiar context for the processes of *self authoring* – that is *being* and *becoming*.

The first ability listed under cross-cultural capability (the ability to communicate effectively across cultures), links directly to intercultural communicative competence. The role which languages have to play within this field is given variable weighting in the literature, with some placing it as central (Byram, 1997, 2006; Matsumoto, 2001), while others are more cautious (Bennett, 2008; Ward, 2001). Set within a UK context in which many of the home student population are only marginally competent in a second language, it is unrealistic (and distracting) to set this down as a necessary attribute. It is also helpful to consider second language proficiency outside of both cross-cultural capability and global perspectives since, in itself, it is no guarantee of inter/cross-cultural communicative

Table 5.1 Cross-cultural capability and global perspectives: Curriculum goals for global citizenship *acting-in-the-world*

	Awareness and understanding	*Abilities*
Cross-cultural capability	An awareness of self in relation to the 'other'. An understanding of one's subject area and professional practice that includes perspectives which derive from other cultures, philosophies, religions and nations.	The ability to communicate effectively across cultures. The ability to apply intercultural awareness, skills and perspectives to one's personal life and to one's professional life. The confidence to challenge one's own values, and the values of others responsibly and ethically.
Global perspectives	An awareness of the relationship between local actions and global consequences (and therefore, how my actions relate to the broader world). An awareness of how global issues relate to one's discipline (and therefore, how my professional self belongs within a global frame). An awareness of how one's discipline may be applied in global contexts.	The ability to reflect upon major global issues (e.g. global warming, world trade, etc.) from multiple perspectives. The ability to critique global issues from a standpoint of social justice.

competence (Jones, 2008: 45), and may in fact mask more significant blocks to cross-cultural capability such as ethnocentrism and insensitivity to alterity. Cross-cultural capability also differs from intercultural communicative competence in two other important ways. First, it is a construct specifically set out for higher education, and as such locates capability within the context of discipline areas and future professional practice. Second, it is based upon an ethical stance in which the norms and values of others are critiqued from a position of respect. Although developed in a much different context and to capture a broader range of 'functionings', it also seems to me now that Sen's (1999) notion of capability as a measure of (comparative global) freedom can enrich the notion of cross-cultural capability as presented here:

> Having greater freedom to do things one has reason to value is (1) significant in itself for the person's overall freedom, and (2) important in fostering the person's opportunity to have valuable outcomes. (Sen, 1999: 18)

When I identify my *self-in-the-world* as one who belongs with the global other, cross-cultural capability accounts for much of that which can offer the freedoms to achieve those things which I, the global citizen, have good 'reason to value'.

The construct of global perspectives is, 'increasingly being regarded as providing the ethical underpinning and values-based ethos for a focus on cross-cultural capability' (Caruana & Spurling, 2007: 27). Specifically, focus on global perspectives seeks to build empathy with the global other through which my sense of *self-in-the-world* may be better envisioned. Much useful work on global perspectives in higher education has been undertaken by the Development Educational Association (DEA), with publications looking at students, curriculum and senior management (Bourn *et al.*, 2006; McKenzie *et al.*, 2003; Shiel & McKenzie, 2008). Shiel proposes that global perspectives, 'alerts students to how their experiences are connected to the experiences of people throughout the world' (Shiel, 2006: 18).

Cross-cultural capability and global perspectives, then, formed the underpinning constructs for an institution-wide curriculum review process, with a notion of graduates as global citizens at its core. To illustrate the challenge of the review process to course review teams, I quote four examples of key questions posed in the review guidelines:

- How are students given the opportunity to analyse and recognise their own tacit knowledge and the influence of their experiences and cultural identity?
- How does the course enable other knowledge/perspectives to be recognised and valued?
- How does the course encourage students to be curious beyond their own cultural boundaries?
- How is a student from this course prepared to interact with, benefit from, contribute to diversity in the world beyond the University? (Killick, 2006: 9–15)

A few responses from review teams serve to illustrate how aspects of provision are seeking to help students develop their sense of *self-in-the-world* and the capabilities to *act-in-the-world:*

From film production

From the induction course onwards, all students are asked to share their experience and point of view on the world. They tell their back-stories[1] and international students' experiences are compared to those of UK students.

From design

Exploring and understanding alternative ethics and value systems is closely related to pursuing an informed response to a design project. This promotes healthy debate in various parts of the course curriculum and in turn helps students develop a rounded personal design philosophy, responsive to contemporary society.

From social sciences

Specifically, the aim of the programme is to enable students to:

- Accept the culture and values of others.
- Respect different views and perspectives on shared issues.
- Be capable of rational and courteous challenge to views and values.
- Be capable of rational and courteous argument to support their own views and values.

From professional training and development

Students are required to critique predominant perspectives from their own personal perspective and from the perspectives of others.

From business

The scheme encourages students to analyse their own values and ethics, understanding those of others and debating issues that arise effectively and peacefully.

From civil engineering

The learning outcomes require students to explore beyond their own social or cultural parameters.

It would have been naive to imagine that a single process such as this could radically change the culture of an institution and transform its practice. However, it has strengthened the global dimension within the university, and encouraged some areas to open up the curriculum to transformation. It has raised the 'status' of our multi-cultural and multi-national student body, enhancing their role within the university home. As this initial review process has drawn to an end, the University's latest Internationalisation Strategy (Leeds Metropolitan University, 2008) commits the whole institution to further curriculum development. Two specific objectives in that Strategy are to conduct an 'iterative review of all pro-grammes for Cross-Cultural-Capability and Global Perspectives' and to 'ensure that global perspectives and skills are assessed across all facul-ties'. As this curriculum internationalisation work is taken forward, I hope we may move closer to realising a model of the international university as a home in which we can enable self-identity and capability development commensurate with global citizenship as individual agency.

Summary and Conclusion

I have proposed that a particular dimension of our 'supercomplex' 'liquid' world is the challenge posed to our sense of self by the increased and increasing interactions with the 'ethnoscapes' of the global 'other'. Such interactions should cause us all to give serious consideration to our relation-ship with those others. This reflects the notion of the global citizen as a marker of personal identity (our sense of *self-in-the-world*) rather than politi-cal status. In turn, this begs questions about the capabilities of the respon-sible global citizen, including those which enable us to *act-in-the-world*.

As a temporary home, a location of global flow, a site of learning and of diverse communities of disciplinary practice, the international university has a legitimate responsibility to ensure that the values it promotes and the capabilities it helps develop are commensurate with ethical being and acting in a globalising world. To attempt a 'neutral' value-free stance, to leave our students at sea in the milieu of their 'international' university and of the globalising world in which it sits, risks producing a disempow-ered generation, able only to act out the roles of tourist and vagabond:

> Unless students find themselves a role to play, there is a risk of disen-franchisement or of disillusionment: that they are aware of global issues but do nothing about them. (Lamb *et al.*, 2007; cited in Bourn, 2010)

Transformative and significant learning theories provide models for the kind of 'accommodative' learning needed to bring about self-identification and the willingness to *be* a global citizen. Through reference to an institution-wide curriculum review project, I have briefly illustrated how one university has sought to initiate curriculum internationalisation as a process to help its graduates author themselves in the context of a lifeworld where the global other is more intimately present.

Higher education has always played a role in helping people dis-cover and transform their identities. On a liquid, turbulent, hot, flat and crowded planet (Friedman, 2008), in which lifeworlds may be set adrift and identities have to shape themselves in uncertain futures, I suggest that the temporary home of the 'international' university can help us all locate our selves *in* a global place, and explore the capabilities that may enable us to act more effectively while we are here.

Notes

1. 'Backstory' is used to denote those significant biographical events that have brought the students to where they are now. In the terminology of this chapter, a backstory would be my personal history as present in my lifeworld at a given point.

References

Anker, C.V.D. (2002) Global justice, global institutions and global citizenship. In N. Dower and J. Williams (eds) *Global Citizenship: A Critical Reader* (pp. 158–168). Edinburgh: Edinburgh University Press.

Annette, J. and Mclaughlin, T. (2005) Citizenship and higher education in the UK. In J. Arthur (ed.) *Citizenship and Higher Education: The Role of Universities in Communities and Society* (pp. 75–95). Abingdon: Routledge Falmer.

Appadurai, A. (1997) *Modernity at Large,* Minnesota, MN: University of Minnesota Press.

Appadurai, A. (2006/1966) Disjuncture and difference in the global cultural economy. In H. Lauder, P. Brown, J-A. Dillabough and A.H. Halsey (eds) *Education, Globalisation and Social Change* (pp. 179–188). Oxford: Oxford University Press.

Arthur, J. (2005) Student character in the British university. In J. Arthur (ed.) *Citizenship and Higher Education: The Role of Universities in Communities and Society* (pp. 8–32). Abingdon: Routledge Falmer.

Barnett, R. (2000) *Realizing the University in an Age of Supercomplexity.* Buckingham: Society for Research into Higher Education and Open University Press.

Barnett, R. (2007) *A Will to Learn.* Maidenhead: Society for Research into Higher Education and Open University Press.

Bauman, Z. (1987) *Legislators and Interpreters: On Modernity, Postmodernity and Intellectuals.* Cambridge: Polity.

Bauman, Z. (1996) From pilgrim to tourist – Or a short history of identity. In S. Hall and P. Du Gay (eds) *Questions of Cultural Identity* (pp. 18–36). London: Sage.

Bauman, Z. (1998) *Globalization. The Human Consequences.* Cambridge: Polity Press.

Bauman, Z. (2005) The liquid-modern challenges to education. In S. Robinson and C. Katulushi (eds) *Values in Higher Education* (pp. 36–50). St Bride's Major: Aureus/University of Leeds.

Baxter Magolda, M. (2001) *Making Their Own Way: Narratives for Transforming Higher Education to Promote Self-development.* Sterling, VA: Stylus.

Bennett, J. (2008) On becoming a global soul. In V. Savicki (ed.) *Developing Intercultural Competence and Transformation. A Path to Engagement during Study Abroad* (pp. 13–31). Sterling, VA: Stylus.

Bennett, M.J. (1993) Towards ethnorelativism: A developmental model of intercultural sensitivity. In R.M. Paige (ed.) *Education for the Intercultural Experience* (pp. 21–71). Yarmouth, ME: Intercultural Press.

Bourn, D. (2010) Students as global citizens. In E. Jones (ed.) *Internationalisation and the Student Voice* (pp. 18–29). London: Routledge.

Bourn, D., Mckenzie, A. and Shiel, C. (2006) *The Global University: The Role of Curriculum*. London: Development Education Association.

Bryant, A. (2007) Liquid modernity, complexity and turbulence. *Theory, Culture and Society* 24, 127–135.

Byram, M. (1997) *Teaching and Assessing Intercultural Communicative Competence*. Clevedon: Multilingual Matters.

Byram, M. (2006) Developing a concept of intercultural citizenship. In G. Alred, M. Byram and M. Fleming (eds) *Education for Intercultural Citizenship: Concepts and Comparisons* (pp. 109–129). Clevedon: Multilingual Matters.

Caruana, V. and Spurling, N. (2007) *The Internationalisation of UK Higher Education: A Review of Selected Material*. York: Higher Education Academy.

Case, R. (1993) Key elements of a global perspective. *Social Education* 57, 318–352.

Colby, A., Beaumont, E., Ehrlich, T. and Corngold, J. (2007) *Educating for Democracy. Preparing Undergraduates for Responsible Political Engagement*. San Francisco, CA: Jossey-Bass.

Collins, G. (2005) Only connect. In S. Robinson and C. Katulushi (eds) *Values in Higher Education* (pp. 216–225). St Bride's Major: Aureus/University of Leeds.

Crick, B. (2000) *In Defence of Politics* (5th edn). London: Continuum.

Crowther, P., Joris, M., Otten, M., Nilsson, B., Teekens, H. and Wächter, B. (2000) *Internationalisation at Home: A Position Paper*. Amsterdam: European Association for International Education.

Delanty, G. (2000) *Citizenship in a Global Age: Society, Culture, Politics*. Buckingham: Open University Press.

Dower, N. (2003) *An Introduction to Global Citizenship*. Edinburgh: Edinburgh University Press.

Dower, N. and Williams, J. (eds) (2002) *Global Citizenship: A Critical Reader*. Edinburgh: Edinburgh University Press.

Featherstone, M. (1995) *Undoing Culture*. London: Sage.

Freire, P. (1970) *Pedagogy of the Oppressed*. New York, NY: Continuum.

Freire, P. (1972) *Cultural Action for Freedom*. Hammondsworth: Penguin.

Friedman, T. (2008) *Hot, Flat, and Crowded*. London: Allen Lane.

Group of Lisbon (1995) *Limits of Competition*. Cambridge, MA: MIT Press.

Heidegger, M. (1998/1962) *Being and Time*. Oxford: Blackwell.

Illeris, K. (2002) *The Three Dimensions of Learning*. Roskilde, Denmark: Roskilde University Press.

Isin, E.F. and Wood, P.K. (1999) *Citizenship and Identity*. London: Sage.

Jarvis, P. (2006) *Towards a Comprehensive Theory of Human Learning. Lifelong Learning and the Learning Society* (Vol. 1). London: Routledge.

Jones, E. (2008) *700 Words on Internationalisation*. Southampton: LIASON, Subject Centre for Languages, Linguistics and Area Studies.

Jones, E. and Killick, D. (2007) Internationalisation of the curriculum. In E. Jones and S. Brown (eds) *Internationalising Higher Education* (pp. 109–119). London: Routledge.

Karsten, S., Kubow, P., Matrai, Z. and Pitiyanuwat, S. (2000) Challenges facing the 21st century citizen: Views of policy makers. In J.J. Cogan and R. Derricott (eds) *Citizenship for the 21st Century. An International Perspective on Education* (pp. 109–130). London: Kogan Page.

Killick, D. (2006) *Cross-Cultural Capability and Global Perspectives. Guidelines for Curriculum Review.* Leeds: Leeds Metropolitan University. On WWW at http:// www.leedsmet.ac.uk/international/Cross_Cultural_Capability_Guidelines. pdf. Accessed 7.4.11.

Killick, D. (2008) Cross-cultural capability and global perspectives: Curriculum development for global citizenship. In C. Shiel and S. Takeda (eds) *Education for Sustainable Development: Graduates as Global Citizens* (pp. 50–55). Bournemouth: Bournemouth University.

King, P.M. and Magolda, M.B.B. (2005) A developmental model of intercultural maturity. *Journal of College Development* 46, 571–592.

Kubow, P., Grossman, D. and Ninomiya, A. (2000) Multidimensional citizenship: Education policy for the 21st century. In J.J. Cogan and R. Derricott (eds) *Citizenship for the 21st Century* (pp. 131–150). London: Kogan Page.

Kurth-Scai, R., Poolpatarachewin, C. and Pitiyanuwat, S. (2000) Using the Delphi cross-culturally: Towards the development of policy. In J.J. Cogan and R. Derricott (eds) *Citizenship for the 21st Century. An International Perspective on Education* (pp. 93–108). London: Kogan Page.

Lamb, A., Roberts, E., Kentish, J. and Bennett, C. (2007) Students as active global citizens. *Zeitscrift für internationale Bildungsforschung und Entwicklungspädagogik* 30, 17–19.

Lave, J. and Wenger, E. (1998) *Situated Learning. Legitimate Peripheral Participation.* Cambridge: Cambridge University Press.

Leeds Metropolitan University (2008) *Internationalisation Strategy 2008–2011. World-wide Horizons at Leeds Met.* Leeds: Leeds Metropolitan University. On WWW at http://www.leedsmet.ac.uk/Revised_Internationalisation_Strategy_2008_–_2012. pdf. Accessed 7.4.11.

Matsumoto, D. (ed.) (2001) *The Handbook of Culture and Psychology.* Oxford: Oxford University Press.

Mckenzie, A., Bourn, D., Evans, S., Brown, M., Shiel, C., Bunney, A., Collins, G., Wade, R., Parker, J. and Annette, J. (2003) *Global Perspectives in Higher Education.* London: Development Education Association.

Mezirow, J. (1991) *Transformative Dimensions of Adult Learning.* San Francisco: Jossey-Bass.

Mezirow, J. (2000) Learning to think like an adult. Core concepts of transformational theory. In J. Mezirow and Associates (eds) *Learning as Transformation* (pp. 3–33). San Francisco: Jossey-Bass.

Mezirow, J. and Associates (eds) (2000) *Learning as Transformation.* San Francisco: Jossey-Bass.

Nilsson, B. (2003) Internationalisation at home from a Swedish perspective: The case of Malmö. *Journal of Studies in International Education 7,* 27–40.

Nussbaum, M. (1993) Non-relative virtues: An Aristotelian approach. In M. Nussbaum and A. Sen (eds) *The Quality of Life* (pp. 242–269). Oxford: Clarendon.

Olssen, M. (2006/2004) Neoliberalism, globalization, democracy: Challenges for education. In H. Lauder, P. Brown, J-A. Dillabough and A.H. Halsey (eds) *Education, Globalization, and Social Change* (pp. 261–287). Oxford: Oxford University Press.

Piaget, J. (1972) *The Psychology of the Child.* New York: Basic Books.

Piaget, J. (1977) *Equilibration of Cognitive Structures.* New York: Viking.

Robinson, S. and Katulushi, C. (2005) The integrity of the university. In S. Robinson and C. Katulushi (eds) *Values in Higher Education* (pp. 242–268). St Bride's Major: Aureus/University of Leeds.

Rogers, C.R. (1961) *On Becoming a Person*. Boston, MA: Houghton-Mifflin.

Sen, A. (1999) *Development as Freedom*. Oxford: Oxford University Press.

Shiel, C. (2006) Developing the global citizen. *Academy Exchange* 5, 18–20.

Shiel, C. and Mckenzie, A. (eds) (2008) *The Global University. The Role of Senior Managers*. London: DEA.

UNESCO (1998) *Higher Education in the Twenty-First Century: Vision and Action*. Paris: UNESCO.

Van Manen, M. (1990) *Researching Lived Experience. Human Science for an Action Sensitive Pedagogy*. New York: State University of New York Press.

Volet, S. and Ang, G. (1998) Culturally mixed groups on international campuses: An opportunity for inter-cultural learning. *Higher Education Research and Development* 17, 5–23.

Ward, C. (2001) The A, B, Cs of acculturation. In D. Matsumoto (ed.) *The Handbook of Culture and Psychology* (pp. 411–445). Oxford: Oxford University Press.

Weber-Bosley, G. (2010) Beyond immersion. Global engagement and transformation through intervention via student reflection in study abroad. In E. Jones (ed.) *Internationalisation and the Student Voice* (pp. 55–67). London: Routledge.

Webb, J., Schirato, T. and Danaher, G. (2002) *Understanding Bourdieu*. London: Sage.

Part 3
The Construction of International Perspectives in 'International' Student Group Work

Chapter 6

Educational Practices in the International University: Language as a Resource for Intercultural Distinction in a Project Group Meeting

D. DAY and S. KJÆRBECK

Introduction

In this chapter our focus will be on the function of language in social and cultural practice and on students' construction of 'internationalism' through language use. We will attempt to answer the following question: What findings in the analyses of language and interactive processes within an academic setting might serve to constitute that setting as 'multicultural' or 'international'?

From an ethnomethodological and conversation analytical perspective, we will investigate the practical, situational use of different cultural backgrounds and different linguistic competencies in a student project group (see also Chapter 7 on the ethnomethodological method). These particular students are enrolled in an undergraduate program in Denmark especially set up to accommodate both local students and students from abroad (see also Chapters 1, 2 and 7 on the Scandinavian perspective). Our task here is to explore what it is on the ground, so to speak, which might warrant a characterization of the program as 'international' or 'multicultural'.

Research in interaction amongst students is still relatively uncommon and typically concerns issues of child socialization (e.g. Ochs, 1988; Watson-Gageo, 1992) or language learning (e.g. Biber, 1996; Cromdal, 2003; Mortensen, forthcoming). International group work has, on the other hand, received quite some attention in organizational studies (see also

Chapter 7 on student group work). The vast majority of these studies, however, do not concern themselves with the practice of such work, much less interaction. Typically their concern has been to explain measured results of efficiency in terms of pre-existing 'national cultures' (see e.g. Cox *et al.*, 1991; Early, 1993).

Taking an ethnomethodological approach, our main interests are the basic organizational features of language use, in this case the methods by which interactants establish and pursue common goals and resources, identities, interpersonal relations, rights and obligations, conflict and conflict resolution, under the affordances of a 'project group meeting' (see Day & Kjærbeck, 2008). This focus on the salient organizational features of the talk implies that even though we are investigating linguistically and culturally diverse study programs, possible intercultural aspects of the data are not assumed *a priori*, and for example, our first study of this project group meeting showed that the intercultural features were not very salient or significant in the practices of the group. However, in this chapter we will take our point of departure in findings that might play a role in constituting the investigated program as 'multicultural' or 'international' as a local achievement and in this way address the intercultural focus of the Cultural and Linguistic Practices in the International University (CALPIU) project (see also Chapter 8 on cross-cultural project work).

In many research traditions the notion of 'multicultural' or 'international' refers to the background of the participants, most often by way of participants having different national origins in the group in question (see e.g. Adler, 1997; Harris & Moran, 1996; Hayashi, 1991; Hendon *et al.*, 1996; Fant, 1992). Thus, interactants of differing national origins are seen as engaging by fiat in 'international' interaction (see also Chapters 3, 4, 5, 9 and 10 on international students; and Chapters 1, 2, 5 and 7 on internationalization 'at home'). And from this, the common-sense inference is often made that the interaction is intercultural. That is to say, national difference is inferably cultural difference.

We take this conceptual understanding of 'international' and the inference to 'intercultural' not as a resource for our study, but as a topic. This is to say that we find such thinking indicative of a 'lay' or 'common-sense' understanding used unreflectively as a theoretical assumption to many investigations, and thus open to the risk of uncovering little more than the analyst's sense-making practices, rather than the people's under study. Instead, we view notions such as 'international' and 'intercultural' as glosses for local, practical work of members in settings. We gloss this work as 'interculturality' which refers to the interactive and endogenous phenomena whereby interlocutors co-construct their interaction as intercultural interaction, specifically in the work interlocutors do to identify themselves and each other as members of different cultural groups (Day, 1994, 1998; Hansen, 2005; Kjærbeck, 2001; Mori, 2003; Nishizaka, 1995) (see also Chapters 4 and 12 on 'interculturality' and intercultural interaction). The interculturality of interaction between individuals with different cultural backgrounds is thus no longer taken for granted. Our focus is on *how* a particular spate of communication becomes intercultural *for* interlocutors. This focus has followed a substantial critique of previous work on intercultural communication on grounds that, to the extent that actual communication was even studied, the interculturality of interaction was rather naively determined by the nationalities of interlocutors, that intercultural communication was inevitably a problem caused by cultural backgrounds often far removed in time and space, and on grounds that these cultural backgrounds were often only considered from a social psychological perspective in terms, for example, of values, attitudes and so forth. In the parlance of Ethnomethodology, interactants were merely 'cultural dopes' (Garfinkel, 1967: 68) (see also Chapters 4 and 12 on intercultural communication).

The position we take towards interculturality is but one example of 'respecification', an Ethnomethodological procedure whereby what is traditionally taken as a resource, or explanum, is turned on its head and taken as a topic, or explicandum (see e.g. Button, 1991). Thus, rather than taking a presupposition of the interculturality of participants as an explanation of phenomena we observe, we seek to find cases where interculturality is practically applied to action within the interaction. The idea of respecification can also be forwarded with the terms 'etic' and 'emic' from linguistic anthropology. Respecification involves taking what may be considered 'etic' – cultural membership, native languages and native speakers, mother tongue, age, gender and other so-called 'background variables' – and respecifying them as something 'emic', that is as local, 'internal' accomplishments of sense making in practical action. These 'variables' thus matter if they are made to matter by interlocutors, and not before, in the sort of analysis we are proffering.[1]

Ethnomethodological conversation analysis (CA) does not question the role of culture in interaction. In fact, for one of its founding fathers, Harvey Sacks, an analysis is always the analysis of 'some culture' (Sacks, 1992: Lecture, 32: 469). But it is important to bear in mind here that this is not a view of culture as some omnipotent determinant of behaviour, rather as a resource for practical action. Sacks likens culture to an apparatus:

A culture is an apparatus for generating recognizable actions; if the same procedures are used for generating as detecting, that is as simple a solution to the problem of recognizability as is formulateable. (Sacks, 1992: 226)

This basic 'culturality' of action of course neither denies that there may be difficulties when people from different cultures interact nor that cultural differences are not discernible or possibly explicative of how interactions get done. The question is more from whose perspective, ours or the interlocutors? Troubles may occur in any interaction, and interlocutors generally bring to bear communicative resources for explaining, clarifying and negotiating so as to facilitate alignment and mutual understanding. It is within these very practices, in troubled as well as trouble-less interaction that we may or may not observe or be able to infer an orientation to interculturality among interlocutors. Thus, our ambition is not to 'correct' or 'deconstruct' interlocutor's judgements concerning the interculturality of their interactions, rather it is to allow them to demonstrate its construction as a locally practical and rational method for pursuing some course of action.

Possibly due to the sociological interest in culturally rather homogeneous data, it was not until relatively recently that a profound interest in analysing foreign language data and investigating cultural matters developed within CA (Bilmes, 1996; Moerman, 1988; Wagner, 1996; Wieder & Pratt, 1990). As mentioned above, the theoretical assumptions of action and interaction as profoundly social and cultural endeavours suggest a certain representational status to the individual participant. But on the other hand, the analytical emphasis on the participants' actions and the local construction and negotiation of meaning leaves the representational aspect out of the account, until proven in data (see e.g. Kjærbeck, 1998).

When we in this chapter deal with phenomena which possibly constitute the project group meeting as 'international' or 'intercultural', we approach data from a particular research interest and our purpose is to categorize the data, say what kind it is or is not and thereby contextualize it. These two endeavours make it relevant to mention a few basic methodological principles of ethnomethodology and CA.

One basic principle is to approach data as openly as possible, ideally with no previous hypothesis or particular interests. This principle is often characterized as 'unmotivated looking' in CA, and it is precisely this methodological principle which mandates closely investigating participants' actions and responses to actions and determining the local logic by which we may analytically reconstruct the interaction step-by-step and demonstrate participant's publicly available sense making.

The other basic principles have to do with the conversation-analytic way of working with context. It is a methodological cornerstone that analytical phenomena must have 'demonstrable relevance to participants' (Schegloff, 1992: 215). Furthermore, not only must they be demonstrably relevant, but also 'procedurally consequential' (Schegloff, 1992: 215). Briefly, these notions stipulate that elements of a distal context, for example, one's profession, gender and ethnicity can be brought to bear in an analysis of a proximate context, that is, the interaction under study, if it can be shown that participants orient to them and that this orientation can be shown to be relevantly tied to particular actions.

Data and Setting

We find it highly relevant for the CALPIU project to study project group meetings because 'Problem oriented project work' constitutes a basic assignment in the students' curriculum, and, moreover, it is recognized as the key component of Roskilde University's profile and pedagogical approach. In project work, the group is given a time-frame within which to conduct and report their investigation, they are appointed a supervisor, and the work is based on the assumption that it should be a collective effort.

We have been working with a corpus of material consisting of video-recorded project group meetings that took place in an international program at Roskilde University.[2] We have specially been looking into a meeting with five participants, a 73-minute-long video recording. The participants have different cultural backgrounds and different language competencies, but the group work is performed in English, with a few code-switches into Danish. There are two females in the group, MAR and LOU, both from Denmark, and three males, JES, ERN and PET, who are from Denmark, Germany and the United States/Denmark, respectively. They are all in their early 20s. The participants are sitting in a conference room at the university around a table, see Figure 6.1. They are in the planning phase of their project.

Extracts from the video have been transcribed with the following CA transcript conventions (Table 6.1).

Our main interest has been to shed light on what a project group meeting is as an accountable social order, in this case as an institutional activity. Using the Ethnomethodological approach, we want to study, as openly as possible, the interactive methods by which interactants establish and pursue common goals and interpersonal relations in a project group meeting. In Day and Kjærbeck (2008), we were concerned with salient activities of the project meeting at hand, namely setting an agenda, legitimizing absences and resolving conflicts. Our results showed that the project

Figure 6.1 The project group and its participants. Beginning of activity

Table 6.1 Transcription conventions

Right	*Speaker emphasis*
yes	Noticeably quieter than surrounding talk
YES	Noticeably louder than surrounding talk
u:	Stretched sound
(.)	Micropause (less than 0.2 seconds)
(0.5)	Time gap in tenths of a second
[yes]	Overlapping talk
xxx	Speech which is not audible
A: hello =	No audible gap between one utterance and the next
B: =hi	
((turns to JES))	Non-verbal actions or contextual remarks
(everything)	Possible hearing
<unless we hire>	Noticeably slower than surrounding talk

group meeting in question is a peculiar mixture of formal and informal activities, and there is a considerable amount of multitasking going on. There is not an agenda established beforehand; but it gets worked out in the process, frequently through questions from individuals to the group concerning what is to be talked about. 'Minutes' are taken throughout the meeting, with a focus on the calendar with deadlines. And the calendar from previous meetings is used in the agenda setting process. Besides the informal treatment and local establishment of the agenda, the talk is also marked by episodes of informal talk, for example, planning social activities, joking or even mocking.

Regarding a specific institutional focus of the talk, in our case the issue of attendance and absence, we found a strong normative orientation to attendance at meetings (Day & Kjærbeck, 2008). Nevertheless, we observed that using work outside the university as a legitimate reason for unavailability is very common and seemingly unproblematic in the sense that it is never questioned by fellow students. We also focused on disagreements and how they are mediated. The analyses show a clear orientation towards conflict resolution: basically the principle is the majority rules and that conflicts should be dealt with immediately.

Summing up, our investigation so far has dealt with some aspects of the social organization of a project group meeting, and we have found an orientation to special constraints and enablements that are normatively maintained. We understand the practices of agenda setting and mediation of conflicts as a way of enacting goal directedness (see Heritage, 1998, 2004, 2005), and we see the normative orientation to attendance as a prerequisite for getting things done, but which, at the same time provides insight into the meeting as part of an institutional context.

Interculturality in the Project Group Meeting

In the following section, we present two examples which we believe document the interculturality of the group as a members' concern.

The translation problem

At the very beginning of the meeting there is a long discussion as to which language, Danish or English, to use for conducting interviews for the project. If the interviews are to be conducted in Danish, the question is how to manage translation into English (see also Chapter 9 on translation). It is a curriculum requirement that the written report is in English. In these sequences, the positions taken on the language and translation issue seemingly correspond with the linguistic background of the participants: The self-ascribed native speaker of English, PET, suggests the interviews be conducted in English in order to avoid translation problems, while the rest of the group (all self-ascribed non-native speakers) think that it is an advantage to conduct some of the interviews in Danish, and afterwards translate them into English.[3] It is not difficult to find possible explanations for this difference of opinion. But let us see how the discussion evolves and decides whether this is an example where the interculturality of the project group is treated as a member's concern.

Extract 6.1

```
1.  PET: i think i'd still rather do it in English because er:m (1.4)
2.       we ran into the same problem (.) last year where we had
3.       some iranian using danish and it's just (.) <unless we hire
4.       a professional translator>
5.  LOU: huh huh hh [xxx
6.  PET: to transcribe them (.) we're just gonna lose so much of the
7.       value (.) by guessing our own translations or by trying to make
8.       our own translations i'd rather still have it in English cause
9.       then that's at least what they said
10. JAN: i'll be back in forty minutes
11. PET: you know we're not changing in any way what they said
12.      that's exactly what they said
13.      ((PET looks down at paper))
14. LOU: but i'm i'm thinking [more that (.) i]
15. PET:                      [that's the way i feel like]
16. LOU: don't know how you used the interviews last year ((turns to
17.      JES)) but i'm thinking this (.) this interview is it's not
18.      that important that it's word for word because we we need to
19.      see a pattern sort of
```

In this extract, lines 3–7, PET expresses what can be heard as a suggestion; he suggests that they hire a translator (lines 3–7). This is said in a serious voice and with emphasis (emphasis on 'unless' and pronounced at a slower pace than the surrounding talk). But LOU's laughter and comment in line 5 suggest that this is completely unrealistic. She is treating PET's suggestion as laughable and not taking it seriously. There is clearly disalignment at this point, and PET responds to this by accounting for his point of view (lines 6–12: 'we're just gonna lose ...'). After PET's long piece of talk, LOU takes the next turn (in line 14). Here, she disagrees explicitly with PET; she does not find the interview that important, and she accounts for her opinion with the words 'we need to see a pattern sort of' (lines 18–19).

It is interesting that PET is the only one who prefers English for the interviews (line 1) and who has serious problems with the group's translation skills. Furthermore, the way PET presents the problem is interesting. He uses the 'we' form, thereby including himself in the problem description and in the group, and blurring his own linguistic competence. PET would probably not have to 'guess', as he says in his problem description: 'we're just gonna lose so much of the value (.) by guessing our own translations or by trying to make our own translations' (lines 6–8). As mentioned earlier, PET is, according to his own assessment, a native speaker of English and has excellent command of Danish. In spite of this, and in light of his manoeuvre with the personal pronoun 'we', his negative description of linguistic competence can be understood as characteristic of the group as a whole. That PET chooses this way of presenting the problem also implicates that his competence is not suggested as the sole resource, even if this might seem an obvious suggestion; he is not going to be in charge of the translation work. In this way, PET's action supports the general orientation to equality in the group.

Extract 6.2

After a while, PET repeats his suggestion of hiring a professional translator. But even though it is prefaced by an account, his suggestion is immediately strongly rejected by his fellow students:

```
1.  PET:  i mean we can also avoid that problem ((the translation))
2.        by all you know (.) paying for someone to transcribe it
3.  JES:  no [way]
4.  PET:     [i] have no problem with that but
5.  JES:  i have a problem with that=
6.  MAR:  =i have a problem with [that]
7.  LOU:                         [hm]
8.  MAR:  and is that necessary (.) transcribing ( everything)
......((sequences cut out))
And only a few utterances later, the following interchange takes place:
9.  PET:  but still
10.       (3.4)
11.       (i don't know) hey i don't i mean i don't know how
12.       good you guys are linguistically so maybe there is someone
```

13.		in this group who can translate perfectly I mean I don't know
14.		(.)
15.		maybe there is
16.		(.)
17.	LOU:	er i can [not translate perfectly]
18.	PET:	[but if there isn't (.)]
19.		some of it is gonna get lost
20.		(1.0)
21.	JES:	but the problem is we er (.) it's it's a general
22.		problem we have when (.) writing in english . . . .

In this extract, PET questions the linguistic competence of the group, pointing to a possible problem of competence. As in the previous extract, he also downplays his own ability. His statement 'so maybe there is someone in this group who can translate perfectly I don't know maybe there is' (lines 12–15), implicates that he is not able to assess his fellow students' abilities – recall again his self-ascribed native speakership – and that he does not possess those abilities. The repetitions of 'I don't know' and 'maybe there is' emphasize his position, but they also emphasize on the face value of his utterance as well as function as prolongations of his turn which invite a response from the other participants.

Given his own linguistic abilities, as well as the 'extreme' formulation of someone who can translate perfectly, his utterance is rhetorical. His question if there is 'anyone' who can translate perfectly in the group sets up the proposition that if there is but one person so able, then that person can do the translations. PET has already excluded himself, and thus he is passing the ball, so to speak, to his fellow students to hear if there is anyone better than he who can, potentially, take sole responsibility for the translations. No one responds to this in the affirmative. In this way, one can hear PET's question as a subtle critique of his fellow students' abilities vis-á-vis his own in spite of the fact that he has set up these abilities as 'group' abilities. There is thus some vagueness here about PET's point, and it is possible, we believe, to gloss this bit of interaction as dealing with the distribution of competences and responsibilities within the group – should a task be the sole responsibility of any one person? Only if that person can accomplish the task perfectly. Otherwise an 'outsider' must be paid to do so.

In line 17, LOU shows that she heard PET's utterance as an indirect question; she says 'I can not translate perfectly.' And building on this action, it is easy for PET to get to his point: 'if there isn't, some of it is going to get lost.' PET sustains his position, overhearing LOU's and MAR's objections that a direct translation is not needed.

Whereas generally we see a strong orientation to equality and 'group spirit' in the group, this last extract shows what some of the problematics of this might be. Even if PET uses an indirect strategy for complaining about the level of competence of his fellow students (in order to account for his suggestion of hiring a professional translator), he is at the same time positioning himself as a linguistically more competent group member. PET's actions are also implying that he is not solely in charge of the translation work – and this point of view is not challenged, nor commented upon at all, by the other participants. So it would seem that the group does not take up the proposition of 'someone being solely responsible for a task if they can not do it perfectly'. At the same time they reject the possibility of an outsider. What is left is that the group members distribute the task among themselves.

We believe that these examples where multilingual issues, such as the participants' uneven linguistic competences, are dealt with are examples of interculturality, resting on a possible common-sense inference from language difference to intercultural distinction (see e.g. Blommaert, 1991; Day, 1999). This is to say that, in its simplest form, if you are a 'native speaker', itself an emic category, of a language different from my 'native language', then the odds are that we are culturally different. As with all such inferences, we note, this is defeasible. We have seen how this difference in linguistic competence brings about different opinions about a language issue, namely which language to use for conducting the interviews of the project. Furthermore, we have seen how the consequences for the project work and the relationships and identities of the group members are negotiated in the talk. These activities show the participants' concern for the intercultural nature of at least some aspects of their collective work.

In terms of 'respecification' we can say firstly that multilinguistic competence is very much a practical concern for the students, and such competence, we maintain, allows an inference of interculturality. Multilingualism feeds into the practical activity of assigning roles for activity in the group and in this way becomes involved in identity and relational work. In this particular instance, we have the case of PET 'playing down' his competence resulting in a leveling of the multilingual field. Thus, we can say that, within a group, something that may mark someone as culturally different, such as multilingual skills, can be ignored for the sake of fitting into the group, or perhaps for avoiding a particular activity related role. Multilingualism functioning as a gloss for such actions becomes much more social and ecological than psycholinguistic in this instance of its practical use.

Mocking

Extract 6.3: Mocking

```
1.   PET:   we've got a lot of stuff to do (my man) we have to prepare
2.          for it too (x)=
3.   ERN:   =we gotta work on saturday
4.   PET:   yeah
5.   ERN:   and we're having (3) then we are having:: on monday
6.          interviews uh the student council
7.   PET:   yeh
8.   ERN:   we gotta xx questions for that on saturday and then we're
9.          having class and then we're having [on tuesday the uhhhh
10.         interviews uh the recruitment of]
11.  ((JES:                               [xxx we gotta send out
12.         emails so I've moved the deadline]))
13.  ERN:   [these people]
14.  JES:   [til the 24th]
15.  PET:   °yeah°
16.         (1)
17.  LOU:   yeah↑
18.  PET:   and then xxx [miss term evaluation]
19.  LOU:                [uhh and it seems so very] short so
20.  ERN:   yea and then we have our mid-term evaluation [right after
21.         that]
22.  PET:                                               [we'll
23.         probably have] to work on wednesday (1) thursday maybe
24.         some day during the weekend (2) it's going be a busy week
25.         dudes so just prepare yourself mentally for it man (.) just
26.         get [pUMPed]
27.  ERN:      [xx mid-term ] evaluation [which DAYS]
28.  PET:                               [do some drugs] if that's
29.         what it takes
30.         (.8)
31.  ERN:   which days days [we have is it two or what]
32.  LOU:                   [but this is my eat pasta ]week
33.  ((JES: pedagogy is))
34.  ERN:   °your what°
35.  LOU:   °I have to eat pasta all week°
36.  ERN:   °why that°
37.  PET:   you gotta me kiddin me (.) you're not on one of those
```

```
38.              stupid diets are you?
39.    LOU:      uh no no no I'm must a I'm just er (.)
40.    PET:      you [broke]
41.    ERN:          [did you] lose a bet?
42.    LOU:      just broke
43.    PET:       yeah ha ha [ha HA HA HA gid]dy e giddy e giddy me::: ↑
44.    LOU:       ((smiles/laughs with PET)) [that's my diet]
45.    ERN:       [(xx)]
46.    PET:       [which] brings us to another subject (1) shouldn't we
47.              arrange like to do something fun with each other again
48.              soon?
49.              (0.5)
50.    LOU:      yea with food ts uh uh uh uh uh
51.    ERN:      ah huh huh huh
52.    PET:      with some food [and]
53.    LOU:                     [yea]
54.    PET:      later maybe doing something like goin to see a movie at
55.              the film festival [or doing something x]
56.    LOU:                        [oh yea that film yea]
57.    ERN:                              [x fuck ] YES [man I'm SO
58.           MUCH x]
59.    MAR:                                         [yeah we
60.           should do it]
61.    PET:      should we do that?
62.    ERN:      OH FUCK ((claps/raises))[DUDE YEAH YOU]((arm movements))GOT IT
63.    LOU:                          [(yesterday)]
```

((throughout line 64-66 JES, LOU, MAR and ERN smile/laugh))

```
64.    PET:      maybe next week ((LOU taps ERN's shoulder)) we're really busy
                 (1)
65.    JES:      that guy's gonna be like [xxx]
66.    PET:                               [maybe] next week   if we work
67.           like really hard one day then maybe we wanna [end that day
68.           with with eating]
69.    LOU:                                                 [and then we'll
70.           have a xxx]
71.    PET:      some dinner [and]
72.    LOU:                  [yeah]
```

Initially in this segment, PET and ERN are engaged in listing the activities the group has ahead of them. The other participants are engaged in

Figure 6.2 LOU and PET laughing

other activities, indicated by italics, what we refer to in the earlier article as 'parallel activities', typically computer work. PET ends this listing by formulating that the long list of activities implies getting mentally ready for the work ahead. He produces this as a joking assessment with extra emphasis and volume, and he uses slangy vocabulary like 'dudes', 'man', 'get pumped' and 'do some drugs' (lines 25–28). His manner of speech changes which we will explicate below as a 'stylization' (to use a term from Coupland, 2001). The group then focuses collectively on a single activity in a jocular discussion of LOU's 'diet' – a comment she has made with regard to PET's comment. PET then follows up this discussion by suggesting they go out, as a group, for some fun, going to a movie, having dinner and so on. ERN then, loudly and with the disruptive exclamation 'fuck'. He sabotages PET and LOU's planning activities (lines 57–62). In doing so, he uses what is recognizably the particular style of speech PET has previously used. This outburst we hear as ERN 'mocking' PET, a sort of 'counter-stylization', which in its performance is an admonishment of PET. Specifically, it can be heard as a critique of PET's manner of speech as a viable linguistic resource for the group. These interchanges we suggest are the making relevant of a cultural distinction; first, it is made relevant by PET's usage of a variety of 'native talk' that highlights his status as a native speaker. And second, the

Figure 6.3 LOU's FUCK DUDE YEA

resource is violently rejected through ERN's exaggerated and 'misplaced' use of it. This will be analysed in detail in the following.

First note that at line 22 PET overlaps ERN's continuation of the list of work ahead. Taking the turn, he adds to the list concerning days on which work is to be done, and then offers his take, in line 24 after the 2-second pause, on what the work will imply and how the group needs to orient to the work. PET's speech here is significantly different from his previous speech, phonologically/phonetically (e.g. higher pitch, increased amplitude and intensity) lexically (e.g. 'get pumped', take 'drugs') and bodily (e.g. rightens up and leans back, opens arms, head tilted upward). This speech stylet can be characterized as reminiscent of 'Valley Girl' or 'Surfer Dude', stylized popular culture renditions of varieties of youth speech in California.[4]

ERN takes a next turn at line 27, carrying on with his list, here concerning the mid-term evaluation, and ignoring PET's action. PET then, at line 28, carries on with his take on what is needed, taking drugs if needed. There is a bit of a pause, followed by ERN again carrying on with the mid-term evaluation. There is thus no uptake by ERN or the others of PET's take, but at a later point LOU steps in, perhaps softening the situation,

Figure 6.4 Orienting to the camera

giving her take on a contingency for her of the upcoming work – that she will be eating pasta.

In the next sequences we see how an imbalance in the relationship between PET, ERN and LOU is established that we believe build up to the mocking episode. After LOU's announcement of her diet in line 35, she gets quick responses from ERN and from PET. ERN's uptake has the form of a question: 'why that?' This question is, however, not answered, and immediately after, PET takes the turn with the quite personal assessment: 'you gotta be kiddin me' followed by the question: 'you're not on one of those stupid diets are you' (lines 37–38). In contrast to the question posed by ERN, this question does get its answer. While delivering her answer, LOU does a word search (39), and once again we see parallel actions from PET and ERN in order to interact with LOU. PET suggests 'you broke' (40), while ERN asks 'did you lose a bet?' PET was right, and LOU's confirmation of this (in 42) elicits a very strong response from PET; he laughs loudly, LOU laughs with him and he starts 'giddy'-ing and moves his fingers as if tickling LOU. As is evident from the inserted picture in the transcript, ERN does not participate in this interchange – he just looks down. We find this narrowing of the participation format and the quite personal and informal interaction between PET and LOU remarkable.

After the joking talk of LOU's diet, PET at lines 54–55 makes his suggestion concerning going out, and LOU immediately provides a positive response to this (line 56). But at lines 57–58 and 62, overlapping with LOU's response, we see ERN's reaction. ERN's mocking is done in two steps. First, at lines 57–58, there is some ambiguity to what he is doing, even though his utterance sounds disruptive, and MAR and PET continue the planning activity. But then, in line 62, ERN upgrades his outburst, he raises, claps his hands and moves his arm in a hip-hop-like manner, while shouting. 'OH FUCK DUDE YEAH YOU GOT IT.' We hear and see this as imitating, in mocking fashion, perhaps due to the general amplitude of his expression, PETs earlier talk of getting pumped and taking drugs. It is delivered as an outburst directed towards PET, and it is remarkable that PET, at line 64 carries on with his suggestion, as if nothing has happened.

After line 62 LOU, MAR, and JES start smiling and laughing quietly, as if embarrassed. And ERN smiles and laughs with them. LOU touches ERN's shoulder, which looks like a tap of consolation. JES points to the camera, and comments on how 'that guy', that is, the researcher doing the filming, is going to understand ERN's outburst (line 65). There is thus some recognition that ERN has been 'extreme', he is consoled and made aware that his outburst will be seen by others. PET at line 66 carries on, and the rest of the group, without ERN, follow with a deliberation of PET's suggestion.

It is our contention that what we have witnessed is the making relevant of cultural distinction by way of a difference of opinion over emically defined cultural resources, namely ways of speaking. PET's 'dude talk' can be seen as a potential linguistic resource for the group. But it emphasizes his status as a 'native speaker' and positions him as culturally distinct. The question, however, is whether it can be shared within the group, that is, how is the positioning action received by the others. As we have already noticed, it was met with no uptake, ERN trying to continue his planning activity, and the others not acknowledging PET's joking assessment, for example, with laughter. We have seen earlier where PET's linguistic abilities have been on the table, but where he manages to forego any obligation to share them with the group. Here we see ERN using PET's 'dude talk' resource, but in a fashion which, we maintain, excludes it as a resource for the group. We can understand ERN's outburst as a 'cultural mocking' and following it we do not observe PET lapsing into 'dude talk'.

Phenomena of the sort we have referred to as mocking has received treatment in sociolinguistics generally. As noted above, Coupland (2001) is responsible for the term 'stylization'. Taking Bauman's treatment of performativity as a point of departure, Coupland sees stylization as a performative social practice in which

> the knowing deployment of culturally familiar styles that are marked as deviating from those predictably associated with the current speaking context. Dialect stylization involves performing non-current-first-person personas by phonological and related means, sometimes in play or parody'. (Coupland, 2000: 345)

While such notions are very helpful for us in appreciating the complexities of what ERN is doing linguistically, our interests in the 'socio' side of things are less well served by variational sociolinguistics. Our concern is with how people in this particular setting accountably organize themselves as part of the setting. We take what they are doing to be precisely that. As stated in the introduction, we are interested in respecifying notions from such theories as potentially member's concerns.

With this in mind the cultural mocking episode deserves further reflection. Mocking is a very uncommon activity in institutional talk, due to the special goal-directedness and general interest in having a professional relationship with each other. The mocking occurs during an informal activity, but even in this sequential environment the other participants clearly treat it as something which is 'out of place'. Recall their concern with its observability by the researchers.

The mocking-episode evidences a tense relationship between PET and ERN, and during the meeting there have been other instances of conflict between the two. In the following, we show an example out of a series of confrontation that were analysed thoroughly in our earlier article (Day & Kjærbeck, 2008). We provide this bit of analysis not as another example of interculturality, rather to demonstrate how the case above is embedded in a local, practical activity, namely the pursuance of conflict between ERN and PET. Interculturality is not a practice. It is our gloss of particular ways of engaging in practices which may very well be accomplished by other means as well, as is the case here.

Usually, the confrontations between PET and ERN appear as opposite opinions about the issues under debate, but they also occur due to opposite attitudes to procedural matters, as is the case in the example below. When a confrontation occurs it is quite systematic that another participant, in most cases LOU, deals with the conflict immediately, thereby assuming responsibility and getting the meeting on track again.

Extract 6.4:

```
1. PET:  when do you wanna meet wednesday=
2. ERN:  =you're you're really really fast I'm (xx) I'd say
3. PET:  well that's
4.            because like we've been doing this (.) for a little while
5.            now [hehh hh hhh]
6. ERN:            [yeah but that's] because you didn't wait until something
7.       else was ↑done so you've got to repeat it
8.            (.)
9. LOU:  o[kay]
```

We see how PET poses a question of when to meet on Wednesday. But latched on to PET's question, ERN complains about PET's action; he produces an assessment reproaching the timing of PET's utterance: he is too fast!

Immediately after, PET answers with an explanation accounting for his action in 1, but he packages his utterance in irony by using understatements: 'because like we've been doing this for a little while now', and by softening his utterance, which really can be heard as a reproach, with laughter (5). The understatement implies that he is sick and tired of spending so much time planning the next meetings. In other words, he is complaining about the time it takes.

In his next turn, in lines 6–7, ERN produces an account for his reproach in 2, which functions as a new reproach. ERN explains that PET should have waited with Wednesday until something else was done, implying that PET can thank himself for the delay.

Of particular interest in this dispute is that LOU simply takes over. She closes the ongoing dispute with an 'okay' (9), thereby opening up for new developments. This is a typical moderator, or chairperson activity, but in this meeting there is no appointed chair. Nevertheless, LOU unproblematically assumes responsibility and overrules the conflict. In the Mocking-sequences we also saw how LOU touched ERN's shoulder as if regulating things with her gesture.

Looking back on other examples of confrontation between PET and ERN we find evidence of ongoing tension between them and the mocking episode seems to be a violent culmination of this conflict. With regard to interculturality, what can this insight provide? How might interculturality be 'respecified' in this instance? Here it would seem that making relevant a cultural distinction, that is, PET's linguistic aptitude, can be used in an ongoing conflict, as a tool for 'putting PET down' in the negotiation of social order in the group. And this is accomplished in the micro-order of deciding if the group should go out together.

Conclusion

In a previous paper (Day & Kjærbeck, 2008), we have discussed some of the ways project members organize themselves in the project group meeting. In this article we are exploring how they are organizing ostensibly multicultural resources and what this may tell us of how they treat each other in this regard. In all our examples, our entrance into this work has been via language. On the one hand, we have seen how the academic work the project team has set for them by their program necessitates their organizing themselves, as speakers of languages, and inferentially as bearers of cultures vis-á-vis a multilingual and multicultural environment. Thus, they must decide which language to use in their interviewing, debate the potential difficulties of translation, the potential loss of understanding one choice or the other implies. As we saw in Extracts 6.1 and 6.2, the group members' language preference corresponds with their linguistic background and competence; PET who has native competence in English prefers English for the interviews, and the non-native speakers prefer Danish. However, we cannot be sure of the reasons for this pattern. In other words, we cannot be sure that the given reasons reflect the real reasons. The only thing we can be certain about is that if personal convenience is the real motivation for the language preference, there is a normative orientation in the group not to mention it. In the same line, we saw that PET was the only person who had serious problems with the group's translation skills. Extracts 6.1 and 6.2 also showed the practical negotiation of rights and obligations in relation to unequal distribution of linguistic competences in the group. We saw how PET downplayed his abilities while excluding himself as a person who could be in charge of the translation work. The group does not treat this as a problem, and PET's 'suggestion' of not doing the translation work is accepted. On the other hand, the group must also organize itself, internally so to speak, as competent members of the team vis-á-vis each other. And here we also find something with regard to them as speakers of languages and inferentially as bearers of cultures, namely a few instances division concerning what sort of language is viable within the group. In Extract 6.3, we saw PET using his native competence and knowledge of 'California style' for joking about the work situation of the group, but at the same time this 'performance' positioned him as a person with distinct linguistic abilities and special cultural knowledge. But PET's stylization received no uptake or

alignment by the rest of the group. In the same extract ERN's violent outburst occurred in which he imitated his fellow student's culturally distinct resources for the purpose of mocking. This was not accepted/was
treated as an unacceptable action.

In all the examples analysed, it is obvious that linguistic and cultural
resources are 'at work'; they are used for a purpose and are expressed
through actions and activities in the talk – be it in strict relation to topics/
issues of the project or regarding the relations in the group. Our treatment
of these resources as 'respecified' topics of investigation demands our attention on their practical utility for interlocutors. And when these resources
are put to work, their local meaning and acceptability are negotiated by the
participants of the interaction. We consider these linguistic and cultural
resource ways of practicing diversity in project work, but they are resources
that are neither enriching nor troublesome per se, rather the function and
influence they have depend on their local use and negotiated meaning.

We set out with the intention of investigating the practical, situational
use of different cultural backgrounds. And this is what we found –
moments of interculturality where the participating students, directly or
indirectly, and as a means for doing other things, identify themselves and
each other as members of different cultural groups. Using CA, we have
dealt with phenomena which the participants made relevant in the talk,
but on the basis of these limited findings of interculturality, we cannot
claim them to be procedurally consequential to the entire project group
meeting at hand, to these people as cohorts, nor to their institution as
such. What we can do, however, is to claim that the procedures they did
use to imbue their dealings with each other with interculturality are
potentially elements in the culture of this group. To what extent this is
general, institutionalized, and available for others in the setting at large is
yet another empirical matter that can only be known by investigating
the actual practices that take place there.[5]

Notes

1. It is undoubtedly already obvious that our position makes using terms such as
   'intercultural', 'language', 'native speaker' and so forth rather cumbersome in
   writing up our analyses as evidenced by the proliferation of 'scare quotes'.
   Henceforth, we will attempt to avoid the scare quotes, hoping that the reader
   will understand what such terms refer to from our position.
2. Janus Mortensen made the recordings for his PhD project, and we are grateful
   to him for allowing us to use his data.
3. The 'self-ascription' referred to here occurred in other data from the CALPIU
   project and it was generally understood in the group that PET was a native
   speaker of English.

4. See Fought, 2002, 2006, as well as the PBS-series 'California English', http://www.pbs.org/speak/seatosea/americanvarieties/californian/. Accessed 5.11.10.
5. For a discussion of such 'wider' context, see Day, 2008.

References

Adler, N. (1997) *International Dimensions of Organizational Behaviour* (3rd edn). Cincinnati, OH: South-Western College Publishing.

Biber, D. (1996) *University Language. A Corpus-Based Study of Spoken and Written Registers. Studies in Corpus Linguistics* 23. Amsterdam: John Benjamins Publishing Company.

Bilmes, J. (1996) Problems and resources in analyzing Northern Thai conversation for English language readers. *Journal of Pragmatics* 26, 171–188.

Blommaert, J. (1991) How much culture is there in intercultural communication? In J. Blommaert and J. Verschueren (eds) *The Pragmatics of Intercultural and International Communication: Selected Papers of the International Pragmatics Conference* (pp. 13–31), Antwerp, August 17–22, 1987, III and the Ghent Symposium. Amsterdam: John Benjamins Publishing.

Button, G. (1991) Introduction: Ethnomethodology and the foundational respecification of the human sciences. In G. Button (ed.) *Ethnomethodology and the Human Sciences*. Cambridge: Cambridge University Press.

Coupland, N. (2001) Dialect stylization in radio talk. *Language in Society* 30, 345–375.

Cox, T.H., Lobel, S.A. and McLeod, P.L. (1991) Effects of ethnic group cultural differences on cooperative and competitive behavior on a group task. *Academy of Management Journal* 34, 827–847.

Cromdal, J. (2003) The creation and administration of social relations in bilingual group work. *Journal of Multilingual and Multicultural Development* 24, 56–75.

Day, D. (1994) Tang's dilemma and other problems: Ethnification processes at some multicultural workplaces. *Pragmatics* 4, 315–336.

Day, D. (1998) Being ascribed, and resisting, membership of an ethnic group. In C. Antaki and S. Widdicombe (eds) *Identities in Talk* (pp. 151–170). London: Sage.

Day, D. (1999) Linguistic ethnic categorizations at two workplaces. Unpublished Ph.D. dissertation, Department of Language and Intercultural Studies, Aalborg University, Aalborg, Denmark.

Day, D. (2008) In another 'messo' context. *Journal of Pragmatics* 40, 979–996.

Day, D. and Kjærbeck, S. (2008) Agendas, excuses of work and assuming responsibility: An exploratory case study of social order in project meetings. In H. Haberland, J. Mortensen, A. Fabricius, B. Preisler, K. Risager and S. Kjærbeck (eds) *Higher Education in the Global Village* (pp. 123–148). Roskilde, Denmark: Dept. of Culture & Identity, Roskilde University.

Early, P.C. (1993) East meets West meets Mideast: Further explorations of collectivistic and individualistic work groups. *Academy of Management Journal* 36, 319–348.

Fant, L. (1992) Scandinavians and Spaniards in negotiation. In A. Sjögren and L. Jansson (eds) *Culture and Management in the Field of Ethnology and Business Administration*. Stockholm: Stockholm School of Economics.

Fought, C. (2002) California students' perceptions of, you know, regions and dialects. In D. Young and D. Preston (eds) *Handbook of Perceptual Dialectology* (Vol. 2, pp. 113–134). Amsterdam: John Benjamins.

Fought, C. (2006) *Language and Ethnicity*. Cambridge: Cambridge University Press.

Garfinkel, H. (1967) *Studies in Ethnomethodology*. Englewood Cliffs, NJ: Prentice-Hall.

Hansen, A.D. (2005) A practical task: Ethnicity as a resource in social interaction. *Research on Language and Social Interaction* 38, 63–104.

Harris, P.R. and Moran, R.T. (1996) *Managing Cultural Differences* (4th edn). Houston: Gulf Publishing Company.

Hayashi, R. (1991) Floor structure of English and Japanese. *Journal of Pragmatics* 16, 1–30.

Hendon, D.W., Hendon, R.A. and Herbig, P. (1996) *Cross-Cultural Business Negotiations*. Westport, CT: Quorum Books.

Kjærbeck, S. (1998) Den etnometodologiske konversationsanalyse som kulturanalytisk metode. [Ethnomethodological conversation analysis as approach to the analysis of culture.] *HERMES. Journal of Linguistics* 20, 139–163.

Kjærbeck, S. (2001) 'Nosotros los españoles' y 'los de afuera': un studio de focus group sobre la identidad cultural y la formación de opinión. ['We the Spaniards' and 'the foreigners': A focus group study of cultural identity and opinion formation.] *Discurso y Sociedad. Lenguaje en contexto desde una perspectiva crítica y multidisciplinaria [In Discourse and Society. Language in Context from a Critical and Multidisciplinary Perspective]* 3, 43–74.

Moerman, M. (1988) *Talking Culture: Ethnography and Conversational Analysis*. Philadelphia: University of Pennsylvania Press.

Mori, J. (2003) The construction of interculturality: A study of initial encounters between Japanese and American students. *Research on Language and Social Interaction* 36, 143–184.

Mortensen, K. (2009) Establishing recipiency in pre-beginning position in the second language classroom. *Discourse Processes* 46, 491–515.

Nishizaka, A. (1995) The interactive constitution of interculturality: How to be a Japanese with words. *Human Studies* 18, 301–326.

Ochs, E. (1988) *Culture and Language Development: Language Acquisition and Language Socialization in a Samoan Village*. Cambridge: Cambridge University Press.

Sacks, H. (1992) *Lectures on Conversation*. Oxford: Blackwell.

Schegloff, E.A. (1992) In another context. In A. Duranti and C. Goodwin (eds) *Rethinking Context: Language as an Interactive Phenomenon* (pp. 191–228). Cambridge: Cambridge University Press.

Watson-Gegeo, K.A. (1992) Thick explanation in the ethnographic study of child socialization and development: A longitudinal study of the problem of schooling for Kwara'ae (Solomon Islands) children. In W.A. Corsaro and P.J. Miller (eds) *Interpretive Approaches to Children's Socialization* (pp. 51–66). San Francisco: Jossey-Bass.

Wagner, J. (1996) Conversation analysis of foreign language data. *Journal of Pragmatics* 26, 215–235.

Wieder, D.L. and Pratt, S. (1990) On being a recognizable Indian among Indians. In D. Carbaugh (ed.) *Cultural Communication and Intercultural Contact* (pp. 45–64). Hillsdale, NJ: Lawrence Erlbaum.

Chapter 7

International Basic Studies in the Humanities: Internationalization and Localization in Four Dimensions

A.H. FABRICIUS

Introduction

This chapter presents a case study of the practice of the so-called international Humanities education at one university within Denmark's borders (see also Chapters 1, 2 and 6 on the Scandinavian perspective). In the discussion that follows, I use Roskilde University's Basic Studies in the Humanities teaching program as a case study of some aspects of internationalization processes in university education in Denmark (see also Chapters 1, 2, 5 and 6 on internationalization 'at home'). In particular, I examine the relationship between a study program's official structure and formalized regulations on the one hand, and the actions and choices that ensue in practice and their unfolding in the work of teachers and students on the other. My observations of this process have led me to investigate processes of international educational frames and localization in a Danish context at work in a particular university pedagogy that aims to submit real-world problems to academic reflection and vice versa.

The study is empirically anchored in the author's one year of participation as a supervisor and the so-called 'house coordinator' (basically, an academic director) within one of Roskilde University's two-year undergraduate programs, International Basic Studies in the Humanities. For this program, as for the other similar study components in Natural Sciences, Social Sciences or Humanities/Technology, students are admitted to the first two years of tertiary study as members of a coordinated four-semester program. Within that two-year framework, half of a student's credit points are earned by carrying out undergraduate-level research-like work in the form of group-based problem-oriented project work within one or more of four Humanities thematic areas each semester. At Roskilde University students have the possibility of choosing between Danish-language and non-Danish language (English-dominated) study programs. It is the latter which is the context of our investigation here.

As a way into an understanding of how the university study regulations and the intentions behind them are implemented in practice, this chapter will describe the process of defining project work topics, from the initial project proposals authored by supervisors to the half-finished product of project papers submitted for the 'mid-way evaluation' that takes place roughly halfway into the term. The study's empirical material consists of student and supervisor documents deposited on a shared cooperative workspace at Roskilde University. It consists of the project work papers produced by one house cohort during the period 2006–2008, when the author was employed as coordinator of the house during its second year of existence.

The study reflects on the extent and manner in which *international themes and questions* are broached in student project work in the context of the Humanities disciplines in which these predominate. These will be contrasted with examples of project topics where students have chosen to negotiate and work with *local Danish topics*, to see the interplay of local and international themes and interests (see also Chapter 8 on local and global alignments). In making this contrast, I seek merely to differentiate between project topics that are anchored in local issues within Denmark's borders, and those which do not (which I call 'international' for convenience without further theoretical implications). Furthermore, I make no claims about the background of individual students (whether born and raised in Denmark or not), since this parameter was not part of my ethnographic knowledge of the whole group, but only in specific cases with students I worked closely with (see also Chapter 6 on the ethnomethodological method). It is no straightforward matter to categorize student backgrounds without detailed knowledge of the individuals, and that was not forthcoming in this case. Instead, the chapter's aims are more modest: to seek to provide an ethnographic window on one aspect of the roles of the local and the international in one example of undergraduate academic interests illustrated by this case study from Denmark (see also Chapters 3 and 11 on role expectations).

Content and Structure of the RU Program[1]

Roskilde University was established in 1972 as a consciously experimental university working within the paradigm that has come to be known as *experiential learning* in the English language literature. Principles of experiential learning are discussed in Kolb (1984), Illeris (1999, 2007) and Weil and McGill (1989).

Following admission to university study in first year at Roskilde University, students are assigned to one of several Basis *houses*, as they are called, that is, they become members of a year cohort consisting of, on average, 100–130 new first-year students. The four-semester program they then embark on entails that each semester's work (30 ECTS points) is equally divided between two courses of $7\frac{1}{2}$ ECTS each, and one project group work assignment, earning 15 ECTS (see also Chapter 6 on student group work). Half of their semester credits are therefore earned through collaborative work in project groups. Each project group in each semester is self-selected around a particular project topic or research question that the group is interested in investigating in depth. These project topics can either be initiated by students or the staff, with the majority being initiated by the staff in the early semesters. At the beginning of each semester, staff and students formulate a number of project outlines that are presented to the group as a whole at an introduction seminar. In the course of two or three days at the beginning of each term, a so-called 'shopping' process takes place whereby students talk to supervisors about project interests, and groups of, ideally, five to seven students begin to congregate into a fixed project group, committing themselves to working together with a particular project proposal for the duration of the term. The social processes that take place during this period of group formation are not the topic of this chapter, but descriptions can be found in publications such as Ulriksen (1997) and Frello (1997).

RU's university pedagogy[2] is also crucially an interdisciplinary one. Broad paradigms such as the Humanities in many universities have a range of clearly delimited disciplinary boundaries that have evolved during the course of the subject's development, and gatekeeping processes around these disciplines at traditional universities can be sharp at times. At RU, however, the ambition is to cross and question disciplinary boundaries as much as possible, since the starting point for much academic work at the university is an anchoring to real-world problems, which requires an intelligent application of theoretical insights that may often stem from different sources. Viewed in this light, the students' project work is intended to tackle such problems and find real-world solutions, utilizing the most suitable theories and methodological approaches, no matter where they may come from in narrow disciplinary terms.

Because of this interdisciplinary approach, each project proposal defined by a supervisor, and each emerging student group project proposal will be 'anchored' or delimited to one of the four Academic Dimensions that are seen as reflecting the methodological and theoretical span of 'the Humanities', broadly defined:

- History and Culture, abbreviated as HC (roughly corresponding to the traditional fields of History, Anthropology, Cultural Studies).
- Text and Sign, TS (roughly, Linguistics, Semiotics, Communication theory, Literary and to some extent Cultural theory).
- Science and Philosophy, SP (all branches of Philosophy and theory of Science, as well as applied disciplines such as Law).
- Subjectivity and Learning, SL (Pedagogy, Psychology and Sociology broadly speaking).

In some cases, students are able to cover more than one Humanities dimension in their project, but this is more common in the first year than in the second year, where projects tend to become more qualified and focused, with inter-disciplinarity defined in a more discipline-based way if it is represented.

Through their project work, students also have to negotiate gradual accommodation to the norms of academic investigative methods and, ideally, to the genres of academic writing (although this is not often taught overtly as a discipline but trained through feedback on written drafts commented on by supervisors). Access to these norms then is moreover enabled by orientation to a so-called *semester progression*, whereby each semester has a focus on one aspect of academic expertise, gradually building up a body of experience that enables students to continuously improve general academic skills. The intention is that they obtain a well-rounded explicit knowledge of the processes involved in project work in groups and the writing of project reports by the end of their four semesters in the program. The elements of the four-semester progression are as follows:

Framework 7.1 Semester progression

Semester 1: Technique/process of academic research
Semester 2: Method/methodology of the humanities
Semester 3: Theory of science/epistemology
Semester 4: Practice, incorporating aspects of all previous semesters

In addition, each two-year house has the option of formulating overarching research headlines that form a unified thematic framework for the duration of the house. The case presented in this chapter, an HIB (International Basic Studies in the Humanities) house from 2006 to 2008, had the following semester themes in the course of its history:

Framework 7.2 Semester themes for this house

Semester 1: Pleasure and pain
Semester 2: Work and play
Semester 3: Knowledge and belief
Semester 4: Citizenship

These broadly defined headline topics help to generate a thematic cohesion across the separate group project endeavors, and in some cases bring in house-wide perspectives that are explored in seminars held for all students.

At the end of the shopping period, each finalized project group is assigned a supervisor whose core research expertise is as close to the project group's interests as possible. The group is then responsible for arranging its meeting schedule such that the group arranges to meet alone, as well as at meetings with their supervisor as frequently as needed, with meetings one or two weeks apart for most of the semester.

Other important principles of RUC pedagogy, autonomy and student directedness consequently result in the actual content and process of production of a student group project being largely independently determined by the group's own wishes and academic concerns. The work is carried out under supervision from a qualified supervisor, so that certain academic constraints will be in operation. But the principle of student autonomy will mean that student-directed initiatives may potentially move the project in other directions than those envisaged by the supervisor, and this process will have to be accompanied by negotiations back and forth.

Supervision meetings can be regarded as examples of specialist, focused teaching sessions with a small group of students, which help to explore and shape their research topic. As well as working theoretically, some groups attempt to carry out fieldwork in Denmark or abroad, while others rely on library study and perhaps a case text to analyze in various ways, depending on the group's academic interests. The final project report goes through a supervised editing process, in that supervisors will read and comment on draft papers during the term. In addition, the group is trained in giving and receiving academic feedback and critique through three scheduled meeting sessions each term: the Problem Definition Seminar, which takes place early in the term, the Mid-term Evaluation and the presentation seminar immediately before the exam, where supervisors (who are also examiners for the project's oral exams) are not present. The final project report, submitted at the end of term, will comprise around 10–12 pages of writing by each student in the group.

Parameters of the Case Study

This chapter is framed around one exemplary case study of a Roskilde University Basic Studies in the Humanities house which existed from September 2006 to June 2008. The present author became the 'house coordinator' in August 2007, having responsibility for the organization of the academic content, staff and procedures during the study semester. While most of the empirical material here is in the form of written texts, the author's knowledge of the practices and history of the house can also play a role in the interpretations presented here.

During one year's participant observation as house coordinator, and as a participant in other Humanities houses since 2000, I observed many times the interesting process of formation and evolution of a student group's project topic during the course of the semester. As I was working in an 'international'[3] HUMBAS house where English and, to a small extent, French and German, are used as working languages, I became interested in the interplay of local Danish and 'international' non-Danish themes in the project proposals the supervisors were offering at the beginning of the term and the project work the students eventually carried out.

This chapter therefore seeks to answer the following questions:

- How do 'Danish' and 'international' topics interact in the processes of supervisor's defining of project topics and student reports-in-progress?
- How often do 'international' academic theories become localized into cases which form students' own research interests?
- To what extent do students maintain an 'internationalized' view of their research interests and academic goals?
- To what extent do students maintain a locally anchored 'Danish' view of their research interests and academic goals?

The discussion will proceed as follows: first, it will examine supervisor project proposals as presented in the published 'semester plans' at the beginning of each academic term and examine student uptake of these topics at the end of the group-formation process that also takes place each term. Second, papers distributed for the 'mid-semester evaluations', which examine progress in academic projects for terms 2, 3 and 4,[4] will be examined to see how the original project topics were transformed during the course of the semester. This transformation takes place through processes of student–staff negotiation, which will not be examined in detail here, but, which are at present being examined as part of at least one large-scale empirical project within the CALPIU research center.

This chapter combines quantitative and qualitative perspectives on the empirical material examined here. A survey approach will present numbers on project work themes and topics, while an exemplary case study will provide a qualitative view of one example of a thematic progression. I have had to eliminate final project reports from the data since these are not always accessible though the RUC library digital archive; instead, this work has had to rely on papers submitted to the house's BSCW electronic archive. Although relying on a comparison between initial project proposals and mid-semester evaluation papers does not give us access to the final products of the students' labours, the mid-way papers do give an indication of the developmental processes that are in focus here. For the purposes of simplicity, moreover, I have chosen to ignore multiple dimensions anchoring awarded at the students' final exams on the basis of the supervisor's recommendations. To avoid identifying individuals the project topics are classified only according to their major disciplinary affiliation and no supervisors or students details are given.

Data

As can be seen from Figure 7.1 and Table 7.1, on average across the four disciplinary areas, around 25% of project topics in supervisors' project proposals have local Danish elements interwoven in the proposal. The greatest representation is found within Subjectivity and Learning proposals,[5] the lowest within Text and Sign projects.

The majority of project proposals on the other hand seem to be anchored in 'non-local' or 'international' topics, orienting to academic literature emerging in other countries than Denmark, and using case study material that did not originate in Denmark.

The picture becomes somewhat different when we turn to considering the project works in progress submitted for the Mid-Semester Evaluation (Figure 7.2).

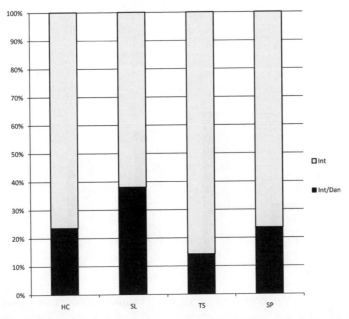

Figure 7.1 Rates of mention of local Danish topics in supervisors' original project proposals in terms 2, 3 and 4, plotted according to disciplinary area. (HC = History and Culture, SL = Subjectivity and Learning, TS = Text and Sign, SP = Theory of Science and Philosophy)

As an average across the four disciplinary areas, 46% of project topics in students' Mid-Semester project topics have local Danish elements interwoven in the proposal, which represents an increase of 20% from the position at the beginning of the semester. Although a large contribution toward this (approximately half) comes from supervisors' initial project proposals as formulated in the original Semester Plan from the beginning

Table 7.1 Number of tokens represented by percentages in Figure 7.1

Teachers	No. of project proposals	Local elements
HC	17	4
SL	21	8
TS	21	3
SP	17	4

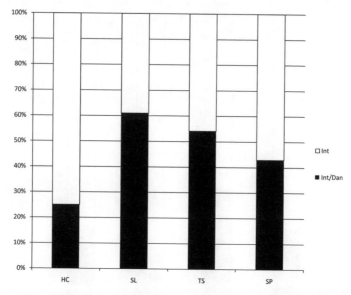

Figure 7.2 Rates of incorporation of local Danish topics in students' Mid-Semester Evaluation papers in terms 2, 3 and 4 plotted according to disciplinary area. (HC = History and Culture, SL = Subjectivity and Learning, TS = Text and Sign, SP = Theory of Science and Philosophy)

of term, student-directed project development seems to a large extent to be aligned towards incorporating local Danish issues into their project work, while at the same time retaining an international perspective through theory choice. In these data, SL projects again dominate, reaching around 60%, while HC projects are those which have least 'Danish' involvement, although the local element does appear in 25% of Mid-Semester papers (Table 7.2).[6]

Table 7.2 Number of tokens represented by percentages in Figure 7.2

Students	No. of project proposals	Local elements
HC	16	4
SL	18	11
TS	23	13
SP	15	6

The quantitative data, then, indicate a large degree of interplay between 'international' and 'locally anchored' elements in student' project work choices in this particular case of a class cohort in the RU program. Even in a so-called 'international' Basic Studies program, then, the potential and realized hybridity of project work in an intersecting non-local/local space is apparent, and is in some disciplinary areas evident in the majority of student projects. While survey figures such as these give us one snapshot view of the result of many conscious and unconscious processes, it is of necessity a limited view in various ways. To expand this view by means of one example, we take a qualitative case study into consideration in the next section of this chapter.

A Qualitative Case Study

In order to flesh out more details of the quantitative data presented above, we now turn to looking at one example study from my own supervisory experience. In Semester 4, the present author was responsible for a range of supervisor proposals anchored within the disciplinary area of 'Text and Sign'. The following proposal was one example:

Citizenship and Language Testing

Several nations around the world have introduced *language testing* in connection with the granting of citizenship. A recent European research network initiative has taken up the issue of *language and citizenship* testing in the light of several European countries' steps towards stricter *language testing procedures*. See http://www.testingregimes.soton.ac.uk/index.html. Accessed 4.4.11.

This project could examine *the ideological underpinnings of such language testing procedures*, and the assumptions held about the knowledge and proficiencies that they test. Is it possible to find a balance between a government's overarching concern for economic viability and growth and the social reality of migrant groups in that national framework? What happens to *linguistic human rights* in these situations? In the context of a still-growing EU, moreover, the complexities involved in this issue can only increase. (italics added)

The student uptake of this project proposal ended with a group of six students who formed a project group for the semester. This was indeed what happened; the students remained together and completed a successful project which they took to examination. Because of my role as supervisor, further documentation was available at the very end of their group process, and so the presentation below will also include documents written after the Mid-Semester Evaluation.

The Problem Definition Seminar paper, which the group formulated some three or four weeks after the beginning of the term, indicates that Denmark had already come to feature prominently in the group's thinking. They had immediately chosen to investigate the issue of (cultural and language) testing in connection with citizenship applications on home ground. The two forms of testing, the language test and the cultural knowledge test, are still in play in early project formulations. It is the latter that ultimately become the project's main focus. The cultural test already features in this initial problem formulation, with an additional interest in the political ramifications of such a testing regime in the current political climate:

Problem Definition Seminar

With this project we want to critically investigate the different requirements that need to be fulfilled to *acquire citizenship in Denmark* and further what *underlying political agendas* are behind these requirements. *We will look into the Danish language test* with the aim of uncovering possible cultural implications and attempt to discuss to what degree language testing is a necessity for integration. Dealing with this issue of language testing in relation to obtaining Danish citizenship there are many possible directions to go in, but seeing as we wish to anchor our project in cultural encounters, *our focus will be on the cultural aspect of the language test, examining possible cultural implications,* as opposed to a language discourse of the test. The above concerns have thus let [sic] us to some questions:

Is language testing the best instrument to measure someone's degree of integration in a given society?

What are the political arguments pro the *language- and 'culture' test?*

Is it possible to say that the Danish language in the context of acquiring a Danish citizenship is used as a political weapon? (italics added)

After further progress during the course of approximately six more weeks, the Mid-Semester Evaluation papers from the group show that the group's focus had shifted to the 'cultural' citizenship test, which seeks specifically to test knowledge of Danish culture and history. This test has been widely criticized in the media in Denmark, both for its form of administration and its contents. The language competence issue has moved to the background in favour of a cultural emphasis, and the Text and Sign dimension of the project instead emerges in a methodological decision to use discourse analyses to uncover the representation of 'Danishness' coming from various textual sources, (including eventually an interview with an influential right-wing figure in Danish politics, Søren Krarup). At the same time, an international, non-Danish perspective remains in their choice of theoretical insights and methodological tools.

In the introduction to the Mid-Semester Evaluation the students present their work so far in this way:

Mid-Semester Evaluation Paper

Our focal point with this project is to investigate the perceptions of Danish culture ('Danishness') which is represented in the test and what the test is a expression of. We have set out to read various materials on the concepts of the nation and nation-states, national identity, citizenship, multiculturalism and so on by reading T.H. Marshall, Yasemine Nuhoglu Soysal, Benedict Anderson, Elana Shohamy etc. We will investigate this representation of Danish culture and 'Danishness' by doing a semiotic discourse analysis of different text such as contributions to the general debate, newspaper articles and interviews with the politicians involved in the creation of the test itself. This discourse analysis will be with point of departure in Norman Fairclough's 'Language and Power', 'Describing discourse' and 'Analysing Discourse' with focus on the use of vocabulary and categorisation, both in the media and in politics. By doing this, we hope to be able to make some assessments on how the Danish culture and being Danish is being represented through the citizenship test. Further, we also aim at making some estimations on how the test will affect the general integration in Denmark in terms of assimilation vs. multiculturalism and how the test can be seen as inclusive or exclusive.

The group's formulation of the research question at this point is:

How is Danish Culture constructed in representations of and reflections on the citizenship test of 2005?

What is the ideology behind the test in terms of being a fellow citizen in Danish society? What is the cultural perception behind the test? To what extent can the test be seen as inclusive or/and exclusive? How is the test being used as a political tool/weapon? Which political processes have led to this particular citizenship test?

Later in the semester as the project hand-in deadline approached, the research question had developed to become:

How does the Danish Citizenship test represent the current Danish integration ideology?

The introductory paragraph shows that this question had arisen from another slight shift in research focus to the cultural test as a tool in immigration and integration policies:

The general tendency in Europe during the last decade, in regards to integration policies, has been very focused on the social integration and differentiation of refugees, where the latter has become more apparent and more desirable to the EU countries.

Through the implementation of citizenship tests, it has been easier for the countries to control how many immigrants apply and are granted citizenship in a given country.

There has been a clear want, as well as for some a need, for limiting the inclusion of refugees and asylum seekers in general (Etzioni, 2007).

The Netherlands, United Kingdom as well as others have implemented the method of testing, although with different approaches to how the specific themes within the tests are weighed.

In Denmark this has come to show as restrictions in the integration policies as well as the implementation of the controversial citizenship test. In this test, the applicant for citizenship has to answer 40 questions and pass in order to have any hopes of attaining Danish citizenship. This initiative has been one of the most heated topics in the Danish media, in the public as well as in the political arena.

Through the extensive debate on the topic, we have chosen to focus on the opinions put forth by the initiators of the citizenship test in order to try and clarify the underlying integration ideology, which becomes evident through their utterances and public statements on the topic.

The texts they have obtained (an interview with a prominent politician, a range of newspaper publications) are now the focus of a critical discourse analysis project that seeks to explore the construction of Denmark's immigration and integration policies as a discoursal reality. The real-world focus on 'one of the most heated topics in the Danish media' carries them through the academic material they are investigating and synthesizing into a relevant and timely academic project.

Conclusion and Future Perspectives

Rather than leaning wholly to one direction or another, either toward the local Danish context or the global, international arena, students in their practice at the International Humanities Basic Studies seem to negotiate an academic education *between* the spheres of the local and the international or 'non-local'. They engage with this interplay between the local and the non-local through their investigations into academic theories, the empirical case studies they choose to embark upon, and the problems they latch onto as needing to be treated, analyzed or solved. Thus, both the local and the international (often English) academic world feature in their project choices and both are valuable in developing academic competences of many kinds. Students clearly see a role for this hybridity and exploit the multilateral perspectives in their educational choices.

As noted above, this chapter's reliance on written sources is a limitation here, but it is hoped that this ethnographic view of a university educational program 'at work' can provide a framework for understanding one version of 'internationalising' processes in the university. Future work could focus on several other aspects of the practice of international educational project work, either those accessible through written documents or those through recordings of interactions. The former could examine for instance the textual treatment of language choice in written work, for example, whether quoted literature in Danish is translated or not, how fieldwork in international settings is tackled and described and so on (see also Chapter 1 on language choice). The latter type of investigation could take many forms: for instance, interviews with long-standing members of HIB teaching staff could shed light on the supervisors' reflections on their role as teachers in an internationalized study program. The type of investigation presented here would also be complemented by investigations of recorded interactions that would give access to the negotiations of students' work processes through the development of a project topic during the semester. Such investigations are currently being planned and carried out within the purview of the CALPIU center (www.calpiu.dk. Accessed 4.4.11). Interviews with students on their work processes and their reflections on ways of negotiating 'problem-orientation' and potential interplays between theory and practice on the ground in Denmark would also serve to illuminate the complexity that students face in learning academic method, disciplinary content and interdisciplinarity through problem-oriented project work in a university curriculum.

Notes

1. http://www.ruc.dk/ruc_en/studying/ has an English language description of the study program at Roskilde University. Accessed 4.4.11.
2. See http://www.ruc.dk/ruc_en/ for detailed descriptions of the study programs and their underlying pedagogical principles. http://studieguide.ruc.dk/ provides a description in Danish. Accessed 4.4.11.
3. As stated above, 'international' here is to be understood as meaning 'not specifically linked to Denmark'.
4. Term 1 documents were not uploaded to the collaborative work server and were thus unavailable to the author.
5. Several proposals within this category sought to apply pedagogical theory directly to Danish case studies, for instance.
6. There is to some extent an individual element to this division within the results: some supervisors are keen to promote links between local situations and theoretical positions, and do so more often, but we lack empirical evidence of this process over and above the data presented here. Ethnography of particular supervisors' practice would be enlightening in this regard and is intended to be a topic of future research.

References

Etzioni, A. (2007) The community deficit. *Journal of Common Market Studies* 45, 23–42.
Frello, B. (1997) *Ny lærer på RUC – møde med RUC kulturen [New teacher at RUC – meeting the RUC culture]* (Vol. 9). Delrapport, UNIPÆD-projektet. Roskilde: Roskilde University.

Illeris, K. (1999) *Læring: aktuel læringsteori i spændingsfeltet mellem Piaget, Freud og Marx. [Learning: current educational theory in the tension between Piaget, Freud and Marx.]* Roskilde Universitetsforlag.

Illeris, K. (2007) *How we Learn: Learning and Non-Learning in School and Beyond.* Routledge: Taylor & Francis.

Kolb, D.A. (1984) *Experiential Learning: Experience as the Source of Learning and Development.* Englewood Cliffs, NJ: Prentice-Hall.

Ulriksen, L. (1997) *Projektpldagogik – hvorfor det? [Project-based pedagogy – what for?]* (Vol. 7). Delrapport, UNIPÆD-projektet. Roskilde: Roskilde University.

Weil, S. and McGill, I. (1989) *Making Sense of Experiential Learning.* Milton Keynes: Open University Press.

Appendix 1

Term no.	Humanities dimension	Supervisors' topic presentations at the start of the semester	Proposal International/ Local
1	HC	Pleasure and pain in the love affair of Abelard and Eloise	int
1	HC	What caused the rise of the West?	int
1	HC	Let's go to the beach. Why?	int/loc
2	HC	Working out migration	Int
2	HC	Adolf Hitler and Joseph Goebbels	Int
2	HC	A miracle of work?	int/loc
2	HC	Play it out on the beach	int/loc
2	HC	NSDAP Propaganda 1934–1935	int
3	HC	Clash or Noma between science and religion	int
3	HC	Kant	int
3	HC	Erasmus vs. Luther	int
3	HC	Reception of Darwinism in Denmark or other country	int/loc
4	HC	Why is Kant's categorical imperative inappropriate to guide civil legislation?	int
4	HC	The idea of citizenship in Plato's Republic.	int

Term no.	Humanities dimension	Supervisors' topic presentations at the start of the semester	Proposal International/ Local
4	HC	An analysis of Tom Paine's *Rights of Man.*	int
4	HC	An analysis of Henry David Thoreau's *Civil Disobedience.*	int
4	HC	Nagorno Karabakh	Int
1	SL	Globalization and education: Towards a new imperialism	int
1	SL	Pleasure and pain of mobile communication	int
1	SL	Technology, self and the body in pain	int
1	SL	Education in an age of neo-liberalism	int/loc
2	SL	Learning at RUC	int/loc
2	SL	Learning at RUC II	int/loc
2	SL	Technology and conduct of everyday life	int
2	SL	Work and identity	int
2	SL	Social currency in extinct civilizations	Int
2	SL	New social movements in Latin America	Int
2	SL	From Summerhill to the Wall	int/loc
3	SL	Learning at RUC	int/loc
3	SL	Contemporary, competing concepts of education and learning?	int
3	SL	Technology, self and everyday life	int
3	SL	Theorizing experience	int
3	SL	San people in Botswana	int
4	SL	Johnny Foreigner	int/loc
4	SL	The individualized citizen: Time, distraction and the conduct of everyday life	int

Term no.	Humanities dimension	Supervisors' topic presentations at the start of the semester	Proposal International/ Local
4	SL	Gender in *Farewell My Concubine*	Int
4	SL	Reform pedagogy, Neill and Summerhill	int/loc
4	SL	Technology, citizenship and influence in everyday life	int/loc
1	SP	The pleasure of reason	int
1	SP	Hedonism	int
1	SP	The sublime	int
1	SP	Abuse	int/loc
2	SP	The ontology of toys	Int
2	SP	Care as work	int/loc
2	SP	Slavery	int/loc
2	SP	Want vs need	int?
3	SP	Does my opinion matter?	int
3	SP	I feel that you don't understand me	int
3	SP	Right and wrong and true and false	int
3	SP	Credibility	int
3	SP	Transhumanism	int
3	SP	Morality and the laws of war	int
3	SP	Is the world eternal?	int/loc
4	SP	Membership	int
4	SP	Citizenship and society	int
1	TS	The concepts of health and happiness, based on an analysis of media texts	?
1	TS	Ethical considerations about killing animals	?
1	TS	Pleasure and pain: Emotive messages in advertising	int

Term no.	Humanities dimension	Supervisors' topic presentations at the start of the semester	Proposal International/ Local
1	TS	Bernard Malamud on pleasure and pain	int
2	TS	Language in play	int
2	TS	Language at work	int
2	TS	Work and play in Dickens	int
2	TS	Second life – Working or playing?	int
2	TS	Play and work in the research interview	int/loc
2	TS	When music went viral	Int?
3	TS	Language varieties on the move in Europe	int
3	TS	Concepts of language in linguistics	int
3	TS	Envisioning theory, project for a visual essay	int
3	TS	Visual culture in the digital age	int
3	TS	Digital rights and wrongs: The new economy of the image	int
4	TS	Language and culture	int/loc
4	TS	What is a speech community? Linguistic Citizenship under the microscope.	int
4	TS	English as a lingua franca: Attitudes and identity	int
4	TS	Citizenship and language testing	int
4	TS	Envisioning theory: Project for a visual essay	int
4	TS	Ways of seeing: Practices of looking	int
4	TS	Digital rights and wrongs: About local and global media politics, citizenship and identity	int
4	TS	The European Union and language learning in higher education	int/loc

Appendix 2

Term no.	Student's project titles at the mid-semester evaluation in four terms of the house	Supervisors specialities	int/loc
1	The letters of Abelard and Heloise	HC	
1	The rise of the west A	HC	
1	The rise of the west B	HC	
2	Play on the beach	HC	int/loc
2	Collapse of the Inca empire	HC	int
2	Documentaries and propaganda	HC	int
2	Goebbels and Hitler	HC	int
3	Science and religion	HC	int
3	The reception of Darwinism	HC	int
3	The reception of Darwinism 2	HC	int
3	Erasmus versus Luther	HC	int
4	The conflict in Afghanistan	HC	int
4	Kierkegaard's attack on the Danish Church	HC	int/loc
4	White man's burden	HC	int
4	Henry Thoreau's *Civil Disobedience*	HC	int
4	Kant's categorical imperative	HC	int/loc
4	The Nagorno–Karabakh conflict	HC	int
4	Dostoyevsky's Super-human	HC	int/loc
4	Plato and contemporary democracy	HC	int
1	Pleasure and pain of mobile communication	SL	
1	Pleasure and pain of mobile communication	SL	
1	Pain and development	SL	
1	Education in an age of neoliberalism: Subculture	SL	
1	Globalization and education	SL	

Term no.	*Student's project titles at the mid-semester evaluation in four terms of the house*	*Supervisors specialities*	*int/loc*
2	SM in LA	SL	int
2	Social movements and media	SL	int/loc
2	Learning 1 ruc	SL	int/loc
2	Learning 3	SL	int
2	Learning 2 summerhill	SL	int/loc
2	Work and identity 1	SL	int/loc
2	Work and identity 2	SL	int/loc
3	Cell phone and sociality	SL	int/loc
3	Transhumanism	SL	int
3	Theorizing experience	SL	int
3	San people in Botswana	SL	int
4	Outside the collective	SL	int/loc
4	Loneliness	SL	int/loc
4	Gender issues in *Farewell My Concubine*	SL	int/loc
4	Multicultural learning in Danish public schools	SL	int/loc
4	Education a global perspective	SL	int
4	Sexual education for ethnic minorities	SL	
4	Sociology, work and organization	SL	int/loc
4	Account of a lost land. Tibet	SL	int
1	The sublime	SP	
1	Free will: Control versus causality	SP	
1	Free will: Control versus causality	SP	
1	Abuse	SP	int/loc
1	The pleasure of reason A	SP	
1	The pleasure of reason B	SP	
2	Trafficking, slavery	SP	int/loc

Term no.	Student's project titles at the mid-semester evaluation in four terms of the house	Supervisors specialities	int/loc
2	Slavery 2	SP	int/loc
2	Want vs. need	SP	int
2	Soldier poet at war	SP	int
3	Does my opinion matter	SP	int/loc
3	I feel that you don't understand me	SP	int/loc
3	Philosophy and sociology	SP	int
3	Is the world eternal	SP	int
3	Jus ad bellum	SP	int
3	Morality and the laws of war	SP	int
3	The fear of Islam	SP	int
3	Honour killings	SP	int
4	Human freedom and the Second World War	SP	int/loc
4	Society and citizen	SP	int
1	Emotive markers in advertising	TS	
1	Online identity	TS	
1	Ethical considerations about killing animals	TS	
1	Malamud	TS	
1	Malamud	TS	
1	Malamud	TS	
2	Business studies communication linguistics	TS	loc
2	Controversial art	TS	int
2	Hip hop identity	TS	int/loc
2	Dickens literary	TS	int
2	Dickens literary	TS	int
2	Music group 2nd life	TS	int

Term no.	Student's project titles at the mid-semester evaluation in four terms of the house	Supervisors specialities	int/loc
2	Research interview	TS	int/loc
2	Research interview 2	TS	int/loc
2	Metafilm	TS	
3	Religion in political discourse	TS	int
3	P3	TS	int/loc
3	The culture of language	TS	int
3	Envisioning theory	TS	int/loc
3	Analogue vs. digital, visual culture	TS	int
3	Digital rights and wrongs	TS	int/loc
4	Political constructions of Danish National Identity	TS	int/loc
4	Language and culture	TS	int/loc
4	Language and culture 2	TS	int
4	ELF a question for the students	TS	int/loc
4	250 years of English	TS	int
4	1984 – An analysis	TS	int
4	Salaam DK – Illuminating cultural diversity	TS	int/loc
4	Envisioning theory – Satire	TS	int/loc
4	Digital rights and wrongs; online bullying	TS	int/loc

Part 4
Academic Writing and Literacy in a Transnational Perspective

Chapter 8

Crossing Borders: The Feasibility of Harmonising Academic Literacy Standards across Europe

C. SEDGWICK

Introduction

The Bologna agreement to harmonise degree qualifications across Europe is an ambitious project aimed at promoting transparency of degree-level qualifications to enable mobility for work and study (see also Airey's discussion on the Bologna agreement in Chapter 1). Through the creation of a European higher education space the agreement also aims to reassert the European university as the prototype for the modern university, the originator of traditions and structures that are still in evidence across the world today. Rüegg notes 'an astonishing unanimity' (Rüegg, 1992: 31) in university practices across Europe towards the end of the medieval period where the 'licentia ubique docendi' (Rüegg, 1992: 17), the licence to teach everywhere, the qualification following examination at the end of university studies, was recognised throughout Europe. Following 500 years of political and economic change, the growth of nation states and the development of the individual identity of the universities, the Bologna project aims to return to the idea of a universal licence. This chapter will report an English language project that seeks to examine some of the challenges to those aims in a small-scale project in universities in two different European countries, Italy and Hungary. The purpose of the study is to investigate what students would need to know and be able to do as writers if they wanted to cross national borders to study in a different linguistic and cultural context in Europe (see also Klitgård's discussion of *academic literacy* in Chapter 9 of this volume).

Needs analyses are commonly used to investigate the language requirements of students in specified contexts of use, so that language programmes and, or, assessments can be developed that will be relevant to students and employers, professional or educational institutions. However, data collection exercises to establish need are problematic. Large-scale surveys in the absence of preliminary small-scale studies risk reflecting the researcher's view about language use in the context(s) investigated because the researcher decides what categories of data they want to collect in advance of the data collection. Such surveys also make an assumption about universality in practices that may not exist. Alternatively, collecting and categorising assignment and examination prompts, advocated by Horowitz (1986a, 1986b), may seem a more direct means of establishing what writers have to do in writing in certain contexts, but there can be problems in interpretation of the task requirements in the absence of the task designer, as Hale *et al.* (1996) discovered. An additional problem, however, is that products and practices developed from task taxonomies in large-scale research analysis exercises are open to local interpretation, as Purves (1992) experienced in a large-scale project involving 14 countries internationally to develop a common framework for the assessment of school writing across national borders. A contributing factor could be that in the development of such common taxonomies a great deal of 'local' information may be lost. Leung (2005) criticises the needs analysis approach that is generally adopted for curriculum development as being too partial, leading to the construction of syllabuses and textbooks based on overgeneralisation and idealisation of genres and stereotypes (see also Chapters 4 and 12 in this volume) that do not necessarily represent communication in the real world. He advocates a fresh approach to investigation of context that is 'ethnographically sensitive', taking more account of the social context: 'Theoretically as well as pedagogically, there is every reason to reconnect with the social world if the concept of communicative competence is to mean anything more than a textbook simulacrum of Englishes in the world' (Leung, 2005: 144).

The current study aims to investigate academic English in the 'real' world by taking a New Literacy Studies perspective towards research design and data analysis. New Literacy Studies are based on the concept of literacy as a social practice. According to Barton (2007) literacy practices reflect attitudes, beliefs and values about writing that are socially situated. Baynham states that literacy practices are '... not just what people do with literacy, but what they make of what they do, the values they place on it and the ideologies that surround it' (Baynham, 1995: 1). This approach to the investigation of writing in context can yield a richer, more holistic view than an atomistic, reductive, taxonomic approach to writing requirements. New Literacy Studies adopt an ethnographic approach to studying literacy in social contexts (for a discussion on ethnographic approaches, see also Chapters 6 and 7 of this volume). Linguistic ethnography problematises the relationship between writing and context. Lillis (2008) advocates an ethnography-as-methodology approach to explore text-making practices in relation to the social context. However, she further proposes an approach which recognises ethnography as 'deep theorising' (Blommaert, 2007). In order to 'close the gap' between text and context in ethnographic research she utilises notions of 'indexicality' and 'orientation', to examine how aspects of context are 'indexed' by certain literacy practices for participants and how they 'orient' subjectively to those practices.

An ethnographic approach that acknowledges Lillis' (2008) interpretations of ethnography is used in the current study to investigate practices surrounding the production and evaluation of postgraduate theses of English language major students in a Hungarian and an Italian university. The thesis was selected because it was the most significant and the most demanding piece of writing that students had to complete in each context. My research questions are:

(1) What academic literacy practices are valued positively on the two programmes in the study?
(2) What similarities and differences in these practices can be identified across the two programmes?
(3) How do these practices relate to the social and cultural contexts?

I carried out a feasibility study in the Hungarian university in 2006. The data collection was made over a two-year period from each university in consecutive years, 2007 and 2008. A preliminary visit to meet staff and students, explain my research and recruit participants for the project was followed by two weeks in each site at the end of the assessment period. The research focused on six theses, three from each site, completed by students who had been successful on their degree programmes because they were predicted to complete theses that would be regarded as 'good practice'. The following data were collected:

- The assessed theses plus drafts with written feedback.
- Interviews: semi-structured interviews concerning each thesis were conducted with student authors; a supervisor and referee in Hungary; a supervisor as assessor, additionally a second reader for one thesis in Italy; Heads of Department.

- Follow-up email exchanges with students and staff.
- Contextual information from the staff and university websites (programme details, thesis instructions and any criteria that were available).

Of major importance in evaluation of the thesis was 'originality'. It was a criterion that was highlighted in all the interviews and in the thesis texts and assessor's reports. It was usually emphasised, given as the first criterion for thesis evaluation, or sought in finding a focus for the thesis, but it was absent from the thesis guidelines in the Italian context and not accorded the same prominence in the criteria for thesis evaluation listed in the Hungarian context. An analysis of the findings in relation to this criterion is reported below.

Originality

Originality was interpreted in terms of presenting new perspectives, new understandings, new meanings, utilising new approaches through thesis research, for a particular academic community. Novelty related to research that had been published in the academic communities that academics aligned to. As experts in the community, but also student mentors, supervisors were expected to identify new possibilities for MA thesis research and encourage new approaches. The students were expected to make a contribution to the work of the academic community by supplying new ideas, new interpretations (see Table 8.1).

Ongstad (2005) proposes a framework to capture meaning-making in text in terms of three dimensions of writer positioning in relation to the evaluation of language use, form and content, respectively. Within this framework, language as a social act is evaluated normatively or 'ethically': form, aesthetically and content knowledge, epistemologically. These dimensions are interdependent, but one or more may be salient in any context. Ongstad based his framework on the concept of positioning as defined by Harré and Van Langenhove (1999), who describe how participants discursively position themselves and others in an act of communication. Positioning accounts for the multiplicity and fluidity of the roles that could be selected from the range that participants, assessors, supervisors and students in the current study perceived to be available to them in their evaluation of the originality of the thesis.

Ongstad's 'triadic' conceptualisation of positioning was identified in the current study in the different participant positions adopted in the data and is reflected in the division of the discussion of the findings with

Table 8.1 Summary of what was regarded as original in each thesis

Case study	Originality	Participants
Case study 1	New interpretation of Wordsworth's 'The Prelude'	HA, HSA, HRA
Case study 2	New understandings of a metafictional novelist's work	HB, HSB, HRB
Case study 3	New perspective on dyslexia in language learning	HC, HSC, HRC
Case study 4	New understandings of an understudied 17th Century English masque	IA, ISA
Case study 5	New method to investigate Virginia Woolf's *To the Lighthouse*	IB, ISB
Case study 6	New method to investigate genre in web texts	IC, ISC, IRC

Note: Key to participant codes: H = Hungary; I = Italy; R = Referee (Hungarian context) or Reader (Italian context); S = Supervisor; A, B, C = Students

regard to the evaluation of originality below. The following section on 'Social Positioning', describes various participant alignments to communities that were assumed to benefit from the thesis contribution: local and global (see also Chapter 7 of this volume), present and invisible, real and imagined. The section on 'Subjective Positioning' concerns participant positions in relation to the form of the work, which could be linked to the moral qualities of the writer. The section on 'Epistemological Positioning' reflects participant stance with regard to the nature of knowledge and how it can be acquired and communicated in their evaluation of the validity of the thesis contribution.

Social Positioning

Participants positioned themselves in relation to academic or non-academic, present or imagined, local or global communities to make and evaluate claims for the contribution of new perspectives, understandings or meanings in relation to a phenomenon of these communities.

Making a contribution

The thesis was framed by academics in four of the case studies in terms of its 'contribution' to a specific disciplinary community. Novelty in terms of contribution to the portfolio of an academic community was identified by Kaufer and Geisler (1989). The value of the contribution was monitored by supervisors who had been selected by students because they were experts in the disciplinary specialism, community members. HA's contribution was to the community of Wordsworth scholars, particularly those interested in his autobiographical poem, 'The Prelude': 'it's most important contribution to this whole topic is this idea itself, that is, of taking a look at how Tengelyi's diacritical phenomenology may be put to use in the reading of the *Prelude'* (HSA interview). HRA, who was also an expert in the Romantic period, proposed that the results of the analysis could 'transform thinking' within the disciplinary community: 'introducing and applying a new set of critical concepts, the author manages significantly to redefine Wordsworth's specific relationship with his autobiography' (HRA written feedback).

ISA is more guarded in her claims for IA's thesis, but, nevertheless indicates its utility for the implied community of scholars who are experts in the literary work of the period in which the 'Raguaillo d'Oceano', the 17th-century masque that was the focus of the study, is situated. Perhaps she is considering an even wider academic audience, because the masque resurrects a work that has been neglected by the academic community. She situates it for future readers in its social, historical and political context: 'Altogether, I think this is useful for anybody who hasn't read 'Raguaillo d'Oceano'. (ISA interview)

However, it is unlikely that these novel ideas would be disseminated to their respective communities unless they are published. Publication was indexed as a goal in interviews with academics in Case Studies 3 and 5. Contribution to the work of a community within the Department but also, potentially, to the wider academic community through publication was also important for ISB. She specifically sought students who could participate in the Department project to investigate meaning in Virginia Woolf's novels through empirical studies involving a systemic functional analysis of the texts: 'I had been looking for people to do this sort of corpus linguistics sort of work with the tagging of Virginia Woolf's texts for various linguistic phenomena' (ISB interview). As project leader she was able to identify gaps in the research:

CS: 'Do you refer students to previous studies?'
ISB: 'Definitely. Definitely. I certainly do, particularly I do because I try
        to do things that fit together because I wanted to be able to put

them all together to see an overall picture ... I usually try to get them to come up with some data of some sort to offer.' (ISB interview)

This 'offer' was framed in terms of a contribution to the work of the Department but also more broadly to the wider community of scholars involved in Stylistics research, or with a specific interest in new applications of the analytic tool. ISB gave me a copy of an international publication in which she had cited systemic functional linguistic research by thesis students in the Department, including IB: 'what is going to happen is that the data is going to be used with reference to her thesis in that bibliography. The data is something that I've published and this is something that has already happened with other theses as well' (ISB interview). She described students' contributions in terms of helping to progress the study, perhaps transforming interpretations and research methods within the community of scholars interested in linguistic solutions to the interpretation of Virginia Woolf's novels: 'they need to do some sort of research project where they are actually moving the discourse forward, moving the theory forward moving the application forward, moving the knowledge in our discipline forward even in some small way' (ISB interview).

HSC asserted that HC's 'contribution' should reach a wider audience through publication but did not anticipate that she would publish as an academic, perhaps because she perceived the thesis would be of value to practitioners, rather than academics:

> I told her that after she has finished at the university, I would like her to think about writing it up in a short version and then publishing it because I think there's a lot in it that other people could learn from, particularly because the parents have never been thought of and they should. (HSC interview)

HRC, on the other hand, had been disappointed that it could not be published as part of the Departmental research project on dyslexia and language learning in the English language publication that she edited because the work did not meet the perceived requirements of the community of applied linguists that the publication would serve:

> we have a big research project on dyslexia and we have looked at all aspects. We have interviewed teachers. We have interviewed students. We have interviewed special ed teachers who have dyslexic children and so on but we have never looked at the parents' views and I was very happy that she chose this topic because I thought, well, that's a perspective we have never investigated, how the parents perceive the problems these students have with language learning and I was

disappointed because I learned very little about actual language learning problems. (HRC interview)

However, the research seemed to fulfil the requirements for a Hungarian publication, which were presupposed, perhaps, to be less rigorous: 'it's a pity because it's a good topic and I actually wanted to publish this in a volume that we edit but I decided no because there is not enough data in here because I mean three students are few anyway but I mean it would be OK for a Hungarian publication' (HRC interview).

Utilising community genres

The thesis texts, with the exception of Case study 4, made appeals for novelty to academic communities through generic structures identified in applied linguistic research on Anglo-American journal articles. According to Hyland (2004), abstracts are an important means of capturing the attention of interested readers, to claim community membership and to promote research. Readers are motivated by 'a search for novelty and relevance to their own work' (Hyland, 2004: 64–65). Berkenkotter and Huckin (1995) examined claims for novelty in American scientific articles over half a century and identified an increase in the inclusion of abstracts in articles, used as a means of showcasing work. They explain this in terms of increased global competition for attention in academia, as well as an ideological shift towards a post-modern promotional, consumerist culture. Abstracts were included in the Hungarian[1] but not the Italian theses. It could be that in this context the abstract was regarded as an important component of the thesis for potential future academics in the spirit of 'initiation' into the global academic community because abstracts are expected for publication in English-medium academic journals. The Hungarian thesis abstracts followed a common abstract structure identified in Anglo-American journals by Hyland (2004: 69): Purpose, Method, Product (outcomes, findings or conclusions). Novelty is highlighted in HA's abstract. She claims that the theoretical framework that she has selected for analysis 'has not been applied to Wordsworth's poetry yet' (HA thesis). HB states that his paper will demonstrate how 'Auster sheds light on a new perspective' in the relationship between fiction and reality. HC does not make any specific claims for originality in her abstract, though she promotes the perspective she is presenting as important. Interestingly, although this text feature may have been regarded as important for the global academic community, it did not seem to be rated as highly by HA's referee: 'I don't care about the abstract very much. I usually skip that' (HA interview). HRA also represented the 'real' local community of referees who could not select which papers to read in her role as assessor, and so the abstract served no purpose for her.

Swales (1990, 2004), Berkenkotter and Huckin (1995) and Bhatia (1993) explained Introductions as a persuasive, promotional tool for academics. Swales (1990) identified move structure in academic article Introductions, in which academics could promote novelty: by indicating a gap in the research, raising questions or providing counter-claims for arguments made in previous research. All except for Case study 4 contained an Introduction in which a gap in the research of an academic community was either explicit or implicit:

- HA repeats her claim made in the abstract for the novelty of the analytical framework that she is using: 'This philosophical background will, I believe, help in answering or answering differently and more appropriately a few long-present questions and theoretical problems that scholars have raised in Wordsworth's poetry.' (HA thesis)
- HB does not make any explicit attempt to establish a niche but states that his purpose is 'to examine this peculiar set of novels .... to explore how and why metafictional devices are used' (HB thesis). By selecting 'peculiar' he makes claims for the rarity of the literary texts and his use of 'explore' indicates the innovative nature of the study.
- HC refers to a gap in her pedagogic studies at university that related to a knowledge gap in the community of practitioners: 'Unfortunately, during my university studies I was not educated on dyslexia at all. However, from my point of view, if teachers want to help dyslexics, they should be aware of the fact that that dyslexic students experience difficulties in several areas of learning.' (HC thesis)
- IB situates her work in relation to earlier studies when she states her aims: 'By analysing conjunction in "To the Lighthouse", this thesis also aims to see whether one of these devices (conjunction) might signal different points of view, and might simplify or help the interpretation of point of view in the novel', thus contributing to the existing interpretations. (IB thesis)
- IC discusses the novelty of the phenomenon of web genres and makes claims for the centrality of her research within this new field. She does not explicitly make a claim for novelty or identify a gap in the research in her text, although the gap is implicit 'it may be interesting to investigate how these genres have been created and how language has been adapted to the new medium' (IC thesis).

In all cases cited above indications of gaps or needs within the academic and/or practitioner communities were framed within existing research and/or practice, which were used to present a positive justification for the thesis. In contrast to the relative modesty discovered by Árvay and Tankó (2004) in *Hungarian Applied Linguistics* journal articles, the Hungarian students emphasised the importance of their research by presenting a positive justification for it and by explicitly or implicitly indicating gaps. IA, perhaps, did not consider it necessary to make appeals to novelty because the text that was the focus of her study was likely to be new to the reader, or, possibly because she was also working within a research tradition where claims for originality were not expected in an academic text.

As Samraj (2008) discovered in her genre research with thesis students of Philosophy and Applied Linguistics in the United States, claims were not necessarily situated within an extensive literature review. HC supplied a separate literature review and repeated the gap or need at the end of the review, but the new perspective she proposed was not explicitly tied to any questions deriving from the literature:

> As we can see a lot of research has been conducted investigating dyslexia, but there are a number of questions left open. My aim is to open up for a new perspective: that of the parents. (HC thesis)

Local and global alignments

HRB reports the dilemma faced by academics who want to identify gaps in community knowledge. He participated on a panel to approve of the new Master's programmes and stated that 'even originality' was included as a criterion for student success, despite the fact that it was impossible to demonstrate mastery: 'It's very difficult to be original now, you see, so we ought to confront this situation that there is so much information available it is impossible to be master of anything nowadays because of just how much material concerning this or that topic there is. So maybe the whole idea ought to be reconsidered' (HRB interview). An academic could not confidently make claims for originality based on what had been published within a disciplinary specialism in which so much published research is now accessible via electronic communications.

Notwithstanding, supervisors and assessors aligned to global as well as local disciplinary communities in their claims for an original contribution in the student theses. Students seemed to understand that novelty was expected in implicitly or explicitly alluding to gaps in the research that they intended to fill. However, they were in the peculiar position of making claims for their work in relation to disciplinary communities, where they were not members, not even legitimate peripheral participants as described by Lave and Wenger (1991) because they did not participate in the daily life of the community of academics as department members or disciplinary specialists.[2] They did not attend Departmental meetings, conferences, publish, teach or participate in online community networks. The communities that supervisors and referees made claims for were imagined or partially experienced by students. Students were expected to demonstrate novelty in relation to existing work and anticipate the value of their contribution in relation to global disciplinary or, in the case of HC, and, possibly, IC, practitioner communities. However, the real communities that would read the theses were local. They were the supervisors, assessors and researchers (student and academic) in each local context. This tension between writing for a global and a local audience was apparent in the student interviews and perhaps reflected the level of experience that they had had with more global communities, an explanation advanced for similar findings by Kaufer and Geisler (1989) and discussed by Bartholomae (1985), Berkenkotter and Huckin (1995), (Ivanic, 1997), Dysthe (2002) and Koutsantoni (2005).

IA and HA seemed to be more confident about their claims for originality with reference to the disciplinary communities in which their work was situated. This confidence could reflect a higher level of familiarity with these communities. IA had won a scholarship to spend four months in the United States conducting research for her thesis and had been able to take on a role as legitimate peripheral participant. She had attended lectures as a student, but she had been able to discuss her thesis with specialists in the same topic area and had delivered a paper on her work at a regional conference there. She reported that her thesis had been of interest to academics in the United States. Her thesis topic had been selected by her supervisor because it was a little-known text. She had been able to take advantage of the opportunity offered by the topic to make a contribution to the literary community because her thesis 'talked about a topic that was not much exploited' (IA interview). IA seemed assured of the originality and importance of her work to the community 'to challenge knowledge and do something original' (IA interview).

HA also made quite confident claims for her perspective, perhaps because she had introduced it to her supervisor as expert, who had assured her that her work was original: 'Well, I think that this topic is quite a new perspective on Wordsworth's poetry and this is the strength of my paper' (HA interview). However, in her interview, she stated that she was not aiming for a specialist audience:

I try to make my own points clear that can be understood by people who like literature and are not experts in Wordsworth's poetry. I think the philosophical part is quite hard to understand but actually I hope that I could write in a way in that everyone who is interested in literature and who reads other papers in literature can understand but I don't think this is very easy reading. (HA interview)

Perhaps she was thinking of the potential audience of local MA students who might read her work.[3]

Despite the fact that IB believed she had performed an original piece of research and had produced original results: 'I have created something which other people have tried but I have created an analysis. I have created some results, I have created a discussion (IB interview), she framed novelty more locally in relation to the Commission[4] who would make the final decision on her grade for the thesis: 'they liked that I had chosen something innovative, something different from the other students' (IB interview). This more local audience is reflected in her comments on the audience for her writing:

By looking at an essay? Yes, essays meaning texts, books ... written by a Prof of Linguistics and by trying to think about the people who could have read my thesis so I tried to think like I was a person who does not know anything about Linguistics or a person who does not know what (?) is what is English linguistics, so I tried to be as clear as possible. Trying to repeat these ideas and so on. (IB interview)

The apparent ambiguity of modelling her essay on a text written by a Professor of Linguistics and writing for a non-linguistic audience, reflects the 'display' nature of these texts, which were expected to be written in a style required by an international audience in the specialism but which needed to be accessible in terms of content for the Commission, who would be composed of non-linguists as well as linguists:

I just tell them that they need to read academic writing and when they for example when they start doing their bibliographies and referring to things and they're coming along putting in footnotes that have their bibliographies in the footnotes then I just pick up the books that we have around here and say, look, this is the way it's done nowadays, in the text with just the author's name and date and page numbers in parentheses, basically showing them how things are done today, showing them the bibliography, when they start putting things in some other order than they should be. (ISB interview)

Interestingly, ISB emphasises 'the way it's done today', presupposing that the same citation requirements had not been required in the past. Perhaps this reflects the fact that students are now expected to address a more global audience for their claims than they would have in the past.

Subjective Positioning

Students positioned themselves subjectively in their descriptions of the process of generating new ideas. HA and HB positioned themselves as creators, discoverers of new ideas through writing. HA contrasted the opportunities afforded by the thesis to develop new ideas with the less creative writing she had experienced in the MA courses:

> I think I did write 2 or 3 argumentative essays in Linguistics and Literature but usually they were not that you found out something but that you had to read many and then to organise the things that you can prove that this is true or not so not being creative or something. (HA interview)

HA contrasted her creative approach to writing with that of tutors who expected students to work out their ideas in advance:

> when I am trying to write an essay, I usually don't know the conclusion before, so I am not the one who writes the conclusion and tries to get to it but I'm starting to write it and then I realise many things, so I can think deeply when I am writing and that's why I can't provide or can't make any drafts many times at the beginning because I don't know what will come out of it and some teachers don't like it. (HA interview)

She was pleased that HRA had been her referee because she was a tutor who appreciated creativity, although there were some tutors who she positioned as more interested in form:

> I was very happy that HRA will be probably my how do you call the person (referee) thank you referee, because I knew that she likes creative ideas and there are other people who like well, the footnotes are good and correct and the paper is well-structured and I hoped that I wouldn't get a referee like this. (HA interview)

She found conforming to the regulatory forms constraining in contrast with the freedom to generate new ideas in her writing. She also equated the opportunity for creativity with Hungarian academic writing, which did not impose such strict rules for form as English:[5]

> it is good to have a sort of international rules how to write a paper and it is very good, I think but I am not very good at obeying rules in this sense because I like to be a bit more creative sometimes and in Hungarian these rules are not so set so in conclusions we many times bring up new ideas and questions that is sort of forbidden in English. (HA interview)

HB described the process of discovering the structure of his thesis through writing:

> I couldn't see the whole thing together, how would it be changed together? How will it be organised as a whole? I couldn't see it, so I had to sit down and write and at some point we came up with the idea of writer, text and reader. What would you call this? (HB interview)

HSB was also a tutor who valued creativity and self-discovery in the process of writing. He believed the unconventional style of HB's paper reflected his adventurous spirit:

> I always try to think what I would do as a next step if I were the author, so where I see that the author is most inclined to go and if there is a good direction then that should be encouraged, very much, but it's always a self-discovery, so while you write you discover what you are interested in and who you are, after all, so what I liked about HB's paper, it was very much like him. (HSB interview)

Although he acknowledged later that HB had probably been too experimental and this had cost him a grade that HSB believed he had deserved: 'so it could have been, I mean he could have written a 5[6] if he had not experimented with this topic. It's a little bit experimental' (HSB interview). HRB had appreciated the freshness of the writing style, but, despite the fact that he had found the experience of reading the text pleasurable, compared to texts he normally had to read, it oriented him towards the student as a lively but not a scholarly personality:

> ... speaks out of the text, addresses his reader, which is a very nice and lively thing so this is a something to be welcomed and there I can go back to again to the liveliness of the language. It is not the stuffy dry as dust kind of writing but it reflects rather agile personality if not very deep, scholarly type of personality. (HRB interview)

This seems to contrast with HB's subjective orientation to the scholarly activities he had to accomplish for thesis writing as pleasurable: 'I enjoyed reading books. I enjoyed synthesising them. I enjoyed coming up with new ideas and writing them' (HB interview).

The juxtaposition of creativity with the constraint of form requirements is also evident in Case study 3. HSC described the process of discovering a conclusion for the thesis that she had shared with HC:

> So as we were talking, she started talking about this, how interesting it was, the behaviour of the parents, how different they were, blah, blah, blah and then we realised that, actually, as she writes up her findings, this is the conclusion she should be driving at, so she did. (HSC interview)

HSC speaks about HC's work in terms of a finding that benefited the student herself as well as the practitioner community: 'she discovered something that has enriched her own thinking, but it is also something that she is happy to present to outside readers' (HSC interview). This perspective conflicted with that of the referee who evaluated HC's work in terms of the requirements of the academic community and found it lacking.

HRC, however, could not support the claims for novelty because the paper did not conform to the expected requirements for empirical research, which signalled lack of 'rigour' in the analysis:

> ... no information is given on the analytic categories. The definition is missing therefore it is impossible to judge. There is not even a description of how she categorised the statements and how she did the data analysis. It is not described at all and it can actually be seen in the Results section that she didn't really think over the data analysis very carefully because there is no – I mean the quotes are not logically arranged and I don't think it's very rigorous. (HRC interview)

IB positioned herself differently with regard to the relationship between creativity and form. She did not perceive form as a constraint but as a means to structure and showcase her creativity, an opportunity afforded by independent original research, so that she was not reporting the research of others, but her own:

> The freedom. The freedom to have written a thesis which doesn't only have an analysis so I said that I have created something which other people have tried but I have created an analysis. I have created some results, I have created a discussion so my personality, my analysis the

work I have made is the central point of this thesis not the ideas of other people. (IB interview)

However, creativity did not feature so strongly in the Italian as in the Hungarian student accounts of the process, perhaps due to the epistemological perspective taken in the theses.

Epistemological Positioning

In five case study theses, new readings, understandings, meanings and interpretations resulted from epistemological approaches that were innovatory in relation to the research focus for the communities to which participants in the study aligned, an influence on evaluations of originality identified by Guetzkow *et al.* (2004). HA's thesis was valued because she introduced a concept from philosophy, diacritical phenomenology, which had not been used before to examine Wordsworth's 'The Prelude'. IA introduced a little-known masque to a contemporary audience of literary scholars by situating the work historically and culturally. IB and IC applied the same linguistic framework to analyse text, but novelty was framed in terms of the quantitative approach taken by IB to the analysis of Virginia Woolf's text, whereas IC's study was regarded as novel because she combined a linguistic with a practitioner framework in a closely focused study of web texts to discover new understandings that could be applied in the 'real' world outside the academy. In Case study 3, the positioning was not highlighted as new but was regarded as important in enabling research that could generate new perspectives on a problem.

However, in Case studies 2 and 3, originality was contested because the epistemological positionings taken by the supervisor and student were not in alignment with that taken by referee. In Case study 2, the referee adopted a different epistemological position to evaluate the thesis, which conflicted with that adopted by student and supervisor. HB had taken a postmodern approach to text analysis and interpretation, seeking new understandings of metafiction through analysis of a metafictional text using theoretical perspectives from other disciplines as metapragmatic tools to re-contextualise the text and discover new meanings. HSB had encouraged this approach. He was disappointed that HRB did not value the new meanings HB discovered through his analysis of the text: 'and the reader and I think he had some very original insights, which the reviewer didn't seem to acknowledge it seems' (HSB interview). According to HSB, HRB questioned the novelty of the ideas in the thesis because he viewed them as postmodern, and, therefore, a resurrection and reconstitution of old perspectives, rather than a set of diverse tools to discover new meanings: 'He said that these things are as always fiction and these are not necessarily novelties, so these are not new insights, but these go together with postmodern theory' (HSB interview). HRB had been disappointed that HB had focused solely on the metafictional features in the Auster text, rather than providing a new perspective on metafiction from an expert view of the concept:

> The particular qualities that make metafiction what it is have been amply catalogued; there is no shortage of information on the metafictional character of TNYT either. Given this situation, the reader naturally expects some new angle or at least the highlighting of hitherto unnoticed or neglected phenomena. The thesis, however, fulfils such expectations only to a limited extent. (HRB written feedback)

He had expected HB to provide evidence of extensive research into the concept and the characteristics he ascribes to it within the discipline so that he could position his findings as novel in relation to existing knowledge within the disciplinary community. As a result, the work appears superficial and he perceives that the community would not find interest or novelty in the thesis:

> My less than lukewarm account of this thesis is due to a number of causes. The most serious of these is its extreme superficiality. The terms in which the author discusses the issues he raises seldom go beyond the banal and the commonplace. Take beginnings and endings, for instance: of course it is true that they may take place at any point in time, but there is always a reason for the choice of that point, so, contrary to the claim the thesis makes, there is nothing arbitrary here; on top of it, this is not a peculiarity of metafiction. The reasons differ, of course; endings in the nineteenth century are not quite the same as they are in the twentieth, but there is a world of meaning in that difference, which, if explored, might have revealed more about the aspect of TNYT than the mere fact. (HRB written feedback)

Originality was contested in Case study 3, although the epistemological positionings do not seem to be so strongly opposed. HC conducted qualitative research to investigate a new perspective on a problem, but it was not valued because she had not followed procedures that were expected by the referee for conducting research and report-writing within a 'reality-oriented'[7] approach to the paradigm. According to HRC, HC had interpreted qualitative research from a positivist positioning, which HRC equated with quantitative research:

> ... she also writes about expected results like you know, hypothesis, which is unusual in qualitative research. You don't have hypothesis. I mean I've never seen a study where you would have a hypothesis just as you would have in quantitative research. That's very mixing qualitative and quantitative research because you know the results emerge from your own data so you don't have hypotheses usually. (HRC interview)

She approved of HC's adoption of data triangulation to strengthen the credibility of her findings, but the questions were not designed to collect sufficient data on language learning and the number of students in the study were too few for the study to warrant inclusion in the Department programme as a new perspective on the problem.

HSC and HC seemed to adopt more of a phenomenological, but also a social positioning as practitioner rather than academic. They wanted to get as close as possible to the parent's perspective. The research reflected HC's own personal interests because she had attended the school that was the focus of her study and her mother had taught there. She was concerned that the parents' voice, which was absent from policy-making should be heard. HC intended to become a teacher. She believed that her research would enable this perspective, which was now silent, to be given a voice in educational policy through her future work in the community:

> I think my aim wasn't to save the world. I just wanted to show dyslexia from another perspective from the parents' one. (So your aim was not to ..) No, I didn't want to do a great research or to get published. I was very interested in this topic and I wanted to show to other people how parents feel and what help they need, what help they don't get and I don't know how it is in Britain, but in Hungary it's sad. I wouldn't have thought that. They don't really get help from anyone. (HC interview)

HSC seemed to share HC's perspective:

> I mean nobody interviews the parent. How do they experience finding out that the kid is dyslexic, that the teachers know nothing about dyslexia, that the kid needs a lot of extra help, that the kid would have rights and then the rights are not granted at school and how do they

know and who are the support groups and who can they turn to and do the teachers talk to the parents and is it worth talking to the parents. (HSC interview)

She added an introduction to the 'Implications and conclusion' section: 'The results of this research allow us to get *an insider's view* of the role of parents in the education of dyslexic children' (HC's thesis, my emphasis).

Conclusion

Originality was a major criterion in the evaluation of the case study theses. However, as has been discussed, interpretations of originality depended on the social, subjective and epistemological positionings of the participants. These three dimensions of positioning were interconnected and interdependent, but have been discussed separately since each was salient at different points in the evaluation of novelty and because examining each separately enriched the understanding of originality in the theses.

Similarities in practice

(1) The mediation by the supervisor of a disciplinary community's understandings of 'originality'. The impact of thesis supervision on the shape of the Master's thesis was highlighted by Dysthe (2002) and reflects the relationship between master and pupil dating back to the first universities in Europe (Verger, 1992).

(2) The ambiguity expressed by students with regard to the audience of the theses. This is consistent with Kaufer and Geisler's (1989) findings that Master's students as outsiders with regard to a disciplinary community need to have access to insider networks and an insider knowledge framework in order to be able to adopt insider identities and insider positions convincingly.

(3) The adoption of Anglo-American academic genres to promote novelty reflects the pressures described by Dysthe (2002) and Curry and Lillis (2004) to conform to 'international' norms for future publication. There is evidence in the Hungarian data to support the view that this could be at the expense of creativity afforded by local or experimental genres.

Differences in practice

(1) Differences in practice with regard to the evaluation of originality relate to different epistemological, social and subjective positionings between and within case studies.

(2) Differences in disciplinary alignments between each social and cultural context reflect differences in Departmental disciplinary interests, as discussed in Becher and Trowler (2001), rather than any regionally or nationally determined concerns.

(3) Local assessment practices are designed to counter these differences. In the Hungarian context, the supervisor can request a third assessor in cases where they dispute the evaluation of the referee. In the Italian context the supervisor grades the work and is supported by the reader. However, here, the oral defence before a Commission of five academics is the ultimate arbitration and check on the final thesis grade.

This chapter reports a very small, closely focused, qualitative study. It was not intended to make generalisations on the basis of common denominators but to expose some of the issues and concerns with regard to the aims for transparency of Master's-degree-level qualifications across Europe. The discussion on practices with reference to originality in the thesis suggests some of the issues and concerns that must be addressed in discussions on elusive 'common standards'.

Notes

1. Required in the school regulations.
2. With the exception, to an extent, of IA and HA, discussed below.
3. All theses would be made available for access in the School library.
4. Students had to defend their thesis orally before the Commission, a panel consisting of members of the Department, representing a variety of disciplines.
5. This accords with the differences identified in journal article introductions by Árvay and Tankó (2004).
6. The top grade.
7. An approach in qualitative enquiry aimed at getting as close to 'the truth' as possible, an approach designed to gain the maximum credibility for a research project, often aimed at informing policy; see Patton (2002).

References

Árvay, A. and Tankó, G. (2004) A contrastive analysis of English and Hungarian theoretical research article introductions. *IRAL* 42, 71–100.
Bartholomae, D. (1985) Inventing the university. In M. Rose (ed.) *When a Writer Can't Write* (pp. 134–165). New York: Guildford.
Barton, D. (2007) *Literacy: An Introduction to the Ecology of Written Language*. Oxford: Blackwell Publishing.
Baynham, M. (1995) *Literacy Practices*. London: Longman.

Becher, T. and Trowler, P.R. (2001) *Academic Tribes and Territories*. Buckingham: Open University Press.

Berkenkotter, C. and Huckin, T. (1995) *Genre Knowledge in Disciplinary Communication*. Mahwah, NJ: Lawrence Erlbaum.

Bhatia, V.K. (1993) *Analysing Genre: Language Use in Professional Settings*. London: Longman.

Blommaert, J. (2007) On scope and depth in linguistic ethnography. *Journal of Sociolinguistics* 11, 682–688.

Curry, M.J. and Lillis, T. (2004) Multilingual scholars and the imperative to publish in English: Negotiating interests, demands and rewards. *TESOL Quarterly* 38, 663–688.

Dysthe, O. (2002) Professors as mediators of academic cultures. *Written Communication* 19, 493–543.

Guetzkow, J., Lamont, M. and Mallard, G. (2004) What is originality in the humanities and social sciences? *American Sociological Review* 69, 190–208.

Hale, G., Taylor, C., Bridgeman, B., Carson, J., Kroll, B. and Kantor, R. (1996) A study of writing tasks assigned in academic degree programmes. *TOEFL Research Report* 54, 1–6. Princeton, NJ: Educational Testing Service.

Harré, R. and Van Langenhove, L. (1999) *Positioning Theory*. Oxford: Blackwell.

Horowitz, D. (1986a) Essay examination prompts and the teaching of academic writing. *English for Specific Purposes* 5, 107–120.

Horowitz, D. (1986b) What professors actually require: Academic tasks for the ESL classroom. *TESOL Quarterly* 20, 445–462.

Hyland, K. (2004) *Disciplinary Discourses*. Ann Arbor, MI: University of Michigan Press.

Ivanic, R. (1997) *Writing and Identity: The Discoursal Construction of Identity in Academic Texts*. Amsterdam: John Benjamins.

Kaufer, D.S. and Geisler, C. (1989) Novelty in academic writing. *Written Communication* 6, 286–311.

Koutsantoni, D. (2005) Greek cultural characteristics and academic writing. *Journal of Modern Greek Studies* 23, 97–130.

Lave, J. and Wenger, E. (1991) *Situated Learning: Legitimate Peripheral Participation*. Cambridge: Cambridge University Press.

Leung, C. (2005) Convivial communication: Recontextualising communicative competence. *International Journal of Applied Linguistics* 15, 119–144.

Lillis, T. (2008) Ethnography as method, methodology, and 'Deep Theorizing': Closing the gap between text and context in academic writing research. *Written Communication* 25, 353–388.

Ongstad, S. (2005) Enculturation to institutional writing: Meaning making in a triadic semiotic perspective. In T. Koustoli (ed.) *Writing in Context(s): Textual Practices and Learning Processes in Sociocultural Settings* (pp. 49–67). New York: Springer.

Patton, M.Q. (2002) *Qualitative Research and Evaluation Methods*. Thousand Oaks, CA: Sage.

Purves, A.C. (1992) *IEA Study of Written Composition*. London: Pergamon.

Rüegg, W. (1992) Themes. In H. De Ridder Symoens (ed.) *Universities in the Middle Ages* (Chapter 1, Vol. 1, pp. 3–34). Cambridge: Cambridge University Press.

Samraj, B. (2008) A discourse analysis of master's theses across disciplines with a focus on introductions. *Journal of English for Academic Purposes 7*, 55–67.

Swales, J.M. (1990) *Genre Analysis – English in Academic and Research Settings.* Cambridge: Cambridge University Press.

Swales, J.M. (2004) *Research Genres: Explorations and Applications.* Cambridge: Cambridge University Press.

Verger, J. (1992) Patterns. In H. De Ridder Symoens (ed.) *Universities in the Middle Ages* (Chapter 2, Vol. 1, pp. 35–76). Cambridge: Cambridge University Press.

Chapter 9
Plagiarism in the International University: From Kidnapping and Theft to Translation and Hybridity

I. KLITGÅRD

Introduction

> Academic language ... is no one's mother tongue (Bourdieu &
> Passeron cited in Angélil-Carter, 2000: 9)

In the Danish newspaper *Information* of 3 September 2007 it is claimed that the increased use of the internet and the increased intake of international students at Danish universities have resulted in an increasing number of cases of student plagiarism in written exams. A number of directors of studies say that Danish study habits and writing conventions are significantly different from those in for instance Spain and countries outside Europe. Students from those places, it is claimed, just do as they are accustomed to doing back home: directly copying from their books and their teachers' notes into their own texts (Richter, 2007: 1–3).

Even though we in Denmark seemingly do not have any specific statistics on cases of plagiarism by Danish *vis-á-vis* international students, the impression that these claims are true seems to thrive in every corner of our universities. These claims support much current teacher dissatisfaction with international students' alleged laziness, their lack of academic literacy, lack of respect for the ownership of words and ideas, lack of meticulous care when writing and, not least, their lack of what we regard as universally ethical ideals.

Since at present I cannot investigate whether this dissatisfaction is warranted, I instead want to ask the following questions: Is it true that international students plagiarise because their different cultural values and practices clash with those of our university system? What differences are we talking about, and how do they manifest themselves in the students' work? Is the cultural factor the only one, or are there other reasons for international student plagiarism? And if we put our trust only in the cultural factor, do we not risk unfairly stigmatising international students as lazy, incompetent cheaters? Does that not create negative teaching situations where students' abilities are predefined by the teacher?[1]

With this article, which mainly analyses and discusses current definitions and scholarly debates on plagiarism, it is my hope to alleviate this dissatisfaction by proposing a new perspective on international student mobility in terms of academic writing. As a teacher of English for Academic Purposes (EAP) (EAP is also discussed in Chapter 2 of this volume) for students attending the international degree programmes at Roskilde University, I need to see beyond easy explanations and thus develop my intercultural teaching skills and 'cultural empathy' (Sercu, 2006: 57) in order to approach the teaching of academic writing and the avoidance of plagiarism in the most appropriate, respectful and 'international' way. Thus, the purpose of this article is twofold: to do away with the 'cultural deficit view' (Ovando, 2003: 213) and to pave the way for new understanding enabling an improvement of the teaching of academic writing in international higher education (see also Sedgwick's discussion on international-ized academic literacy in Chapter 8).

Due to both demanding cultural and educational clashes when travelling abroad, and due to difficult linguistic dilemmas when working with academic English as a foreign language, international student writing cannot, as I see it, only be classified as culturally right or wrong, as culturally accepted or rejected. The traditional perception of culture as something isolated and distinctly 'Chinese', 'African' or 'Spanish', for example, is a fallacy. Culture is 'a deep, multilayered, somewhat cohesive interplay of language, values, beliefs, and behaviours that pervades every aspect of a person's life, and that is continually undergoing modifications' (Ovando, 2003: 188). International student writing, then, must be seen as an even deeper and more multilayered hybrid space-in-between in which the 'transcultural' (Risager, 1999: 212) encounter and an inevitably *translational* language use are in constant motion – hence the term 'student mobility' as it were (for a contrasting, micro-perspective on translation in this volume, see Chapter 6).

In order to argue for this perspective most convincingly, I suggest that we first look at problematic ethnocentric definitions of plagiarism, both in reference tools and in international university regulations. Then I discuss plagiarism as both a cultural problem and a language problem, based on findings from a major Scottish survey, supplemented with significant recent literature on the two strands of ideas. Finally, I argue for a pedagogical approval that academic writing in English as a foreign language is a cultural and linguistic hybrid which calls for revised subject teaching and EAP instruction in the international university.

Plagiarism as a Crime: Kidnapping and Theft

But what is plagiarism, actually? Searching for a succinct definition of 'plagiarism' in the popular free online dictionary Dictionary.com, often used by students to my knowledge, we get the following:

(1) The unauthorised use or close imitation of the language and thoughts of another author and the representation of them as one's own original work.
(2) Something used and represented in this manner.

We also get a reference to the Online Etymological Dictionary:

- 1621, from L. *plagiarius* 'kidnapper, seducer, plunderer', used in the sense of 'literary thief' by Martial, from *plagium* 'kidnapping', from *plaga* 'snare, net', from PIE base *p(e)lag- 'flat, spread out'. *Plagiary* is attested from 1597.

And finally, we are directed to the Encyclopaedia Britannica:

- The act of taking the writings of another person and passing them off as one's own. The fraudulence is closely related to forgery and piracy practices generally in violation of copyright laws (all references are from http://dictionary.reference.com/browse/plagiarism. Accessed 4.4.11).

In total, we are presented with definitions which emphasise the criminal intent of plagiarism, that is, unauthorised and fraudulent kidnapping or piracy. A look in the related Thesaurus.com supports this impression:

- appropriation, borrowing, counterfeiting, cribbing, falsification, fraud, infringement, lifting, literary theft, piracy, stealing, theft (http:// thesaurus.reference.com/browse/plagiarism. Accessed 4.4.11)

Consequently, if teachers ask their international students to look up 'plagiarism' in online resources on the internet, they will most likely be faced with definitions which may scare them to such a degree that their work may be damaged by their fear of accidentally plagiarising. In other words, our ethical ideals of non-plagiarised texts rest on a scare tactic about moral corruption and guilt and do in no way take linguistically unintentional or culturally situated imitation into consideration. Even when checking a classic students' English–English dictionary, *The Oxford Advanced Learner's Dictionary*, we get:

Plagiarise: to copy another person's ideas, words or work and pretend that they are your own.

I think this definition is highly problematic as 'pretend' implies a wilful action, but that is not always the case with international student plagiarism. This is one of the main points I am going to make in this discussion.

When we turn to international universities' explicit definitions of plagiarism in handbooks, university regulations and guides to academic misconduct, we get the same picture. In her article 'Plagiarism and International Students: How the English-Speaking University Responds' (2001), Diane Pecorari refers to an international survey that establishes a common core of institutional definitions based on an examination of 140 universities: 72 in the United States, 42 in the United Kingdom and 26 in Australia. In all, 54 universities responded with material revealing serious accusatory attitudes to the matter. Pecorari, for instance, refers to a typical definition such as 'Plagiarism is defined as the use of other people's work and the submission of it as though it were one's own work' (Pecorari, 2001: 233) and various other recurrent phrases, such as 'stealing' and 'taking credit falsely' (Pecorari, 2001: 234). One of the more extreme cases is the following explanation from a British University:

> Plagiarism is the substantial use, without acknowledgment and with intent to deceive the examiners or knowing that the examiners might be deceived, of the intellectual work of other people by representing, whether by copying or paraphrase, the ideas and discoveries of another or of others as one's own work submitted for assessment. (Pecorari, 2001: 233)

Paradoxically, not many of the documents in the survey stated why it is wrong to plagiarise, and information about the issue was often randomly scattered around in the material making it difficult for the students to get the right information (Pecorari, 2001: 236–237).

Surprisingly, no more than 11 documents in the survey recognised that plagiarism may be unintentional, but not without emphasising that such cases are rare. An Australian University admits that plagiarism may 'sometimes occur unintentionally, but is more frequently a deliberate attempt to deceive' (Pecorari, 2001: 236). And only six documents out of 74 documents in total from the 54 universities suggested that plagiarism may be a writing practice problem: three universities described the so-called inadvertent plagiarism to be due to 'sloppy writing', and three universities acknowledge that a lacking knowledge of citation rules may be the cause (Pecorari, 2001: 236).

Apart from these findings, the survey also reveals that the discourse applied in describing the seriousness of the matter is strongly judicial. Plagiarism is 'an act of academic fraudulence', 'fraud' and 'nothing less than an act of theft' (Pecorari, 2001: 237). On top of this, a study by Ali R. Abasi and Barbara Graves documents how some universities not only attack international students in their regulation discourse, they also physically pursue them with the self-same regulations. An international student in Canada complains:

> Every day before I started classes there was like this international students' session, and there was the general one, the graduate studies one, the barbecue one. And in every session they give you this yellow sheet about plagiarism saying, 'It's a crime; you don't do this.' (Abasi & Graves, 2008: 279)

This unfortunately happens concurrently with the growing Anglo-American 'gotcha industry' of websites and text matching tools, such as Turnitin.com, that will help 'catch the culprits': 'In our stampede to fight what some call a "plague" of plagiarism, we risk becoming the enemies rather than the mentors of our students; we are replacing the student–teacher relationship with the criminal-police relationship,' and thus, fatally, we cannot see that it is our own pedagogy that needs reform – 'Big reform' (Howard, 2002: 47). (On the student–teacher relationship, see also Chapter 11 of this volume.)

The dictionary definitions and the results from the studies above underscore a most unfortunate perspective on the claimed rise in plagiarism among international students: they are nothing but lazy or corrupt offenders – nothing but 'persistent plagiarists' (Juwah *et al.*, 2006: 5) who have to be policed and condemned by teachers and other guardians of the high morals of academia. Pecorari is correct in seeing two problems with such narrow-minded conceptions:

> First, students who have no intention of breaking the rules may not understand that the crime they are warned about is something they are likely to do. Second, students and teachers may feel uncomfortable about discussing the embarrassing possibility that the student is an academic criminal. When this happens, students who use source material in inappropriate ways may not get the help they need. (Pecorari, 2001: 239)

Going through my own institution's guidelines, those of Roskilde University in Denmark, I do not find as harsh a tone as in the above, but I find a puzzling refusal to use the word plagiarism at all. This is the full description of everything there is to say about 'Examination fraud and misconduct' at Roskilde University:

> There is no absolute definition of examination fraud and misconduct, but below are examples of what is considered academic dishonesty.
>
> Any attempt at cheating in an examination will be treated under the rules governing examination irregularities, irrespective of whether the attempt is successful or not. The rules governing examination fraud and misconduct apply regardless of the type of examination.
>
> Examples of examination fraud and misconduct:
> Before the examination:
>
> * To falsify data or other examination material.
> * To obtain unauthorised prior knowledge of the contents of an examination paper.
> * To fail to provide proper citation and/or source reference – also when you submit work you have previously presented, for example, in projects that form the basis of the examination.
>
> During the examination:
>
> * To falsify data or other examination material.
> * To use unauthorised aids during an examination.
> * To receive help during the examination.
> * To help or assist another candidate during the examination.
> * To use the work of others in a way that suggests the work is your own.
> * To fail to provide proper citation and/or source reference – also when you submit work you have previously presented.
>
> After the examination:
>
> * To continue writing an examination answer when the examination time has expired.
> * To change the basis for assessing your examination paper when the examination time has expired – for example, by attempting to hand in additional sheets.
>
> (http://www.ruc.dk/ruc_en/studying/regulations/examination_fraud/. Accessed 4.4.11.)

The sentence 'To fail to provide proper citation and/or source reference' is the closest we get to a concession that there may be practical writing problems when using sources, but the explanation is still categorised under the heading of 'fraud and misconduct', thus in fact making no allowances for inadvertent plagiarism.

It is about time we begin to view the problem from a different angle. It is my claim that in the international university we need to see the problem as both culturally and linguistically demanding, not only as an ethical or legal issue beyond dispute. This claim is going to be the crux of the following two sections. Here I want to present, describe and discuss two categories of recent conceptions within the fields of EAP and English as a Foreign Language (EFL), namely the cultural issue and the linguistic issue, in order to do away with the before-mentioned simplified myths of international students being nothing but 'persistent plagiarists' – as *we* see them. I claim that what is needed in order to do away with these myths is a greater intercultural awareness among both teachers and decision-makers and the willingness to open mindedly and explicitly help international students understand the habits and conventions of the particular university in question. In fact, we need to understand that the international university is a fast-expanding space of transcultural hybridity where we no longer can uphold a distinct divide between cultures, languages and writing traditions, but have to accept a) diversity as a constituting factor of international education (see also Chapters 4, 5, 10 and 12 of this volume) and b) cultural translation as a constituting factor of academic English writing to non-native speakers of English.

Plagiarism as a Cultural[2] Issue

A recent investigation into the relationship between plagiarism and international students by a research team in Aberdeen speak for much research on this topic. Based on student questionnaires, they wanted to identify the reasons as to why international students plagiarise, which cultural factors influence on these reasons and how to find strategies enabling students to overcome the cultural barriers. Conclusively, in this study the team identify (and I quote):

- 'intercultural uncompetence' [sic] evidenced by lack of understanding of the concept of plagiarism from the western construct.
- Previous educational experience in which respect for authority 'figures' was given high prominence.

- Lack of understanding of referencing systems and the belief that referencing and attribution was not necessary unless materials were already available in the public domain such as the internet. (Juwah *et al.*, 2006: 1)

According to this study, the traditional definitions of plagiarism, such as the ones opening my article, may be highly incomprehensible to some international students: In Confucian-based societies, such as China, Japan and Korea (see further Chapter 11 on Confucianism), 'the individual ownership of spoken or written word or ideas is not the norm as is the case in Western countries. In those cultures, learning which involves analysis or original thought and deviation from the original text is not highly valued, and the individual may be referred to as being egoistic and non-conformist' (Juwah *et al.*, 2006: 4). To this can be added Sharon Myers' thought-provoking quotation from a Chinese teacher: '... knowledge belongs to society, not to ourselves. If you have knowledge, it is your duty to give it to others. Students ... cannot view their talent as private property. You don't lose any of your knowledge if you share it with others' (Myers, 1998: 9).

Besides this, in these cultures, including African and Arabian cultures according to the Scottish survey, learning is mostly carried out by way of 'memorisation and folklore (story telling)', and therefore rote learning, recitals and quoting verbatim are regarded as marks of high standards and great respect for the authorities (Juwah *et al.*, 2006: 4). This view is supported by Carolyn Matalene (1985) who relates her personal experiences as an American writing teacher in China. She, for instance, brings a poignant quotation from one of her Chinese students reflecting on the newly learned Western concept of plagiarism:

> After our teacher's explanation, we understand that in her country or some others plagiarism is forbidden. Whenever you want to quote a passage from an essay or article, you must be permitted by its author, or else you will be accused as a criminal. This is clearly made by their laws. However in our country, things are a little different. We may perhaps call what our teacher calls 'plagiarism' as 'imitation', which is sometimes encouraged, especially for a beginner. Imitation is usually considered to be one of the secrets for a greenhand in writing. So there are many printed books which consist of many kinds of good models to follow for learners. I remember when I was in middle school, I wrote a Chinese composition by imitating several model writings that were suitable for my topic. I also employed some of the same words and phrases in them. I was praised by the teacher for this writing. (Matalene, 1985: 803)

These views are resonant in a number of other studies on the difficulties of acculturating Asian students in Western higher education. In one such study titled 'Cultural Orientation and Academic Language Use', Lixian Jin and Martin Cortazzi explain Chinese culture as a collectivist culture where they focus on 'we' for their identity, whereas the British culture, for example, is individualist focusing on the 'I' as the world's solar plexus: 'In individualist cultures people look after themselves and their immediate family only, whereas in collectivist cultures, people belong to in-groups or collectivities which look after them in exchange for loyalty' (Jin & Cortazzi, 1993: 85).

Jin and Cortazzi interview and collect questionnaires from Chinese postgraduate students and visiting scholars at six British universities and one polytechnic about their expectations of students and teachers followed by a comparison with a similar survey among 37 British academic staff. This comparison yields the following data about expectations (Jin & Cortazzi, 1993: 87):

BRITISH SUPERVISORS:	CHINESE STUDENTS:
Students should develop –	*Teachers should provide –*
- independence - individuality - creativity - openness to alternatives - processes of investigation - critical thinking	- acquisition of knowledge - guidance - imitation, models for/of learning - a single answer - results and solutions - new methods to learn, ways to reach - advanced technical levels
Students should	*Teachers should*
- think for themselves - know what to do - express themselves when they need help - take responsibilities academically, and for everyday activities	- be moral leaders - know everything in their area of expertise - should ask students if they have any problems - plan for and instruct students - be sensitive, sympathetic, helpful and know our problems - act as parent supporting children

Some unreflected responses might take all these testimonies from Chinese learners as an easy ideological proof that they are more immature, passive, illiterate and less sophisticated than Western learners. Indeed, in his published objections to Glenn D. Deckert's inquiry about

Chinese students' perceptions of plagiarism carried out in Hong Kong (1993), Alastair Pennycook deplores the tendency in such studies to, on the one hand, acknowledge Asian students' high performance in academic work, and, on the other hand, ridiculing them as undeveloped 'rote-learners' (Pennycook, 1994: 281). We need to 'differentiate between memorization as rote learning and memorization as a means to deepen and develop understanding', he proclaims (Pennycook, 1994: 281). In a more elaborate article on understanding plagiarism from a historical and cross-cultural point of view, Pennycook emphasises that 'the memorization of texts [in China] is not a pointless practice [...] because the issue is not one of understanding the world and then mapping language onto it but rather of acquiring language as texts as a precursor to mapping out textual realities' (Bloch, 2001: 214; Pennycook, 1996: 222).

Picking up on this idea, I do in fact see neither mindless nor infantile approaches to learning in the above examples. The collectivist sharing of knowledge, where knowledge hereby is never lost, but simply passed on to more than one person, facilitates an environment where teachers, it is proposed in the Chinese student questionnaires, are sensitive and sympathetic towards their students' 'greenhand' imitations of writing as a way to learn the skills of a best practice. Nowhere in the quotations and findings above do we get the impression that students are automatised or subdued by way of senseless drills. And as Kam Louie points out, in Confucian-heritage cultures such as China, repetition and rote learning eventually leads to inspiration, enlightenment of the mind and deep learning – something all sports people know as a fact: 'practice makes perfect' (Louie, 2006: 22).

Other voices object to the critical tendency towards a clear-cut and categorical distinction between 'us' and 'them': the West vs. the Orientals. In their contrastive study on the use of citations in American and Chinese academic discourse from 1995, Joel Bloch and Lan Chi argue that even though their use of citations and previous knowledge differ from our writing, Chinese writing is by no means less rhetorically complex than Western writing (Bloch & Chi, 1995). And the concept of intellectual ownership does indeed exist in China. It has just taken a different shape than ours due to a different historical development (Bloch, 2001: 213.)

In fact, if we want to understand our Chinese students' educational background, we need to understand that China is a 'translation society' where translations are valued as much as original work (Quian, 1985 quoted in Bloch, 2001: 213.) Bloch explains:

> Since many Chinese academics do not know other languages, and since, compared to the West, there are significantly fewer researchers

in China to create original research and far fewer places in China to publish research, the translation of foreign articles has become an important academic activity. Financial rewards for translations of articles are similar to those for original articles. (Bloch, 2001: 214)

The same is the case with literary translation. In contrast to the West where literary translators are hardly every celebrated, or even mentioned, Chinese literary translators have a high standing in society. Here the voice of the author merges with the voice of the translator into a 'collaborative voice' demonstrating 'a shared sense of audience but not necessarily a different view of intellectual property' (Bloch, 2001: 214–215).

However, due to recent political and economic changes in China, many aspects of Chinese higher education seem to be radically changing (Coverdale-Jones & Rastall, 2008) – including the concept of plagiarism and the concept of intellectual property. In order to keep up with the West, in 2002 Beijing University was the first Chinese university to adopt a written rule on plagiarism (Juwah *et al.*, 2006: 4). And Bloch testifies that plagiarism is now as 'repugnant in China as in the West'. In, for instance, three highly publicised cases, Chinese scholars were caught plagiarising and were given extremely severe punishments (Bloch, 2001: 215).

All this evidences the banal but nevertheless rarely considered proposition that when trying to understand the cultural backgrounds of our international students, we should refrain from putting our trust in bits and pieces of anecdotal evidence that make *our* habits the norm and *their* habits unlearned and primitive, but instead try to grasp the complexity of the students' cultural heritage.

What seems to be an even more complex, but nonetheless more tangible point in identifying the dilemmas of plagiarism among international students, is the language issue. And this is the factor many university teachers and policymakers forget to consider when they readily accuse international students of cultural poverty.

Plagiarism as a Language Issue

The Aberdeen research group mentioned earlier concludes that a majority of international students are non-native speakers and have English as a second or third language, and thus they have great difficulties navigating and communicating in English. On top of this, academic discourse is often 'underpinned by subtleties of the discipline, concepts, terminologies, jargons, etc.' (Juwah *et al.*, 2006: 3). To this can most certainly be added the previously mentioned hidden agendas of unspoken codes of academic honesty and integrity which keep international students in the dark rather than enlightening them – and the Enlightenment, I think, was puzzlingly one of the prime movers behind our so highly valued Anglo-American and utilitarian conceptions of academic honour codes. The academic community discourse paradoxically becomes 'a gatekeeper, denying access to social goods to those who do not succeed' (Angélil-Carter, 2000: 11).

When it comes to linguistic proficiency, the obstacles seem to be abundant. Mastering correct or even just adequate written English proficiency at an advanced level takes a large vocabulary, a good understanding of grammatical structures and an overall idiomatic and communicative competence. So what do the students do if they fail to meet the requirements? From fear of showing their ignorance they may begin to parrot – to copy or memorise – exact expressions, 'apt terms' or even large chunks of text in what they are reading and more or less deliberately paste them into their own writing without due acknowledgment – either to a less severe extent resulting in 'patchwork' or 'paraphrase plagiarism', or to a far more serious extent resulting in 'outright plagiarism' (Hamp-Lyons & Courter, 1984: 161–166).

This imitation strategy is paradoxically a traditionally fully legitimate foreign language acquisition strategy. *Say after me!*, the international students' perhaps audiolingual (Richards & Rogers, 2001: 156–157) language teachers back home may have told them at some point – or *when in Rome do as the Romans do.* Therefore, when we get a new international student 'learning how to write in a discipline ... what may manifest itself in their writing is the unsuccessful conflictual hybridization[3] of prior school (or other) discourses and new academic ones' (Angélil-Carter, 2000: 38). According to the Russian psychologist Lev Vygotsky, imitation is, however, no crime, but the cornerstone of cognitively acquiring and later transforming a language: 'development based on collaboration and imitation is the source of all the specifically human characteristics of consciousness that develop in a child' (cited in Lantoff & Thorne, 2007: 207–208). Thus, imitation is not just an unmindful copying process, but a reasoning process (Lantoff & Thorne, 2007: 213), echoing Pennycook's rationale for the Chinese writing tradition of imitation models described above.

As Diane Schmitt tells us: 'Language acquisition is not about creatively developing one's own idiosyncratic method of speaking or writing; rather, it is about learning to use the conventionalised language of the community one finds oneself in and learning to appropriate others' language to establish group membership' (Schmitt, 2006: 68). Hence, EAP instructions in using the many conventional and formulaic academic phrases as can be found in for example, the celebrated Academic Phrasebank from

The University of Manchester. And here they thoughtfully emphasise that, 'The phrases are content neutral and generic in nature; in using them, therefore, you are not stealing other people's ideas and this does not constitute plagiarism' (http://www.phrasebank.manchester.ac.uk/. Accessed 4.4.11).

A more serious matter is expressed in one international student's laments in Jude Carroll's slides for the 2006 conference 'Moving towards the internationalisation of the university': 'When I get nervous about writing up my thoughts in poor English even when I know the subject OK, I can't think. So I use other people's words' (cited in Carroll, 2006, slide 5). This incontrovertible dilemma when writing from sources is impressively demonstrated in practice in Diane Pecorari's study 'Good and original: Plagiarism and patchwriting in academic second-language writing'. Her purpose is to examine how extensive unintentional textual plagiarism is in academic texts written by novice writers of English as a second language (ESL is also discussed in Chapter 1 of this volume). Through qualitative text analysis and interviews Pecorari explores to which extent non-native speakers of English happen to copy/repeat the language of the sources they are using in their works. Pecorari is motivated by the apparent clash between on the one hand the 'conventional wisdom' that international students often fall prey to plagiarism, and that their 'crime' is most certainly intentional (Pecorari, 2003: 318).

One of the terms Pecorari applies in her study is Rebecca Moore Howard's concept of *patchwriting* to describe the 'source-dependent composition' of L2 writing in which the voice of the non-native speaker of English merges with the voice of the source, through chunks of copied/ repeated language, in an attempt to gain control of the text (Pecorari, 2003: 320). Patchwriting, then, is not to be categorised alongside what is conventionally regarded as prototypical plagiarism, that is, intentional cheating, but in contrast to be regarded as an essential, 'developmental stage' novice L2 writers go through before they can begin to manifest their own voices in their academic writing (Pecorari, 2003: 320).

In the attempt to provide a snapshot of L2 student patchwriting as comprehensive as possible, Pecorari's research embraces both textual analysis and interviews. It is divided into two phases involving the writing of 17 international non-native speakers of English from the areas of science, engineering, the humanities and social sciences at three British universities.

In the first phase, students finishing their master's degrees supplied writing samples from their dissertations in draft form and participated in interviews. The purpose was kept a secret as the students and their supervisors were only told that they were to participate in a study of general academic writing skills. Besides, in order to do away with potential personal implications, they never had any contact with Pecorari while providing the samples. Their supervisors told them to select samples they believed would be suitable, and by doing so, Pecorari prevented that students and supervisors might find samples that would either blatantly confirm or reject any declared claim on Pecorari's part.

In the second phase similar text samples (of 10 consecutive pages) were provided from eight selected completed PhD theses from the university library catalogues as Pecorari wanted to compare novice MA dissertation writings with texts at the PhD level where a greater mastery of English language skills, citation and source use skills are expected.

All samples were then compared with the sources mentioned which Pecorari had to retrieve from university libraries. On the basis of her statistical material, Pecorari analyses and discusses the texts' levels of (a) *transparency of language* and (b) *transparency and the presence of citation*. Transparency is defined as the way a text accurately signals the relationship between the source and citing text.

The results of the textual analyses demonstrate that there is a wide tendency to use sources in an opaque, or occluded, way to such an extent that both the MA and PhD students might be accused of the so-called 'default assumption' of prototypical (intentional) plagiarism (Pecorari, 2003: 333). In contrast to this, surprisingly, the subsequent interviews with the nine MA students demonstrate that no students ever intended to either plagiarise or 'patchwrite'. The observations provide profiles of the students as 'diligent, motivated, and engaged students, and second, that they made no apparent effort to conceal the source use strategies' (Pecorari, 2003: 334). Paradoxically, the observations also prove to be at odds with much speculation on (inter)cultural dilemmas as the reasons for plagiarism as all the MA students in the study were aware of the British conventions of appropriate source use.

The article concludes that even though this qualitative study is in no way conclusive nor quantitatively representative, it nevertheless supports the many anecdotal accounts that unintentional patchwriting is a fact, and if this is accepted, 'then deceptive plagiarism cannot be the default assumption' (Pecorari, 2003: 336).[4]

Another major and related work on these dilemmas is Ling Shi's comparative study of whether the type of task and first language have an effect on undergraduate students' use of source information. 39 students were American students at an American university, whereas 68 students were Chinese students studying English as a second language at a Chinese university. Half of each group completed a summary task, whereas the other half completed an opinion essay task. Both groups were given a specific text to use in their assignments. The investigation proves that students in general used much more textual borrowing when writing summaries than when writing opinion essays. But more significantly, Chinese students borrowed far more words from the source texts than the native English-speaking students. And they also generally refrained from using references, both when citing directly and when paraphrasing the original. In contrast, the native English-speaking students used source texts mostly with citations for either task (Shi, 2004: 190).

Shi concludes that 'University professors need to understand the genuine concern of many international students to appropriate language when writing using unfamiliar words for new ideas. By punishing those who copy or integrate others' words in their own writing, we actually deprive them of the only strategy or natural resource that many L2 students rely on' (Shi, 2004: 191). And furthermore: 'there is a need to distinguish legitimate appropriation of language from dishonest copying so as to make ways for novice L2 writers to traverse the boundary and become members of the academic community' (Shi, 2004: 191).[5]

This impasse can be explained from a genuinely foreign language pedagogical point of view suggesting that

There are four stages in the development of academic writing. These are *repetition*, which involves extensive copying without citation; *patching*, which also involves extensive copying but with appropriate citations; *plagiphrasing*, in which students blend copied sections, quotations, paraphrases, and their own words, and, finally, *conventional academic writing* ... [T]he third stage, plagiphrasing, shows that students are beginning to speak with their own voices, and is an important stage on the way to developing the appropriate academic writing style. (Wilson cited in Schmitt, 2006: 69)

This is a systematic continuum reflecting foreign language acquisition in general as we know it from the concept of interlanguage: a foreign language learner's developing grammar that may differ from the standard grammar of the foreign language in question. Consequently, both EAP teachers and subject teachers have to keep this developing stage in the back of their minds both when teaching, providing feedback on their students' texts, and when evaluating written exams. Ignorance – or negligence – of such profound reasons for textual borrowing may be disastrous to the individual international student, and to the idea of student mobility as a whole as these students will be suspected of cheating and of undermining the so-called learned standards of Anglo-American-oriented higher education.

Plagiarism as Transcultural Translation and Hybridity

In the international university the term *plagiarism* has to be redefined. The definitions found in dictionaries, online reference tools as well as printed books, and in a great deal of international university guidelines and stipulations, belong to a distant past when words were regarded as individual intellectual property. I am, however, not advocating downright cheating in the sense that it is alright to deliberately pass off others' words or ideas as one's own, but I am advocating an 'internationalised' outlook on the problem that includes greater awareness of plagiarism as a cultural and linguistic dilemma to international students. If we want to earn money from visiting students, we certainly have to give them – and thus in the end ourselves – value for money and refrain from welcoming them as potential criminals.

I propose that we regard these cultural-linguistic dilemmas as expressions of 'transcultural translation', that is, as cultural encounters in which cultural changes take place induced by the introduction of 'foreign' elements in the 'domestic' sphere. Thus, international students' academic English writing processes and products should rather be perceived as a dynamic *transculturation* than as the conventionally expected *acculturation* where the international student has to adjust to the norms of the host culture (Ortiz, 1995: 102–103).

As with the Chinese celebration of merged voices in translation, we, too, might begin to understand and accept that international student writing constitutes a cultural and linguistic translation of previous educational strategies into a new textual practice where native and various foreign language voices and discourse styles collaborate in a hybrid patchwork – or *patchwriting*. Academic literacy in the international university is no longer to be defined as the ability to read and write according to the homogenous standards of a single culture, here predominantly the Anglo-American one, but to be defined as the ability to merge practices in what a British interviewee in Jin and Cortazzi's study calls 'cultural synergy': 'what you need to do, to benefit from the experience, is to try to pick out the best parts of the British way of doing things and at the same time resort to or retain the best ways from [for instance] the Chinese, and then you might actually be benefiting in a way that no one who hasn't experienced both systems could do' (Jin & Cortazzi, 1993: 95).

This outlook has bearings on the way English is taught to these students. As it is explained in the British Council's report on the fate of English, the 19th century EFL tradition

> positions the learner as an outsider, as a foreigner, one who struggles to attain acceptance by the target community. The target language is always someone else's mother tongue. The learner is constructed as a linguistic tourist – allowed to visit, but without rights of residence and required always to respect the superior authority of native speakers. (Graddol, 2006: 83)

The student is constantly measured against native standards and is thus bound to fail. This approach may be predominant in English-speaking countries, obviously, but does not have to be the norm in a non-English-speaking educational system, where the mother tongue is Danish, not English. Danish international programmes have the opportunity to take a different path towards more culturally flexible approaches. Owing to the growing literature on these matters, as demonstrated in this chapter, I sense a timely willingness to change old habits and old viewpoints within EAP and EFL. The major obstacle will probably be to make subject teachers realise the need for a greater cultural awareness and a greater cooperation with EAP teachers. Not all international students attend EAP programmes, and thus they may be left at the mercy of many subject teachers' ignorance of or unwillingness to either learn about their international students' backgrounds or the intricate foreign language acquisition problems which influence the students' writings.

In agreement with Celia Thompson and Alastair Pennycook, I suggest that we try to abandon both 'homogenisation', making all diversity succumb to standardisation, and 'polarisation', pointing out the sharp divide between cultures, such as the traditional Western/Oriental divide, in favour of a 'hybridisation' process – or 'third space' (Bhabha in Montgomery, 2008: 22; Kostogriz, 2005: 195) – of mixing and borrowing:

> Hybridization may occur with the forces of homogenization and polarization to create a transformational learning environment in which new cultural forms and practices can emerge. Being able to engage in pedagogically effective ways with such hybrid forms of text or knowledge production poses yet more challenges for educators working in the transcultural university classroom. (Thompson & Pennycook, 2008: 133–134)[6]

This may be compared with the American folk singer Pete Seeger's paradoxical saying that 'plagiarism is basic to all cultures' (Ovando, 2003: 190), meaning that throughout history societies have always *borrowed* from each other. Ovando elaborates: 'This borrowing has been a principal source of the instability of culture and the constant development of cultural patterns "apart from" the original ones. This perpetual state of becoming – of new beginnings crafted on old ones – gives culture its dynamic and fascinating character.' (Ovando, 2003: 191)

Again I want to stress that I am not advocating the teaching and acceptance of a more or less creative English language use in university writing, such as the radical proposals for a new ELF (English as a lingua franca) where, for instance, certain grammatical and phonological deviations from *standard English* (see also Chapter 10) are accepted and encouraged (Graddol, 2006: 87). So far, I find it impossible to distinguish between systematic traits of a virtually recognisable ELF and systematic traits of foreign language learners' various interlanguages. Besides, an authorisation of ELF will endanger international standards for language testing and examining. And finally, the students *themselves* may be resistant to such a radicalisation of the English language since they are dependent on their language skills for professional purposes after graduation, and they are no doubt well aware that international workplaces in their home countries or abroad may not be as welcoming of deviating English as are university intellectuals.

What I *am* advocating, though, is a widened cultural and linguistic horizon in subject and EAP teachers working with international programmes and international students in higher education. We cannot subscribe to international student mobility as a period of formation in the students' lives where they are treated as thieves and kidnappers, but as a period of formation where they are actively assisted in developing their hybrid 'greenhand in writing' so that they may blossom as citizens in a global world.

Conclusion

To sum up, my discussion here proves the biting truth of the epigraph of this text: 'Academic language … is no one's mother tongue', and especially not so to international students if it is in the alien version called academic English. Becoming accustomed to this foreign tongue does not happen overnight. And most students struggling with this foreign tongue certainly do not *kidnap* the words of their host language with evil intents, as my discussion suggests in refutation of the claim that international students are persistent plagiarisers owing to educational backgrounds in less competent cultures, such as the 'Chinese' culture. These students rather find themselves in a process of transcultural translation and hybridity which both their subject teachers and EAP teachers should recognise and assist convincingly in a climate of mutual respect.

Notes

1. The same problem is encountered in much research on language-minority students in the United States. Ovando, for example, explains that 'educators and policymakers in the past all too often pointed fingers in the direction of the students' sociocultural backgrounds, suggesting that students possessed deficiencies that impeded academic success'. A gross example is the fact that Hispanic students were often placed in classes of the mentally retarded due to IQ test scores that were rather influenced by language problems than intelligence problems, but no one seemed to take that into account (Ovando, 2003: 211).
2. Here 'culture' is defined as in Juwah *et al.*: 'value systems, customs, traditions, norms and the way of life of a people (comprising the socio-technical, political, economic and education systems). To survive in a culture, individuals need to be acculturated – that is, acquire new norms, knowledge and strategies of coping to enable them to adapt to the new community or environment' (Juwah *et al.*, 2006: 3).
3. Angélil-Carter defines hybridisation as 'the contestation between different discourses, past and new, as represented in student writing' (Angélil-Carter, 2000: 102).
4. The study is reprinted in Pecorari's later volume on plagiarism (2008a).
5. Similar examinations and discussions can be found in Johns and Mayes (1990), Bloch and Chi (1995), Howard (1999), Roig (2001), Moon (2002), Keck (2006), Abasi and Nahal (2008) and Pecorari (2008b).
6. In Kostogriz, a so-called 'Thirdspace pedagogy of literacy' is promoted in second language learning environments for minority and migrant students, advocating a collaborative and 'political strategy of "reassembling" educational knowledge to bring about the active involvement of minority students in literacy learning. This activity is simultaneously critical and productive' (Kostogriz, 2005: 205).

References

Abasi, A.R. and Graves, B. (2008) Academic literacy and plagiarism: Conversations with international graduate students and disciplinary professors. *Journal of English for Academic Purposes 7*, 221–233.

Abasi, A.R. and Nahal, A. (2008) Are we encouraging patchwriting? Reconsidering the role of the pedagogical context in ESL student writers' transgressive intertextuality. *English for Specific Purposes 27*, 267–284.

Academic Phrasebank, The University of Manchester. On WWW at http://www.phrasebank.manchester.ac.uk. Accessed 4.4.11.

Angélil-Carter, S. (2000) *Stolen Language? Plagiarism in Writing.* Harlow: Pearson Education/Longman.

Bloch, J. (2001) Plagiarism and the ESL student: From printed to electronic texts. In D. Belcher and A. Hirvela (eds) *Linking Literacies: Perspectives on L2 Reading–Writing Connections.* Ann Arbor, MI: The University of Michigan Press.

Bloch, J. and Chi, L. (1995) A comparison of the use of citations in Chinese and English academic discourse. In D. Belcher and G. Braine (eds) *Academic Writing in a Second Language: Essays on Research and Pedagogy* (pp. 231–274). Norwood, NJ: Ablex Publishing Company.

Bourdieu, P. and Passeron, J-C. (1994) Introduction: Language and the relationship to language in the teaching situation. In P. Bourdieu, J.C. Passeron and M. de Saint Martin (eds) *Academic Discourse.* Cambridge: Polity Press.

Carroll, J. (2006) Supporting international students by deterring, detecting and dealing with plagiarism. Staffordshire University. On WWW at http://www.staffs.ac.uk/uniservices/cpd/conferences/previous/internationalisation/index.php. Accessed 4.4.11.

Coverdale-Jones, T. and Rastall, P. (2008) *Internationalising the University: The Chinese Context.* Houndmills: Palgrave Macmillan.

Deckert, G.D. (1993) Perspectives on plagiarism from ESL students in Hong Kong. *Journal of Second Language Writing* 2, 131–148.

Dictionary.com On WWW at http://dictionary.reference.com/browse/plagiarism. Accessed 4.4.11.

'Examination fraud and misconduct', Roskilde University, Denmark. On WWW at http://www.ruc.dk/ruc_en/studying/regulations/examination_fraud. Accessed 4.4.11.

Graddol, D. (2006) *English Next: Why Global English May Mean the End of 'English as a Foreign Language'.* British Council. On WWW at http://www.britishcouncil.org/learning-research-english-next.pdf. Accessed. 4.4.11.

Hamp-Lyons, L. and Courter, K.B. (1984) *Research Matters.* Rowley, MA: Newbury House.

Howard, R.M. (1999) The new abolitionism comes to plagiarism. In L. Buranen and A.M. Roy (eds) *Perspectives on Plagiarism and Intellectual Property in a Postmodern World.* Albany: State University of New York Press.

Howard, R.M. (2002) Don't police plagiarism: Just TEACH! *The Education Digest* 67, 46–49.

Jin, L. and Cortazzi, M. (1993) Cultural orientation and academic language use. In D. Graddol, L. Thompson and M. Byram (eds) *Language and Culture: Papers from the Annual Meeting of the British Association of Applied Linguistics* (pp. 84–97). Clevedon: Multilingual Matters.

Johns, A.M. and Mayes, P. (1990) An analysis of summary protocols of University ESL students. *Applied Linguistics* 11, 253–271.

Juwah, C., Lal, D. and Beloucif, A. (2006) *Overcoming the Cultural Issues Associated with Plagiarism for International Students.* The Robert Gordon University, Aberdeen. On WWW at http://www.rgu.ac.uk/files/ACF52AC.doc. Accessed 4.4.11.

Keck, C. (2006) The use of paraphrase in summary writing: A comparison of L1 and L2 writers. *Journal of Second Language Writing* 15, 261–278.

Kostogriz, A. (2005) Dialogial imagination of (Inter)cultural spaces: Rethinking the semiotic ecology of second language and literacy learning. In J. Kelly Hall,

G. Vitanova and L. Marchenkova (eds) *Dialogue with Bakhtin on Second and Foreign Language Learning* (pp. 189–210). Mahwah, NJ: Lawrence Erlbaum Associates.

Lantoff, J.P. and Thorne, S.L. (2007) Sociocultural theory and second language learning. In J.P. Lantoff and S.L. Thorne (eds) *Theories in Second Language Acquisition* (pp. 201–224). Mahwah, NJ: Lawrence Erlbaum Associates.

Louie, K. (2006) Gathering cultural knowledge: Useful or use with care? In J. Carroll and J. Ryan (eds) *Teaching International Students: Improving Learning for All* (pp. 17–25). London: Routledge.

Matalene, C. (1985) Contrastive rhetoric: An American writing teacher in China. *College English* 47, 789–808.

Montgomery, C. (2008) Global futures, global communities? The role of culture, language and communication in an internationalised university. In H. Haberland, J. Mortensen, A. Fabricius, B. Preisler, K. Risager and S. Kjærbeck (eds) *Higher Education in the Global Village* (pp. 17–34). Roskilde: Department of Culture and Identity, Roskilde University.

Moon, Y. (2002) Korean University students' awareness of plagiarism in summary writing. *Language Research* 38, 1349–1365.

Myers, S. (1998) Questioning author(ity): ESL/EFL, science, and teaching about plagiarism. *Teaching English as a Second or Foreign Language* 3, 1–16. On WWW at http://www-wrting.berkeley.edu/TESL-EJ/ej10/a2.html. Accessed 4.4.11.

Ortiz, F. (1995) *Cuban Counterpoint: Tobacco and Sugar*. Durham, NC: Duke University.

Ovando, C. (2003) *Bilingual and ESL Classrooms: Teaching in Multicultural Contexts*. New York, NY: McGraw-Hill.

Pecorari, D. (2001) Plagiarism and international students: How the English-speaking university responds. In D. Belcher and A. Hirvela (eds) *Linking Literacies: Perspectives on L2 Reading–Writing Connections* (pp. 229–245). Ann Arbor, MI: The University of Michigan Press.

Pecorari, D. (2003) Good and original: Plagiarism and patchwriting in academic second-language writing. *Journal of Second Language Writing* 12, 317–345.

Pecorari, D. (2008a) *Academic Writing and Plagiarism: A Linguistic Analysis*. London: Continuum.

Pecorari, D. (2008b) Repeated language in academic discourse: The case of biology background statements, *Nordic Journal of English Studies* 7, 9–13.

Pennycook, A. (1994) The complex contexts of plagiarism: A reply to Deckert. *Journal of Second Language Writing* 3, 277–284.

Pennycook, A. (1996) Borrowing others' words: Text, ownership, memory, and pla-giarism. *TESOL Quarterly* 30, 201–230.

Richards, J.C. and Rogers, T.S. (2001) *Approaches and Methods in Language Teaching*. Cambridge: Cambridge University Press.

Richter, L. (2007) Globaliseringen øger snyd på studier [Globalisation increasing cheating at universities]. *Information* 3 September. On WWW at http://infor-mation.dk/print/145414. Accessed 4.4.11.

Risager, K. (1999) Kulturtilegnelse og kulturundervisning [Culture learning and culture teaching]. In A. Holmen and K. Lund (eds) *Studier i dansk som andetsprog* (pp. 207–231). Copenhagen: Alfabeta.

Roig, M. (2001) Plagiarism and paraphrasing criteria of college and University Professors. *Ethics & Behavior* 11, 307–323.

Roskilde University's Rules and Regulations: Examination fraud and misconduct. On WWW at http://www.ruc.dk/ruc_en/studying/regulations/examination_fraud. Accessed 4.4.11.

Schmitt, D. (2006) Writing in the international classroom. In J. Carroll and J. Ryan (eds) *Teaching International Students: Improving Learning for All* (pp. 63–74). London: Routledge.

Sercu, L. (2006) The foreign language and intercultural competence teacher: The acquisition of a new professional identity. *Intercultural Education* 17, 53–72.

Shi, L. (2004) Textual borrowing in second-language writing. *Written Communication* 21, 171–200.

Thesaurus.com http://thesaurus.reference.com/browse/plagiarism. Accessed 4.4.11.

Thompson, C. and Pennycook, A. (2008) Intertextuality in the transcultural contact zone. In R. Moore Howard and A.E. Robillard (eds) *Pluralizing Plagiarism: Identities, Contexts, Pedagogies*. Portsmouth, NH: Bonton.

Part 5
East and West at the International University

Chapter 10

International Students at China Three Gorges University: A Survey

HU X. and CHEN Y.

Economic globalization has brought about the global use of English, which in turn has made the internationalization of higher education possible all over the world. Yet, true internationalization in higher education is also concerned with the relationship between many different cultures and languages within the same educational institution, and with the possibility of international students (cf. also Chapters 3–6, 9) practicing linguistic, social and academic diversity. An increasing number of transnationally mobile students are living and studying in international universities. Therefore, issues related to language choice, cultural identity, cultural differences, teaching and learning, and administrative management are receiving much attention. This chapter, based on a survey, attempts to measure and evaluate the social and academic diversity international students experience in a Chinese university, and what problems and difficulties both the students and the university encounter (for cultural diversity, see also Chapters 3–5, 9 and 12).

Kachru's Concentric Circles

As English is being spoken by hundreds of millions of people now, its varieties are increasing as well. British English and American English, which have been traditionally regarded as the only two varieties of 'standard' English (cf. also Chapter 9), are in fact but two World Englishes among many. According to Kachru (Crystal, 2003: 61), 'World Englishes' fall into three categories:

(1) The Inner Circle, where English is a mother tongue and includes countries such as Australia, Canada, Ireland, New Zealand, South Africa, Britain and the United States.

(2) The Outer Circle, which uses English as an additional institutional-ized, official language, though it is not a mother tongue – these coun-tries include, for example, Bangladesh, Ghana, India, Kenya, Malaysia, Nigeria, Pakistan, the Philippines, Singapore, Sri Lanka, Tanzania, Zambia and Zimbabwe.
(3) The Expanding Circle, which refers to English as a foreign language, countries being, for example, China, Korea, Nepal, Russia, Saudi Arabia, those of continental Europe, South America and so on.

English is now *the* international language, and students from the Expanding Circle countries are frequently seen at the educational insti-tutions of the Inner and Outer circle countries. At the same time, as edu-cational programs are increasingly taught in English in the Expanding Circle countries, more and more students from the Inner and Outer circles go to study in the Expanding Circle countries. The authors' university, China Three Gorges University (CTGU), accepts students from many countries, in particular from the Outer Circle countries.

The International Students at CTGU

CTGU came into being in June, 2000, with the amalgamation of the former University of Hydraulic & Electric Engineering and Hubei Sanxia University. It is located in Yichang, in central China. This city is the hydro-electric capital of the world and home to the Three Gorges Dam Construction Project. CTGU offers the full range of disciplines and enrolls students from all over China as well as from abroad. Our university has admitted students from a number of countries, including India, Nepal, the United States, Vietnam, Korea, the Maldives, Denmark, Norway, Germany and Italy. At the time of the survey, the number of international students stood at 441, most of whom were from the Outer Circle, for exam-ple, India and Nepal (see Table 10.1). The great majority were studying clinical medicine at the Medical College of CTGU while a very small minority were studying Chinese at the Humanities College. Of these 441 students, 150 were in Grade 4, 135 in Grade 3, 87 in Grade 2 and 69 in Grade 1. They had thus been attending classes at CTGU for periods rang-ing from almost four years to less than one year.

As the great majority of the international students at CTGU come from the Outer Circle and the Expanding Circle, the authors of this chapter set out to investigate the academic and campus life of this group of students at CTGU. To do this, we conducted a survey to obtain information relating to their classroom learning, use of languages, the culture differences they

Table 10.1 The international students at CTGU in 2007–2008

Country	Major	
	Chinese	*Clinical medicine*
India		301
Nepal		115
Maldives		2
Vietnam		3
Italy	3	
Denmark	4	
Norway	3	
Germany	4	
South Korea	4	
United States	2	
Total	20	421

encounter, other problems and any suggestions they might have for improving their conditions.

A Survey of the Academic and Life Experience of the Outer Circle and Expanding Circle Students at CTGU

Subjects

From the 441 students mentioned above, the authors chose 251 (56.9% of the total) to take part in the survey. They were from 20 to 24 years old and all spoke the language of the region or country from which they came. Of these, 40 were first-year students, 52 second-year students, 74 third-year students and 85 fourth-year students. There were 158 male students and 93 female students. Eighteen of them were studying Chinese at the Humanities College while the rest were studying Clinical Medicine in the Medical College (see Tables 10.2–10.5).

Questionnaire

The authors designed a self-reporting questionnaire consisting of two parts. Part 1 collected the subjects' basic information: their name, gender, age, nationality, major, first language and other languages, and their level in Chinese. Part 2 consisted of questions concerning their studies, campus life, language and cultural differences, teachers' instruction, problems

Table 10.2 Students' length of time at CTGU

Length of stay	Number of students
4 years (the fourth-year)	85
3 years (the third-year)	74
2 years (the second-year)	52
1 year (the first-year)	40
Total	251

and difficulties, future plans and suggestions (see the Appendix for the questionnaire; cf. also Chapters 2 and 3).

As the international students were studying in two colleges of CTGU, namely, the Medical College and the Humanities College, the authors went to the Medical College first and asked 233 students, with the help of their subject teachers and the administrators, to answer the questionnaire. In order to ensure the reliability and validity of their answers, we divided them into six smaller groups so that they could answer the questionnaire in separate classrooms. Four teachers and administrators were asked to help the authors. Each was responsible for administering the question-naire in one classroom and supervising the students. On another day, the authors went to the Humanities College. With the help of a Chinese teacher, the questionnaire was completed by the 18 students. It took the students about one-and-a-half hours to finish the questionnaire. Then all the 251 answer sheets were collected, all of which were retained as they were all completely and carefully answered.

The quotations on the following pages are the original responses writ-ten by the subjects. There were obviously some errors, but the authors did not correct them in order to preserve them as authentic examples of lingua franca English (cf. also Chapters 1, 3–5 and 9).

Results and discussion

The personal information about the students in Part 1 of the question-naire are given in Tables 10.1–10.5; so the authors now present the results of Part 2, the questions, which are divided into four sections.

Table 10.3 Students' gender

Total	Male	Female
251	158	93

Table 10.4 Students' majors

Major	*Students*
Chinese	18
Clinical medicine	233

Section One: Language-related issues
Question 1: Do you attend Chinese classes? And do you want to improve your Chinese? Why or why not?

Of the 251 students, 238 (94.8%) attended Chinese classes. CTGU provides a three-year optional Chinese course for international students. Among the 251 students, 172 students (68.5%) said that they wanted to improve their Chinese, although for different reasons. Of these, 112 (44.6%) had a strong instrumental motivation (Ellis, 1994; Gardner & Lambert, 1972). These students reported that if their Chinese was good, they could pass Chinese exams, find jobs or do their jobs more easily:

- I want to improve my Chinese to get my MBBS (Bachelor of Medicine and Bachelor of Surgery) certificate and pass the HSK (The Chinese Language Testing System) exam.
- We must deal with people here in Chinese and we can't deal with hospital problems without Chinese.

Table 10.5 Students' nationality

Nationality	*Students*
India	160
Nepal	68
Maldives	2
Vietnam	3
Italy	3
Denmark	4
Norway	3
Germany	4
South Korea	4

- Nowadays, there are more and more good job opportunities world-wide. The Chinese language is getting stronger than before due to China's economic development, so I want to improve.
- I want to stay in China for future studies.

And 82 (32.6%) are intrinsically motivated. These students took a genuine interest in China, Chinese people, Chinese language and Chinese culture.

- I love Chinese, China and kind Chinese people.
- I want to talk with Chinese people and learn the culture of China.
- I feel the language is beautiful and I want to speak it fluently.
- I just like the language.
- I like studying different languages.
- My spoken Chinese is quite good, but not written. I want to improve my written Chinese so I can learn more about Chinese history and culture by reading the amazing language.

The rest of the students who wanted to improve their Chinese had a mixture of both instrumental and intrinsic motivations:

- I want to improve my Chinese cause I think that Chinese language is interesting and would be useful in any part of my future life.
- ... to pass HSK exam and to make friends and get more knowledge about China.
- I can understand Chinese people, their culture, do well in clinical medicine.
- I'm eager to be fluent in spoken Chinese and I'll know more about Chinese culture and find a better job.
- I'm interested in Chinese and I think it'd be great capital if you had a good command of this language.

Of the 238 students who attended Chinese classes, 66 (27.7%) of them did not want to improve their Chinese and they reported that they had no motivation at all. They could not see any point in learning the language as they knew that after they returned to their own countries, the language they learned here would be of no use at all.

- No, no, I don't want to learn the language at all, for our education, Chinese language is not necessary.
- No, no use back in my home country India.
- No, not interested.

- I don't actually want to improve my Chinese as I am not going to stay in China after my course gets over. I came to China to study medicine not Chinese.
- I'm not sure if I have to improve it because this language is no longer useful to me after I return back to Nepal.

Interestingly, all the 14 European students who were studying Chinese at the Humanities College reported that they were highly motivated to learn Chinese. Six of them wanted to do business in China and said that China was the largest market for Europe; four of them were interested in the Chinese writing system; one wanted to find a Chinese wife; two were keen on settling down in China in the future and one wanted to study Chinese history.

Question 2: What languages do you use here both in class and after class? And what languages do you use when you're with the students from your country?
    The results showed that, with the exception of the 18 students who were studying Chinese in the Humanities College, all of them used English in class with their teachers but, at the same time, some of them used some simple Chinese with their Chinese teachers and some used their mother tongues when discussing in class with those from their own country. After class, most of them continued to use their own language with their fellow countrymen, and when they were with Chinese people, they used English and Chinese.
    Almost everyone was either bilingual or multilingual. A number of them could speak Chinese well. They used a total of 23 languages both in class and after class. The languages they spoke on the campus are shown in Table 10.6.

Question 3: Do you understand the local dialect?
    Mandarin (Putonghua, standard Chinese) is usually the language used on campus. Chinese students from different parts of the country speak it both in and after class, but to the authors' surprise, 113 of the international students (45%) said they understood some or a little of the local Yichang dialect and a few of them even said they spoke quite a lot of the local dialect. When asked how they learned it, they said that they learned it from the local students and local people working in the markets, supermarkets, shops, restaurants and so on.
    Haberland (2008) found that foreign students who came from other than the Scandinavian countries usually worked through English when

Table 10.6 Languages used on CTGU campus

In-class languages	English
	Chinese
	Their mother tongues for class discussions with their native teachers
After-class languages	Hindi
	Nepalese
	English
	Bengali
	Chinese
	Korean
	Malayalam
	Tamil
	Newari
	Maithlay
	Arabic
	French
	Bhojpuri
	Telugu
	Languages of Pakistan
	Spanish
	Italian
	Danish
	Norwegian
	German
	Vietnamese

they came to study in Denmark. At Roskilde University, for example, he found that many (but not all) of these students learned Danish rather quickly and often went on to finish their studies in Danish. In this way, Danish became their language of internationalization. The options of choosing between languages to learn and languages to use, and the motivation behind these choices are worth further study.

It has been suggested that language choice toward audiences with very diverse language resources will follow Van Parijs' 'maximin' principle: people tend to favor the use of the language that is best known by the members of the audience who know it least (Haberland, 2008).

Question 4: Do you make friends with Chinese students? If you do, what languages do you use to communicate?
Although the international students have their own classrooms and are not mixed with Chinese students, 184 (73.3%) out of the 251 reported that they had Chinese friends ranging from 'a few' to 'many'.

- I have so many Chinese friends that I use Chinese language in phones and messages too.
- I like to make Chinese friends.
- I have many Chinese friends and get used to communicate both in Chinese and English in order to improve the standard of languages of both.
- I mostly use Chinese with them.

The survey showed that mainly English and Chinese were used when they were with their Chinese peers. Out of the 184 students who had Chinese friends, 124 (67.5%) reported that they used both; 37 (19.9%) used English; 23 (12.6%) said 'we only use Chinese' (see Table 10.7).

When talking about language choices, Van Parijs (2004: 114) uses the term 'probability-sensitive learning' to refer to this phenomenon. The expected usefulness of learning a language determines a person's desire to improve their ability in the language. If they are motivated by a need to communicate they will expend more effort in learning. In addition, less effort is needed if one is in a location where the language is actually used. These two elements, motivation and usefulness, reinforce each other. Motivation leads the student to take opportunities for language practice, and the student is rewarded by its usefulness, enabling him to actively engage, understand and be understood in conversations with native speakers.

Question 5: Have you ever encountered any language difficulties on the campus? If yes, can you list as many examples as possible?
One of the greatest obstacles that the authors expected could cause problems should be the language barrier due to language differences and language shock. Language shock refers to learners' feelings of doubt and

Table 10.7 Language use with Chinese peers

Language choice	*Students*	*Percentage*
English and Chinese	124	67.5
English only	37	19.9
Chinese only	23	12.6

confusion when they use another language. This is an affective phenomenon in which the learners fear that their language use does not reflect
their meaning accurately, or that they may appear comical, childlike or
dependent when using the L2 (Schumann, 1986). Language shock is particularly likely to occur in adults who often worry about being misinter-
preted or seen as less competent than they really are. Before conducting
the survey the authors hypothesized that the great majority of the international students would have encountered language difficulties on the
campus. As expected, 225 out of the 251 students (89.8%) reported that
they had 'some' or 'many' language difficulties and shocks.

For some students, the biggest obstacle in class was the language problem. They complained that either they could not understand the Chinese
teachers' English or the teachers had difficulties understanding their
English as they spoke different kinds of English; therefore, sometimes
they had to spend so much time trying to understand each other that
communications broke down:

- The way we speak Chinese and actual Chinese pronunciation are
  very different so they don't understand much of what we speak and
  we don't understand much of what the Chinese say.
- Sometimes when I ask a question of the Chinese teachers they can't
  even understand what we are saying.
- Lots of time we have to use English but many of them don't understand English, so communication is very difficult; then we are forced
  to speak Chinese but it is very difficult and the pronunciation which
  we have doesn't match with theirs.

Apart from the language difficulties they encountered in class, the students reported that they were amused by some of the translated menus
and public signs. They found that some of the bilingual menus in Chinese
restaurants in Beijing were very entertaining: one of the dishes 'fried
young chicken' was translated into 'chicken without a sex life', 'toilets for
the disabled' translated into 'deformed man toilet' and in a taxi, the
Chinese expression which meant 'don't forget to take your things with
you' was mistranslated into 'don't forget to take your thing'.

Another language shock, reported particularly by the European
students, comes from the Chinese sound system, which is very different
from English in that Chinese is a tone-based language. The four tones in
the language (the first, the second, the third and the fourth) are the students' 'biggest headache' as each tone represents a character that has at
least one different meaning. For instance, the four tones for 'ma' mean
four totally different words. An Italian student reported that she asked

the university cafeteria for some 'tāng (soup)', and was given 'táng (sugar)'. The character 'tang' for soup is spoken in the first tone, whereas the one for sugar is spoken in the second tone. The student simply used the wrong tone. A Danish student wanted to tell his Chinese friend 'my suit (xīfù) is in my bag', but instead he said 'my wife (xífù) is in my bag'. More amusingly, a German student ordered a Chinese dish, braised spare ribs, and meant to say 红烧排骨 *hóng shāo pái gǔ*. Unfortunately, he pronounced it as 红烧屁股 *hóng shāo pìgu* which means 'braised buttocks', which created embarrassment for the waitress and made her feel insulted and angry. Another student, a Norwegian, wanted to have Chinese ravioli (饺子 *jiǎozi*), but what he said was understood as 轿子 *jiàozi*, a palanquin.

All these misunderstandings are largely attributed to the fact that the students neglected to learn the tones, which are integral to Chinese speech. We are reminded of the British writer Susan Barker's experience in China: When she thought she was asking a passer-by for directions to the internet cafe, she was actually calling him a 'son of a turtle' (very strong swear words in Chinese). When she said, 'I've caught a cold,' others heard, 'I have sex with cats.' (Barker, 2008).

On the other hand, Chinese teachers and administrators complain also that they find it difficult to understand the students who mainly come from the Outer Circle countries where English is used as a second language. Their English sounds so different from the Inner Circle English that they had been taught and are more familiar with. For instance, some Indian English speakers pronounce certain RP voiceless consonants in word-initial position (as in *try* and *thank* you) in a way that could be heard by Chinese speakers as /d/. Chinese teachers and administrators are not used to this and wonder at the meaning of 'have a dry (try)' and 'dank (thank) you'.

Section Two: Teaching-related issues

Question 6: Do you prefer the Chinese teachers' teaching or teaching of the teachers from your own country? What seems to be the major problems with the Chinese teachers?

All the 18 students studying Chinese at the Humanities College said that they enjoyed their Chinese instructors' teaching very much. Quite a few European students even said they enjoyed Chinese teachers' instruction more than their own teachers' back at home. They said that the teachers were very friendly, helpful, patient and experienced and even better than the teachers in their own countries. One Italian student wrote:

- among the Chinese teachers and teachers in my own country, I like my Chinese teachers more. They are very good companion to me and treat me as their son.

The other European students all thought highly of their Chinese teachers:

- They are very helpful and dedicated.
- When we have problems or questions, our teachers are always happy to help us.
- They are like our family, caring and concerned.

At CTGU some of the medicine-related courses are taught by Chinese teachers who know some English and some are taught by teachers employed from India and Nepal. Of these students, 60.9% (142 out of the 233 students) said that they preferred the teachers from abroad. They thought that they could understand their own teachers more easily as they spoke the same kind of English and shared the same culture. Also they were familiar with their own teachers' teaching styles that made them feel more comfortable. What is more important, their own teachers knew them better.

- It's easier to understand the teachers and the teachers understand our problems and difficulties. There's no language barrier.
- Our own teachers have got a good accent.
- I enjoy our own teachers' classes most of time but when the Chinese teachers take the classes I don't enjoy it much because it is really different from the way it is done in my country.
- We're more familiar with our own teachers' teaching styles, teaching approaches.
- When our own teachers come to teach a class, we will have the feeling that he can speak better English, has greater knowledge and so on.

Thirty-six percent of the students (91 students) enjoyed both the Chinese teachers' and their own teachers' instructions. They said that both the Chinese teachers and the teachers from their own countries were trying very hard to teach them, and that they were impressed by their professionalism and kindness. Some students even showed their understanding and patience with the Chinese teachers whose English could not be easily understood.

- They provide good information and new knowledge which are based on courses and out of courses.
- Our own teachers are trying their best to help us and improve ourselves. Chinese teachers put a lot of hard work in teaching us. They are very much dedicated to their profession but the language problem makes it difficult for us to be comfortable in class.
- They are both very educated and helpful. They provide us with valuable information regarding our subjects and various other important

aspects of our life. I know it's very difficult for the Chinese teachers to speak English in class but they're trying hard.

From the above results, we can see that the biggest problem with the Chinese teachers is the language. Not many teachers in China are truly bilingual. Since 2001, bilingual teaching has been accepted by most Chinese universities including CTGU and a great deal of work has been done. New bilingual courses have been opened, especially in fields such as computer science, medicine, business, information technology, biology, management and law. However, bilingual teaching is still in its initial stage, and many problems are yet to be solved. It is generally believed that the key factor for carrying out bilingual education is having teachers who are proficient in both the subject and the foreign language. In CTGU, teachers capable of bilingual education are very rare. This is the major reason for CTGU having to pay the high cost of employing a number of foreign teachers from India and Nepal.

Section Three: Culture-related issues
Question 7: Have you ever experienced any cultural differences or culture shocks here either in class or after class? If yes, please list as many examples as possible.

Culture shock (see also Chapter 3) is associated with feelings in the learner of estrangement, anger, hostility, indecision, frustration, unhappiness, sadness, loneliness, homesickness and even physical illness (Brown, 1994: 170). Schumann describes culture shock as 'disorientation encountered upon entering a new culture' (Schumann, 1986: 383). It occurs particularly when routines used in the L1 context no longer work in the new environment. The learner, in attempting to find a cause for his disorientation, may reject himself, his own culture, the organization for which he is working and the people of the host country. Under such conditions the learner is unlikely to make the effort necessary to become bilingual. Archer (1986, in Jiang, 2001) uses the term 'culture bump' to refer to cases where an individual from one culture finds himself or herself in a different, strange or uncomfortable situation when interacting with persons of a different culture. A culture bump/shock occurs when an individual has expectations of one type of behavior, and gets something completely different.

We expected that all the international students who answered the survey had encountered culture shocks in the new environment. To the authors' surprise, over half of the students (52%) reported that they had not experienced any cultural shocks. They said that they enjoyed the cultures and customs very much and had had no shocks or bumps. We assumed that it might be due to their ambiguity tolerance (Brown, 2000) in the sense that they were cognitively willing to tolerate Chinese ideas and propositions that ran counter to their own belief system or structure of knowledge. The following is a handful of the surprises that the international students experienced.

One of the immediate major shocks that some of the international students experienced was the food. 'Food is one of the most obvious of the familiar cues that remind us of the environment we are in' (Hu, 2008: 102). Some Indian students found it odd to eat raw or half-cooked vegetables, such as green beans or carrots, which must be well cooked in their own country, and they complained that:

- Indian food here in the city is too expensive; Chinese people eat too many eggs almost every day which is rare in India; 10% of Indian people eat eggs.
- We use the right hand to eat instead of chopsticks; we feel we are not eating if we use chopstick; Chinese people feel it's not hygienic but we declare we wash our hands.
- We don't use toilet paper, instead we use our left hand to clean ourselves after using the toilet, so we use the right hands to shake hands with people or touch children on the head.

One Danish student thought it incredible and disgusting to put rice in soup, which is like mud to them but very common for Chinese people. Most of the European students complained that the food was too spicy. They also reported that the table manners were very different. In Europe, everyone is given a plate in which all the food is offered (meat, vegetables, potatoes etc.), but in China, different kinds of food are placed in plates on the table so that everybody shares all the food until they are full. Usually, there is much more food available on the table than needed. The European students were also amused by the noise that Chinese people make while eating, and restaurants are often very noisy places. People eat noisily to show that they enjoy the food and the company. Hosts persuade their guests and friends to eat and drink as much as possible, and the hosts often cook or order much more food than they can eat to show their generosity and hospitality. In Europe, however, when people eat, they chew with their mouths closed and talk quietly with no food in their mouths. These students from Europe reported that it took them quite some time to get used to this difference.

Another culture shock to the international students was the different ways Chinese people were dressed. In India and Nepal, people wear the traditional saris, churidars and slippers. At CTGU they do likewise. The students even wear slippers in all seasons and walk to class in slippers, which shocked the Chinese students. They explained that they wore slippers instead of shoes in order to be able to take them off more easily when they worshiped their God. Chinese girls wore miniskirts or 'wear very little' in summer which some Indian boys reported that they did not like. They said, 'Chinese girls show too much of their body which is not graceful in our culture'.

The European students said that they felt uncomfortable being stared at by the Chinese because they looked different, and sometimes they felt 'people here see us as strangers, as they fear to speak English'.

Regarding smoking, a Korean student reported: 'I notice that when I have a meal with Chinese friends, sometimes they throw cigarettes to their friends, but in Korea if someone throws something to people it is really rude'. In China, if you throw a cigarette to somebody, it means that you are 'brothers' or very close friends.

The differences were felt by subject teachers and administrators too. They told the authors that many of the international students were often late for class. The authors asked the students why. Some Indian students explained that they were late for class because, in their culture, the VIPs were usually late in order to show their importance and they wanted to look like VIPs.

Section Four: Other issues
Question 8: Do you enjoy your campus life here in general? What do you enjoy the most? And what are the main problems you have here?

Of the 251 students, 188 (75%) reported, from different perspectives, that they enjoyed their campus life. They told the authors that they were amazed and impressed by the diversity of after-class activities and various kinds of culture-based performances. They also found, to their great satisfaction, that life was easy and convenient at CTGU.

- Life here becomes very easy and convenient. We can use credit cards for shopping which is real cool.
- I do enjoy my campus life here. I enjoy learning new things like culture and other people's lifestyle along with my study.
- I like the cultural programs such as performances on special days and holidays. The library here is real good.
- Yes, I do. I enjoy classes, picnic, watch cricket play, hospital visits; no much problems.
- I like the cultural activities, dance, music, sports, library, cinema, TV, football, basketball. Climate is the main problem.
- There are many interesting seminars.
- Both of us (Indian and Nepali students) like the country CHINA very much!

Of the total, 63 (25%) of the students did not enjoy their campus life because of language and food problems:

- I don't enjoy it. Language barrier.
- I don't have much friends.
- Some of the Chinese students showed their negative thought about foreigners and refuse to talk, we feel like hurting.
- We know Chinese but Chinese don't know English.
- We don't get the type of food which we eat.
- It is difficult for a vegetarian to survive here.
- It's not fair that we are not allowed to cook.

Other complaints such as 'too many rules at CTGU', homesickness and HSK pressure were reported by only a few students.

Question 9: What are your suggestions for the University?
While the international students in general felt happy with their academic and campus life, they also offered some suggestions in the hope that CTGU would make the international program more effective:

(1) Introduce more foreign teachers to CTGU to teach specialty courses.
(2) Hold more culture-oriented activities.
(3) Improve Chinese teachers' English.
(4) Abolish the HSK examination or do not make it compulsory.
(5) Organize more study tours.

Question 10: What are you going to do and where are you going after you finish your study here?
Out of the total of 251, 191 (76%) said that they would go back to their own countries, of whom half were going to continue to study and the other half were planning to find jobs. Twenty-five students (10%) wanted to stay in China either to work or to study Chinese, and the rest were going to other countries to work or for further study.

Conclusion and Suggestions

Generally speaking, most of the international students felt happy with their stay at the university and thought that the international program had been successful overall due to the effort that CTGU, the subject teachers as well as the administrators had made, and due to the international students' positive contribution. Research shows that it is common for international students to face many difficulties in their adjustment to higher education in another country (Myles & Cheng, 2003). In general, their main challenge is to become acculturated into a new academic and cultural community. In addition to language barriers and academic challenges, which can impede effective communication, a number of these students face psycho-social challenges, such as making new friends, isolation, loss of social status and understanding the rules that apply in specific social situations. But these problems can be minimized in the future with the provision of more detailed preparation. One important factor that can determine the success of a program like this is the participants' attitudes. When their attitudes are open and positive, they can overcome all the difficulties and enjoy their stay in a new culture. For CTGU, this survey offered a clearer picture of the international students' life and study. Based on the feedback of the survey, CTGU can improve the program by acting on the following suggestions:

(1) Subject teachers should try to improve their English competence so that they can make themselves understood and communicate with students both in and after class. CTGU should send their teachers to English-speaking countries or get special training in English language schools in China.

(2) Culture-oriented courses should be created for international students. On arrival at CTGU, the international students should take courses in Chinese culture to help them avoid cultural conflicts. CTGU can also organize more culture-based activities so that both Chinese and international students can participate and have the opportunity to know each other's culture and reach international understanding.

(3) CTGU, as an international university, should establish a set of systematic teaching and management models suitable for international students including specially trained teaching and administrative staff, teaching materials, teaching methods, testing, assessment and extracurricular activities. This requires CTGU to think globally and act locally.

References

Archer, C. (1986) Culture bump and beyond. In J.M. Valdes (ed.) *Culture Bond: Bridging the Cultural Gap in Language Teaching.* Cambridge: Cambridge University Press.

Barker, S. (2008) The orientalist and the ghost. *The Guardian* 12 May.

Brown, H.D. (1994) *Principles of Language Learning and Teaching* (3rd edn). Englewood Cliffs, NJ: Prentice-Hall, Inc.

Brown, H.D. (2000) *Principles of Language Learning and Teaching* (4th edn). Pearson Education: Addison-Wesley Longman, Inc.

Crystal, D. (2003) *English as a Global Language* (2nd edn). Cambridge: Cambridge University Press.

Ellis, R. (1994) *The Study of Second Language Acquisition*. Oxford: Oxford University Press.

Gardner, R. and Lambert, W. (1972) *Attitudes and Motivation*. Rowley, MA: Newbury House.

Haberland, H. (2008) Danish as the language of internationalisation. Conference paper presented at the international conference *Language Issues in English-Medium Universities: A Global Concern*. University of Hong Kong, 18–20 June.

Hu, X. (2008) The culture shock that Asian students experience in immersion education. *Changing English* 15, 101–105.

Jiang, W. (2001) Handling culture bumps. *ELT Journal* 55, 382–385.

Myles, J. and Cheng, L. (2003) The social and cultural life of non-native English speaking international graduate students at a Canadian university. *Journal of English for Academic Purposes* 2, 247–263.

Schumann, J.H. (1986) Research on the acculturation model for second language acquisition. *Journal of Multilingual and Multicultural Development* 7, 379–392.

Van Parijs, P. (2004) Europe's linguistic challenge. *Archives européennes de sociologie* 45, 111–152.

Appendix

Questionnaire

Part 1: Your basic information:
Name:_____ Gender:_____ Age:____ Country:__ Your major:_____
Your Grade_____
Your mother tongue or first language:_____
Other languages you can speak fluently: _____
_____

Your Chinese level: very good; good; poor; very poor (tick one of the choices please)

Part 2: Questions
1. Do you attend Chinese classes? And do you want to improve your Chinese? Why or why not?
2. What languages do you use here both in class and after class? And what languages do you use when you're with the students from your country?
3. Do you understand the local dialect?
4. Do you make friends with Chinese students? If you do, what languages do you use to communicate?
5. Have you ever encountered any language difficulties on the campus? If yes, please list as many examples as possible.

6. Do you prefer the Chinese teachers' teaching or the teaching of teachers from your own country? What seems to be the major problems with the Chinese teachers?
7. Have you ever experienced any cultural differences or shocks here either in class or after class? If yes, please list as many examples as possible.
8. Do you enjoy your campus life here in general? What do you enjoy the most? And what are the main problems you have here?
9. What are your suggestions for the University?
10. What are you going to do and where are you going after you finish your study here?

Chapter 11

How Far Can Face and Hierarchy Affect Developing Interaction between Korean University Students and their Supervisors in the United Kingdom?

J. BACK

Introduction

Among a range of problems that many East Asian overseas learners, and particularly Korean students, are likely to confront while studying in English-speaking countries, culture-related issues deriving from student–teacher relationships (cf. also Chapter 9) between Asian learners and Western teachers have been discussed. This is based on the assumption that, from an East–West cross-cultural perspective, cultural differences may generate a whole series of mismatches in expectations between Asian students and Western tutors or universities in an academic context, as well as in their social life. This chapter aims at examining how cultural factors stemming from Confucianism may affect Korean students' learning when they use English in a different educational context, focusing on their progress and specific patterns in adjusting into supervisory meetings on one-year programmes. Also, their reactions to the problems and difficulties throughout one year are discussed.

Background

Cultural mismatches in the student–teacher relationship

In as much as 'age' and 'social status' are the major factors affecting hierarchical relationships generally in Korea (Shin & Koh, 2005), the interpersonal relationships between the members of the teaching staff and between staff and students show how hierarchical authoritarianism permeates Korean higher education (for hierarchical relationships, cf. also Chapter 3). Students show a strong tendency to respect and obey their lecturers, and the lecturers in turn tend to take care of their students in a manner similar to parent–child relationships (Janelli, 1993; Lee, 1997, 1998, 1999, 2001). Lecturers can be considered 'rulers' in class, with a role similar to that of a king, or a father (Shin & Koh, 2005: 2). Both ethical values in this sort of relationship and the teacher's social authority underpin the student–teacher relationship in Korea (Janelli, 1993; Lee, 1997, 1998, 1999).

Furthermore, students' respect towards their lecturers is also traditionally based on the high value placed on the teaching profession in Korean society (Yum, 2000, cited in Shin & Koh, 2005). The teacher in Korea as in other East-Asian countries is regarded as an important authority figure, respected by students as a 'dispenser of knowledge' and a 'moulder of character' (Siu, 1992; Strom *et al.*, 1981, cited in Shin & Koh, 2005: 2). This may lead students to unconsciously believe that the lecturer is always right and his or her authority should never be challenged. The teacher, in general, plays a role in guiding students as a moral model and a transmitter of knowledge:

> CHC student–teacher interaction is not lubricated with the democratic oil of warmth and first names, but with the oil of respect, which is a more effective lubricant in a hierarchical, collectivist culture. (Biggs, 1998: 730)

Indeed, it seems clear that respect towards, and the authority of, teachers in Korea still remain highly valued in the Korean educational system (Egeler, 1996). This leads in many cases to 'passive' learning, in which students are very hesitant to suggest their opinions voluntarily to their teachers. The link with Confucianism was noted by Kolrarik (2004: 3),

> [p]assivity is not attributed to low English proficiency or lack of cooperation, but rather a reticence based on a cultural form of respect (Boyle, 2000a). A student's quiet behaviour is a sign of a learning attitude which entails respect to teachers, classmates and superiors as guided by Confucian belief (Cortazzi & Jin, 1997).

As 'face' is also a significant factor in hierarchical relationships, and is related to age, status, rank and seniority, this passivity can be explained by a belief that giving unsolicited comments or asking questions may interrupt teachers and thus cause a loss of the teachers' face (for the influence of Confucianism, cf. also Chapter 12; for '(loss of) face', cf. Chapter 2). Korean students tend to listen to teachers rather than express their ideas

(Cortazzi & Jin, 1997), which in turn leads to teacher-centred classes and learning. The learners are more familiar with internalising information given by the teachers, that is, with memorising rather than being critically analytical. The belief is that the teacher is always right and his or her authority should not be challenged (Flowerdew, 1998). As a result, since students may often behave in ways that they have been familiar with in their native culture, they may not actually recognise 'clues' that they are being given by a teacher in the host country to offer their ideas or opinions (Lim & Griffith, 2004, cited in Back, 2009b).

In Western academic culture, however, learners are encouraged to voluntarily express their own ideas and actively interact with teachers (Cortazzi & Jin, 1997). This is supposed to lead to learner-centred learning through which learners are expected to develop autonomy and independence.

The following is a summary of Cortazzi and Jin's points about the contrasting perceptions of teachers' and students' roles in higher education in

SUPERVISORS	CHINESE STUDENTS
Students should develop ...	*Teachers should provide ...*
independence individuality creativity	acquisition of knowledge guidance imitation, models for/of learning
openness to alternatives processes of investigation critical thinking	a single answer results and solutions new methods to learn, ways to reach advanced technical levels
Students should ...	*Teachers should ...*
think for themselves know what to do	be moral leaders know everything in their area of expertise
express themselves when they need help	should ask students if they have any problems plan for and instruct students be sensitive, sympathetic, helpful and know our problems
take responsibilities academically, and for everyday activities	act as a parent supporting children
mix with British	no money to go out with them

(Cortazzi & Jin, 1993: 87)

English-speaking countries, especially between Chinese students and British teachers (see also Cortazzi & Jin, 1993: 87).

These mismatches in role expectations (cf. also Chapters 3 and 7) between Western teachers and Chinese students may cause a degree of conflict in the learning and teaching context, and Korean students can also be assumed to experience this cultural conflict while studying abroad in the United Kingdom. Western teachers are likely to feel that Asian students have a low level of participation in classroom activities and show a lack of autonomy (Wong, 2004).

On the other hand, Chinese students may feel that teachers from Western countries are not sufficiently prepared to transmit their knowledge in a lecture or a seminar, and that asking for active participation and involvement is not really teaching (Li, 1999). The evidence would suggest that such mismatches can be generalised to other Asian students including Koreans, but this requires further research into cultural gaps between Korean and British perceptions of teachers' and students' roles. It might be beneficial to examine which aspects of these gaps Korean students find more salient and of greatest concern.

To summarise, role expectations of Western teachers and international students in an English-speaking country differ: while teachers advise or guide students, encouraging students' autonomy and independence in a student-centred approach, the students may expect their teachers to advise them on all steps of the learning process as authoritative 'mentors' (Chan & Drover, 1997: 56). Accordingly, both teachers and students from different cultural backgrounds need to be sensitive to each other's expected roles. In particular, it seems clear that Asian students who are familiar with teacher-dependent, 'spoon-fed' learning need to assimilate more of the interactive and independent learning styles of the Western educational context.

Methods

The aims of the study

The in-depth interviews (cf. also Chapters 1, 3, 4, 8 and 10) were undertaken with six Korean Master's students at a northern British university from 2005 October to 2006 October. Thus, qualitative research in a 'real-life setting' (Gillham, 2005: 3) was needed to examine the pace of students' progress in developing social interaction skills and adapting to the academic culture of British universities, especially on short one-year Master's programmes. The in-depth interviews aimed at answering the following questions:

(1) What is specifically problematic to Korean Master's students in the areas of social integration into their host environment?
(2) What caused key social problems and challenges?
(3) To what extent and how did the students adjust to a different academic culture within the UK university system across the year?
(4) What attempts did the students make to solve their problems?

Adopting a case study approach whereby each individual could be tracked in reasonable detail across the three terms and the summer vacation, the study thus includes individual histories of each participant, which could be built up as long as the appropriate checks were made, allowing comparisons to be made term by term.

Sampling and procedures

Despite my failure to balance between students in science-based courses and those studying non-science-related subjects (which was not possible as there was only one 'science' student available), the six participants studying at the MA level at a northern British university were recruited as they all agreed to participate in the interviews. Their relevant information is summarised in Table 11.1.

Each participant had six interview sessions and thus altogether 36 interviews were conducted over the three academic terms and the summer vacation. Throughout the three terms, the basic structure of the interview time frame consists of two interview sessions of each participant across each term, although the final sessions, which include summarising and discussing all the information from each participant, were conducted during the summer vacation. This function of final interviews as 'review stage' (Gillham, 2005) was a device for checking the credibility and objectivity of the data and minimising the researcher bias.

Toyoshima's (2007) 'structured conversation' method (Conteh & Toyoshima, 2005) was adopted and modified: Toyoshima (2007: 120) developed 'a semi-structured format which I called structured conversation' to trace her university students' learning history (Back, 2009a). The in-depth, longitudinal interviews with six Korean students developed a large amount of conversation within theme-based structured questions.

Table 11.1 In-depth interviews: Summary of baseline information on the six participants

ID	Sex	Age	Subject
NJ	M	36*	MA in Social Policy
BK	F	26	MA in Linguistics
YJ	M	35*	MA in Social Policy
JM	M	28	MSc in Financial Mathematics
MK	F	29	MA in TESOL
HC	F	43*	MA in TESOL

*Participant was older than the researcher.

As I adopted 'data triangulation', two other ways of collecting data, alongside of data from the 36 interview sessions, were used between and across the interview sessions: informal talk by phone, informal or any social meetings, or emails from the participants. I tried to check their adjustment to a new life by asking them to email me in case of specific experiences or problems. I also arranged several informal meetings or participated in social meetings with them to create natural conversational settings where we discussed their experiences or anecdotes. This worked positively and thus gave me abundant data.

Findings and Discussions

Investigating each participant's progress in adjusting to supervisory meetings in British higher education, the interview data from each interview are summarised in Tables 11.2–11.7.

Although there were some individual variations in the students' adaptation to supervisory meetings in the United Kingdom as summarised in the tables above, the key point is that none of them appeared to know initially what the meetings were for. In Korea, although all the subjects had experienced at least an undergraduate degree, none of them were aware who their own supervisors had been, they had not, in most cases, actually met their supervisors, or understood why supervisors are necessary. Consequently they did not have any background knowledge of supervisory

Table 11.2 In-depth interviews: Problems with and reactions to the supervisory systems: NJ

Interview sessions	Problematic areas and reactions
I1	• He did not understand supervision sessions: he met his supervisor only once at the beginning of the first term in Korea. (He had no experience of supervisory meetings in Korea.) • He was waiting until his supervisor contacted him, but he was rather concerned about this matter.
I2	• He discussed a 'practice essay' in the second meeting and this proved very useful to him. He sent emails to express his gratitude for the day's meeting after he got back home. • He found several communicational difficulties in English when he needed to express himself in detail/in depth. • He never contacted his supervisor, even when he had a question or academic problem: he was very hard to contact. He thought even using emails would disturb his supervisor. • He was not clear how far he could request any academic advice.
I3	• He felt the supervision meetings were always useful to him, but still hesitated to contact him: He expected his supervisor to send emails for the meetings and take care of him with academic advice. • He sent emails rather than ask questions in face-to-face interactions.
I4	• Not much had changed. • He met his supervisor to discuss his dissertation topic.
I5	• He met his supervisor very rarely.
I6	Overall self-evaluation: • He expected his supervisor to manage all the supervision meetings. • He hesitated to contact him many times, even when he desperately needed to request academic advice.

systems. This shows quite clearly that there are cultural differences in the concept of supervisor between the two different academic contexts.

Because of this lack of experience and understanding, the students said that they felt very reluctant to contact their supervisors at the beginning of the first term and could not overcome this passivity. This can be explained by the cultural assumption that the Korean students had experienced a more hierarchical and vertical relationship between teachers and students in Korea. In the first interview sessions, although they

Table 11.3 In-depth interviews: Problems and reactions in supervisory systems: BK

Interview sessions	Problematic areas and reactions
I 1	• She did not know what the supervision sessions were for in the UK educational system; she had no experience of supervisory meetings in Korea. • She was not encouraged to contact her supervisor frequently. She hesitated to ask questions. • She had met her supervisor only once at the beginning of the first term.
I 2	• She met her supervisor twice during the first term. • Although she understood the supervisory meetings more than in I1, she was not familiar with them. • She had only a very short conversation with her supervisor. Overall, she did not actively ask questions, even though she needed to clarify some points.
I 3	• She was not satisfied with the supervisory sessions: she thought that the supervisions she had did not guide her towards deciding on a topic for her dissertation.
I 4	• She received quite useful and satisfying advice from her supervisor.
I 5	• She felt that supervisions in the United Kingdom were not very useful overall. • She was dissatisfied with the supervision system itself, which seemed to rely on students' independent research and voluntary contact. She expected to meet her supervisor regularly and frequently.
I 6	Overall self-evaluation: • She expected the supervisions to take the form of regular meetings. She found it hard to adjust to voluntarily contacting her supervisor. • She hesitated many times to contact her supervisor when she needed to request academic advice because she was afraid that she would disturb him. This did not encourage her to improve herself academically.

found out who their supervisors were and wanted to meet them, NJ, HC and YJ reported being very concerned about not contacting their supervisors, instead waiting until their supervisors first contacted them. They were not clear about whether this was the more courteous procedure or not and were also concerned about what they needed to prepare for their

Table 11.4 In-depth interviews: Problems and reactions in supervisory systems: YJ

Interview sessions	*Problematic areas and reactions*
I 1	• He did not understand what the supervision sessions were for in the United Kingdom: he had not experienced them in Korea. • He emailed his supervisor once and was very grateful to receive useful advice about the reading lists and useful courses.
I 2	• He met his supervisor twice. • He was more confident in, and had adjusted to, contacting his supervisor, and felt he understood the supervision system better. He was still not very clear what the supervision was about, though found that supervision meetings were very useful as long as he was active about making contact and asking questions. • He was satisfied with his supervision meetings and grateful for his supervisor's caring attitude. • He still hesitated to ask his supervisor any questions. • He generally used emails to ask questions rather than the face-to-face discussions, because he was not confident about his communication skills.
I 3	• He tried to use polite linguistic devices both in discussions and email letters (He was always worried if he needed to say' how are you' or use 'could/would'). • He discovered cultural differences in the relationship between students and supervisors: it was less hierarchical and vertical in the United Kingdom; he felt less unwilling to ask questions or request academic advice from his supervisor than previously. • He was very impressed with his supervisors through regular supervisory meetings.
I 4	• He was 70% satisfied with his supervision meetings. • He still struggled with verbally expressing his in-depth ideas to his supervisor.
I 5	• He discussed his dissertation with his supervisor once, but he had communication problems; his supervisor could not fully understand what he thought.
I 6	Overall self-evaluation: • He had adjusted well to the supervision system in the United Kingdom and thus he did not hesitate to ask questions, although he still had problems with communicating fluently with his supervisor. • He found that he could approach his supervisor more in the United Kingdom and thus supervisory meetings could benefit his academic achievement, but he still hesitated to contact him in many cases.

Table 11.5 In-depth interviews: Problems and reactions in supervisory systems: JM

Interview sessions	Problematic areas and reactions
I 1	• He did not understand the supervision sessions in the United Kingdom; he had not experienced them in Korea. • He really hesitated to email his supervisor for cultural and language reasons; he was concerned about being impolite to ask the supervisor for academic advice and had a fear of speaking in English. But he tried to email his supervisors to ask some questions.
I 2	• He met his supervisor three times using the advertised office hours: he still had a lot of difficulty with using English when discussing things with his supervisor.
I 3	• In most cases, he only sent emails to ask questions, instead of interacting face to face. • He thought most supervisors in UK universities were less authoritative than in Korea and he thus hesitated less to email his supervisor than in the first term.
I 4	• He often sent emails to ask questions. • He was quite satisfied with his supervisors' help both psychologically and academically: he felt that his supervisor was very caring and considerate about his lack of competence in spoken English.
I 5	• He sent emails to his supervisor to ask questions about his dissertation and he was satisfied with the supervisor's guidance and comments.
I 6	Overall self-evaluation: • Supervision meetings across the course were very useful to motivate and encourage him to study hard. • He was very positive about the relationship between supervisors and students, which was he thought more rational, open, independent, and equal than in Korea.

first supervision meetings. HC commented that a psychological distance from her supervisor as an authority figure led her to hesitate to contact her supervisor. She unconsciously expected that the relationship between her and her supervisor in the United Kingdom would be hierarchical, of the sort she was accustomed to in Korea.

Alongside this cultural reason, the students all agreed that they were not confident about speaking with their supervisors. NJ was very reluctant

Table 11.6 In-depth interviews: Problems and reactions in supervisory systems: MK

Interview sessions	Problematic areas and reactions
I 1	• She did not know what the supervision sessions were for and had not experienced them in Korea. • She was just waiting until her supervisor contacted her first.
I 2	• She understood what the supervision systems in UK higher education were for after meeting her supervisor three times. • She felt more adjusted to the meetings: she was satisfied with the guidance and advice about the outline for the essay by her supervisor, and felt more confident in interacting with her supervisor. This encouraged her to study.
I 3	• Her supervisor was so caring that she felt psychologically more comfortable talking to her and asked questions more actively or requested academic advice.
I 4	• She felt supervisory meetings were very satisfying and settled down both psychologically and academically.
I 5	• She discussed her dissertation with her supervisor and this was useful to her, although there was still a language barrier when it came to expressing herself in detail.
I 6	Overall self-evaluation: • Interacting with her supervisor was a very good experience, in that she learned a different academic culture as well as improved her academic and language skills.

to communicate verbally with his supervisor because he often experienced misunderstandings when conversing with him. However, their lack of oral language skills did not cause serious problems as three cases showed: NJ, YJ and JM preferred to email, and thus mostly emailed to ask questions or request academic advice, especially when they needed to clarify details. This may also imply that these students were more accustomed to written than to spoken English.

In terms of their level of satisfaction with interacting with their supervisor, it is inevitable that there would be variation resulting from the different personalities involved, and the different situations of the supervisors, courses and departments. However, it was clear that each of the students reacted differently when they became dissatisfied with their supervisory interactions; BK gave up actively contacting her supervisor when she was not very satisfied with her supervisory meetings, finding that they did not

Table 11.7 In-depth interviews: Problems and reactions in supervisory systems: HC

Interview sessions	Problematic areas and reactions
I 1	• She did not understand what supervision sessions were for; she had not experienced any in Korea even though she had completed a Master's course. • She was concerned about when she could contact her supervisor. • She felt psychologically distanced from her supervisor, which made her panic when meeting him.
I 2	• She had met her supervisor three times and now she felt it was clearer how supervision meetings worked in the United Kingdom, but she did not think they were very useful, because of the very limited time for a meeting. She also tried actively to ask the other academic staff questions whenever she needed to know something.
I 3	• She felt less satisfied with supervision meetings than she had expected, so she tried to rely on the other lecturers. This did not meet with positive reactions, in part, because she was not accustomed to asking questions of lecturers or seminar leaders. The problem was that she felt that her supervisor was not very caring or considerate in view of her cultural or language barriers.
I 4	• She felt very dissatisfied with her supervision meetings, so instead of asking her supervisor for academic help, she tried to rely on doing literature research on her own or asking the other academic staff after class, using emails.
I 5	• She felt her supervisor was more open than in previous terms when discussing dissertation matters, but she was not very satisfied with her supervisor's advice.
I 6	Overall self-evaluation • She thought that supervision meetings were more systematized than in Korea, even though her supervision meetings were not useful in encouraging her to work hard or improve her study skills. • She was not satisfied with her supervisory meetings and was not very active in solving the problems with supervisory meetings overall.

encourage her to improve her academic skills. HC on the other hand relied, from the end of the second term, upon self-study and research, making several attempts to actively contact other academic staff when she needed to ask a question.

The interview data make it abundantly clear that all six participants found it hard to adjust to supervisory meetings in the United Kingdom within the framework of a year. By the end of the year, they were still being quite passive instead of contacting and interacting with their supervisors, even though they had tried to improve the situation and resolve their problems. In order to understand why the six students all appeared to express little satisfaction with their interactions with their supervisors, it is necessary to examine the range of specific behavioural patterns.

First, all six participants reported that they were very concerned about being polite in terms of using language and meeting the role expectations of their supervisors. In other words, they tried to use polite linguistic devices with formal expressions, such as 'could you', or 'would you' when verbally communicating with them or writing emails. They were also very hesitant to ask their supervisors for academic advice, in order not to disturb them or cause them to lose face in the event that the supervisor was unable to help them. Even when the students came to understand the academic expectations of supervisory meetings and the relationship between students and supervisors in the United Kingdom, this tendency to be concerned about being polite did not change very much. For instance, NJ noted,

> As I experienced in the first term, I think I bothered my supervisor, making him open such a silly email I sent as soon as I got home after I finished my supervision meeting in the first term. The email was to express my gratitude for the meeting with him: 'Thank you very much for giving me your time for the meeting today. I hope that I did not bother you …'. Although I realised what a useless email he would think it was, I still hesitated about whether I needed to express my gratitude whenever I had a meeting with him. (NJ, I5)

YJ commented similarly on using linguistic devices to express politeness:

> I think I always used 'would you … , could you … ,' whenever I talked to my supervisor or emailed her. Also, I was always hesitant; clearly, it is not the best way to start with 'How are you' in such an email. I think it can be rude to make direct requests in an email. Although I think this derives from politeness – involving values that I am not accustomed to in Korea and thus it is difficult to understand that I do not need to think about the question of politeness so much here. I am always worried about being rude. (YJ, I3)

His comment shows that politeness was a serious problem when it came to communicating with supervisors and requesting academic advice from them. In addition, his attempt to be polite before making a request comes from pragmatically culture-specific behaviour in the Korean communicational context (on the cross-cultural differences in 'making a request' between Korea and America).

Second, all the interviewers reported that they had discovered differences between the two countries in how far students' rights to request academic advice are guaranteed. However, it needs to be borne in mind that while the interviews were able to highlight areas of concern to all the six students, there was a limit to the extent to which they were in position to directly compare the United Kingdom and Korean systems, as only two (YJ and HC) had undertaken MAs in Korea.

Despite the above limitation, I made an attempt to examine particular areas that contrasted, based on the data from YJ and HC, who had experienced MAs in Korea. As HC noted,

> I did not have any regular supervision sessions in Korea when I did my Master's course, although it depends on the department. During the course in Korea, I always felt a psychological distance between my supervisor and me, which discouraged me from contacting him, even though I needed to discuss my dissertation with him. During the course in Korea, in many cases, I contacted my seniors more often than my supervisor; they were mostly to be found in the PhD courses, when I needed to discuss things and request academic advice. (HC, I1)

HC's comment neatly illustrates the finding by Prasad *et al.* (2004) that a vertical relationship between students and supervisors, deriving from Confucian values concerning the relationship between students and teachers, makes it difficult for students to contact their supervisor. Rather than attempting to interact with their supervisors, students tend to rely more on interaction with their seniors. The relationship between juniors and seniors does not only relate to getting jobs, but seniors also play an important role in handing down information and their university experience to their juniors. Thus, it is unsurprising that HC would have felt more comfortable about asking her seniors in the department for academic advice than about contacting her supervisor either in Korea or the United Kingdom.

Due to a lack of experience with supervisory meetings in Korea, HC said she did not know how to prepare for her UK supervision meetings at the beginning of the first term, and was very unsure about whether or not to wait until her supervisors contacted her first. She asked me several times in the first and second interview sessions whether it was preferable to wait until her supervisor first emailed her. Although she felt more adjusted to the supervisory sessions in the second and final term, she was still concerned about whether she would disturb her supervisor or not whenever she asked him for academic advice on her work. Although YJ was less concerned about meeting his supervisor than HC, he also asked me for some advice on his supervision sessions during the year, as he too was unfamiliar with meeting and discussing things with a supervisor:

> Initially, I thought I would bother my supervisor if I contacted him before he emailed me. I had been just waiting until he had time and thus could email me. I was very worried if I was doing the right thing or not. I am very unfamiliar with meeting and discussing things with my supervisor. I was concerned that I would make a mistake during the first supervisory meeting. (YJ, I1)

Although the two students expected their supervisors to contact them first, which was in fact the right thing to do, the important point is that they were not clear about what to do and what would be polite and courteous. It is, in particular, noteworthy that both participants tended to discuss the matter of their supervision sessions, and the relationship between them and their supervisors, with me first, rather than directly discussing the question with their supervisors. They tended to depend more on my suggestions or advice to sort out their initial worries in the first term, considering me as a senior who was experienced at the MA level. Like HC and YJ, the other participants also frequently tried, from the first interview to the fifth, to ask me about supervision matters, such as how many times they could meet in a term, or how often it is acceptable to email one's supervisor to ask questions. This tendency was particularly extreme during the first term, but continued, albeit at a lower level, throughout the year.

Having grown accustomed to the non-existence or formality of Korean supervisions, NJ was not aware of the supervisory role in the United Kingdom or of students' and teachers' responsibilities, and thus he did not initially have any understanding of what his supervisor could do for him during the academic year. BK similarly reported that she did not understand the supervision system in the United Kingdom, pointing out at the beginning of the course,

> I do not expect my supervisor to do anything for me, and I do not try to actively contact him or rely on the meetings when needed. In fact, I guess it would be impossible for my supervisor to care for his students individually. (BK, I1)

In short, none of the students initially perceived how UK supervision sessions are organised and run, or understand the role of a supervisor with respect to their overall academic achievement. They were not aware of cultural differences in the supervision system between the two countries and were still accustomed to a strong vertical relationship with their supervisors.

Interestingly, this finding does not completely correspond to the expectations expressed by Asian students in Prasad *et al.*'s (2004) study, also discussed by Cortazzi and Jin (1999): they mostly expected their supervisors to take care of them like parents, a view which may well lead to quite a different series of cultural mismatches between international students and their supervisors in the host country. The confusion on the part of the six Korean students changed when they developed a greater understanding of the UK supervisory system. Although they did not anticipate their supervisors caring for them in the first term, by the second term BK did complain that her supervisor did not seem very caring.

As previously discussed, the confusion about the function of UK supervision sessions seems to have led to considerable uncertainty by all six participants about how far they could request academic advice from their supervisors. Moreover, even when the students had experienced supervision, their reluctance to ask for advice persisted. Thus, YJ noted,

> I feel I am getting more confident about contacting my supervisor now in the second term, but I am still unsure if I can request any advice from him or not. In the first term, I asked him to guide me in making an outline for my assessed essay, but I am not sure if I can ask him again to give me some guidance for another essay this term. (YJ, I3)

Lastly, the interview data make it clear that, as the year progressed, all the participants except for BK reported that they were increasingly able to discuss things with their supervisors, based on a more equal and open relationship between the two of them. As JM put it,

> I felt that the authoritarian position of supervisors and other academic staff in Korea made me hesitate to approach them. However, in the UK, supervisors appear more approachable and open to the students. (JM, I5)

Despite having a favourable attitude towards an atmosphere where they could discuss things freely with their supervisors, the students were nevertheless unable to fully overcome the cultural barriers which discouraged active interaction. They remained in general fairly passive rather than contacting their supervisors even at the end of the year, though YJ and JM attempted to contact and interact with their supervisors more actively and voluntarily than the other four. This problem only serves to highlight the difficulty of adapting to very different cultural norms within the space of a one-year programme.

Conclusion

None of the six participants were able to overcome their passivity about contacting and interacting with their supervisors and other academic staff and showed reluctance to react to the problems they had encountered. This could be partly explained by their lack of knowledge about what the supervisory meetings were for and their concern about being polite in relation to using language and meeting the role expectations of their supervisors. They were all still accustomed to a hierarchical relationship between them and their supervisors, which affected their passivity about contacting supervisors. In particular, it was notable that all the six students said that they had a high level of uncertainty about how far they could request academic advice from their supervisors and thus their reluctance to ask for academic advice continued to the end of the course.

Added to these cultural reasons, their language problems also appeared to contribute to their passivity about interacting with their supervisors, and being responsible for the preference by NJ, YJ and JN to email their supervisors. This passivity and reluctance continued over the year; even though their reactions to solving their problems with supervisory meetings differed across and between participants, the students tended to ask for my suggestions or advice, which also showed the cultural assumption that they relied on the senior – junior relationship deriving from Confucian values in Korean higher education.

References

Back, J-H. (2009a) Korean students' progress in developing social interaction with native speakers in the UK. *English Language and Literature Teaching* 15, 1–31.
Back, J-H. (2009b) Korean students' perceived difficulties in the diffident academic situations of UK universities. *The Journal of English Education* 39, 25–46.
Biggs, J.B. (1998) Learning from the Confucian heritage: So size doesn't matter? *International Journal of Educational Research* 29, 723–738.

Boyle, J. (2000a) Education for Teachers of English in China. *Journal of Education for Teaching* 26,147–155.

Chan, D. and Drover, G. (1997) Teaching and learning for overseas students: The Hong Kong connection. In D. McNamara and R. Harris (eds) *Overseas students in Higher Education: Issues in Teaching and Learning* (pp. 76–90). New York: Routledge.

Conteh, J. and Toyoshima, S. (2005) Researching teaching and learning: Roles, identities and interview processes. *English Teaching: Practice and Critique* 4, 23–34.

Cortazzi, M. and Jin, L. (1997) Communication for learning across cultures. In D. McNamara and R. Harris (eds) *Overseas Students in Higher Education: Issues in Teaching and Learning* (pp. 76–90). London: Routledge.

Egeler, R.M. (1996) *What are the Cultural Differences between Asian Countries and Western Countries?* On WWW at http://www.omf.or.kr. Accessed 12.2.04.

Flowerdew, L. (1998) A cultural perspective on group work. *ELT Journal* 52, 323–329.

Gillham, B. (2005) *Research Interviewing: The Range of Techniques.* Maidenhead: Open University Press.

Janelli, R.L. (1993) *Making Capitalism: The Social and Cultural Construction of a South Korean Conglomerate.* Stanford, CA: Stanford University Press.

Jin, L. and Cortazzi, M. (1993) Cultural orientation and academic language use. In D. Graddol, L. Thompson and M. Byram (eds) *Language and Culture: Papers from the Annual Meeting of the British Association of Applied Linguistics* (pp. 84–97). Trevelyan College, University of Durham, September 1991. Clevedon: Multilingual Matters.

Kolrarik, K. (2004) *Loosening the Grip on the Communicative Ideal: A Cultural Perspective.* Paper presented at the 17th Educational Conference, Adelaide, 2004.

Lee, J.K. (1997) A study of the development of contemporary Korean higher education. Unpublished doctoral dissertation, The University of Texas at Austin.

Lee, J.K. (1998) A comparative study of leadership and ethical values in organizational culture revealed in the thoughts of Confucius and Aristotle: From the perspective of educational administration [Korean]. *The Journal of Educational Administration [Korean]* 16, 76–107.

Lee, J.K. (1999) Historic factors affecting educational administration in Korean Higher Education. *Higher Education Review* 32, 7–23.

Lee, J.K. (2001) *Korean Higher Education: A Confucian Perspective.* Seoul: Jimmundang Publishing Company.

Lim, H-Y. and Griffith, W.I. (2004) Successful classroom discussions with adult Korean ESL/EFL learners. *The Internet TESL Journal* IX.

Prasad, R., Mannes, M., Ahmed, J., Kaur, R. and Griffiths, C. (2004) *Adjusting Teaching Style and Practice to Accommodate the Needs of International Students.* Working Paper No. 8.

Shin, S. and Koh, M. (2005) *Korean Education in Cultural Context* On WWW at http://www.usca.edu/essays/vol142005/koh.pdf. Accessed 12.2.04.

Siu, S.F. (1992) *Toward an Understanding of Chinese American Educational Achievement*: *A Literature Review.* Report No. 2. Center on Families, Communities, Schools, and Children's Learning. The Johns Hopkins University.

Strom, R.D., Griswold, D. and Slaughter, H. (1981) Parental background: Does it matter in parent education? *Child Study Journal* 10, 253–260.

Toyoshima, S. (2007) Evidence from learning histories elicited through structured conversations: Continuity in English language learning in Japan. Unpublished doctoral dissertation, The University of York, York.

Wong, J.J.K. (2004) Are the learning styles of Asian international students culturally or contextually based? *International Education Journal* 4, 154–225.

Yum, J.O. (2000) Korean philosophy and communication. In D.L. Kincaid (ed.) *Communications Theory: Eastern and Western Perspectives*. Academic Press. On WWW at http://www.byuh.edu/courses/comm360/reserves/yum.pdf. Accessed 8.6.06.

Chapter 12

Intercultural Interaction: Teacher and Student Roles in the Classroom of Portuguese as a Foreign Language in Macau, China

R. TEIXEIRA E SILVA and C. CAVACO MARTINS

Introduction

One of the implications of globalization is the fact that it increases dramatically the contexts for teaching and learning foreign languages. So far, English has held a dominant role in this discussion, but there is a new trend of academic research, such as that represented in this volume, which has a wider focus.

Our work aims to shift the focus away from English to the investigation of a context where Portuguese is considered an international language with a specific role in a globalized world.

We want to contribute to expand the knowledge about the impact of cultural diversity in classroom interactions, which can and should be built on different languages within the international university (for cultural diversity in other contexts within the international university, see e.g. Chapters 3–5, 9 and 10).

Cultural and linguistic diversity marks most of the Asian socio-cultural contexts, where Macau is no exception. This chapter analyzes how cultural diversity can coexist in the same learning environment, reshaping inter-locutors as well as being reshaped by them. Analyzing an interactional situation in a foreign language class of Portuguese in Macau, we under-stand that a second language is the ground where cultural exchange is possible and is negotiated.

The Asian tertiary educational context is a learning environment usually characterized as being different from Western learning contexts

(Grosso, 2007; Scollon, 1999; Stephens, 1997; Watkins & Biggs, 2001), both in terms of teacher and learner roles. What seems to be at stake in this statement of 'difference' regarding the Asian learning context is the cultural background. From a Western perspective, Chinese students are usually viewed as passive (Cheng, 2000; Grosso, 2007). However, this perspective is on the one hand, culturally biased and, on the other, does not consider that in the classroom of foreign languages the linguistic and cultural identities of both teachers and students with different cultural backgrounds are in a process of negotiation (Goffman, 1959; Gumperz, 1982a, 1982b). From our experience, given the appropriate interactional conditions, Chinese students not only interact, but also show, during class, that they are motivated, interested and stimulated.[1] We believe that to consider cultural traits as determinants for students' and teachers' behavior is to forget that we exist, create and recreate ourselves in language. Interactions occur in a space of cultural, religious, ethnic, age, linguistic, social class, gender and power diversity (Teixeira e Silva, 2009). Therefore, taking those traits into account, our investigation draws on the principles of Interactional Sociolinguistics (IS) (Goffman, 1959, 1967, 1974, 1991; Gumperz, 1982a, b, 2001, 2008; Ribeiro & e Garcez, 2002; Schiffrin, 1994, 1996; Teixeira e Silva, 2008, 2009). In terms of language and education, IS can be used both as a methodology to understand what is happening in the interactions in the classroom, and as a theoretical orientation in order to plan and organize the teaching – learning process.

Within the context of language teaching, especially in the past decades, the concept of culture has become an important and integral part of second and foreign language teaching. The communicative approaches to language learning and teaching have emphasized the importance of culture for communication. Not only is the knowledge about the culture one learns vital for the learning process but also that knowledge has to be built up through interaction. This construction of cultural and linguistic knowledge is vital in the process of L2 learning, since it strengthens and (re)shapes the beliefs and attitudes about the other culture and language, simultaneously fostering confidence in one's language abilities. The concept of culture is broad (Cortazzi & Jin, 1999: 197; Hinkel, 1999: 1), since it deals not only with the cultural beliefs of those who learn, but also with the cultural beliefs of those who teach. Furthermore, the concept of 'target culture' has also become a focus of most L2 syllabi. But if the teaching of the target culture can be viewed as a positive aspect of L2 teaching and learning, cultural values and beliefs, including learning cultures and beliefs (Nae-Dong, 1999: 515), can pose problems for the participants in the process, whenever they are considered to be at odds. This mismatch, according to Cortazzi and Jin (1999: 213) '(…) can be improved if the teacher understands the students' culture of learning'. Nevertheless, this is only part of the picture, since from an interactional sociolinguistic approach the classroom context creates the conditions for role and identity reconstruction of both teachers and students.

In this chapter, we shall start by setting the learning context, focusing on a brief historical perspective on the teaching of Portuguese as a foreign language in Macau. Since two different cultural backgrounds come together in this learning context, we will discuss the possible values of the concept of culture and their importance for the conception that Chinese students have of teacher and student roles in the foreign language classroom. We shall then present the main tenets of the IS approach. In the final part, we shall discuss and analyze qualitatively the data collected.

The context

Macau, nowadays a Special Administrative Region of the People's Republic of China, was until 1999 a territory administered by Portugal. Until then in Macau, Portuguese was the official language, although spoken by a minority of the population. The use of Portuguese in Macau was basically restricted to the sphere of Government and Civil Servants, who in general were required to learn Portuguese. Language policies for Macau had been nonexistent until the 1980s, the period when Portugal and China signed the Handover Joint Declaration. With very little tradition for teaching Portuguese as a Foreign Language, or even as a Second Language, Portugal launched a campaign of teaching Portuguese in primary and secondary schools in the territory, especially in Luso-Chinese schools.[2] The lack of expertise in the field of SLA[3] led to a rather deficient start of the language teaching programme in Macau. The teachers that had been involved in the teaching of Portuguese until the 1980s were usually primary school teachers. After the 1980s, Portugal hired teachers in Portugal, most teaching Portuguese as L1, to meet the large demand of teachers at the time. The approach that was sometimes implemented in terms of teaching strategies and also in terms of teaching materials was that of Portuguese as L1. This perspective can be justified by the experience of teaching Portuguese in the ex-colonies in Africa, but also by the fact that most of the teachers involved in the programme were used to teaching Portuguese as L1, never having had any training in the teaching of foreign languages. This rather conservative stance in the teaching of Portuguese that had been adopted in Macau gave rise to several specific conceptions of what it meant teaching Portuguese in Macau to Chinese learners. These conceptions were based on two principles: (1) the cultural differences that existed between those who taught and those who learned, held as striking by those involved in the teaching process; (2) the specificity of Chinese learners who, influenced by Confucius' doctrine (Ho & Crookall, 1995; see also Chapters 9 and 11 of this volume), were seen as passive in their attitude toward the learning process.[4]

One of the issues that has been the focus of debate in the past decades in terms of the teaching and learning of Portuguese in Macau, is the fact the majority of students very seldom reach high standards in their level of proficiency. Many factors contribute to the difficulties in teaching and learning Portuguese in Macau, according to Grosso (2007): (1) the Chinese community was ignored for decades by the Portuguese administration in terms of education – only in the 1960s did the Macau Government make it compulsory to learn Portuguese for those who wanted to join the Civil Service; (2) Portuguese is not learned in a Portuguese speaking context; (3) teachers ignored the local learning culture; (4) Western teachers who have been teaching in Macau have had very little contact with the Chinese learner and have been making use of Western methodologies; (5) the pedagogical intervention of Western teachers teaching in Macau is, in general, not well adjusted to the Macau socio-educational context.

Nowadays, together with Mandarin Chinese, Portuguese still remains one of the official languages of Macau. To date, we can identify some changes to the panorama of teaching Portuguese as a Foreign Language in Macau. Although politically the importance of Portuguese may have decreased, we have seen a greater demand on the part of students to learn Portuguese, not only in Macau, but especially in Mainland China, where the financial prospects that can be achieved by trading with the Portuguese-speaking countries, namely Brazil and Angola, have led to this surge in the interest to learn Portuguese.

As a consequence of these facts, in the context of the learning–teaching process, we find two strong ideological constructions in Macau about the classroom of Portuguese as a foreign language (within and outside of tertiary contexts) (Rodrigues da Silva & Teixeira e Silva, 2009):

- Chinese students are different from Western students.
- Western teachers do not know how to teach Chinese students.

The former statement may seem obvious; all students are different, of course. However, this ethnically based generalization is actually quite dangerous. Many teachers believe that they have to adopt special pedagogical methodologies. This has led, in general, to the adoption of very traditional approaches to teaching language due to the myth that communicative/interactive approaches do not work with Chinese students (Grosso, 2007: 90).

The second statement leads us to question whether communication is possible in intercultural interactions (for intercultural interaction, cf. also Chapters 4 and 6).

These beliefs have been the basis for the organization of interactions in the classroom and have had a fundamental influence on what teachers and students say, and what teachers and students do. We consider these beliefs to be stereotypes (Scollon & Scollon, 2001: 168; cf. also Chapters 4 and 8), which need to be analyzed from an intercultural perspective.

Theoretical and Methodological Base

Theoretical framework

Interactional sociolinguistics

The theoretical basis of our research builds on IS (Goffman, 1959, 1967, 1974; Gumperz, 1982a, 1982b; Ribeiro & e Garcez, 2002; Schiffrin, 1994, 1996; Tannen, 1984; Teixeira e Silva, 2008, 2009), which analyzes language as the place where interactions and our world are built. It is through language that we learn how to be man, woman, Chinese, Brazilian, students and teachers.

It is through processes of socialization that we learn how to understand and differentiate types of interactive events (a lesson, an informal conversation, a work meeting, a business meeting etc.). Through these processes we learn how to understand and differentiate their different moments (the greetings, the jokes, the insults, the justifications, the farewell moments etc.). It is based on this process of interpretation and understanding of events that we become engaged in the social game.

Thus, we build a social cognitive model (schema, cf. also Chapter 5) that leads us to making inferences about the situations (frames) that we experience. According to the world knowledge and experience we have acquired, we create certain expectations when faced with our interactants and interaction situations. These expectations affect both the 'how we will react' and the 'how we expect the other to react'. If these expectations are not met, it may lead to conflict in the interaction situation. This will necessarily force us to rethink our attitude and posture.

In this case we are dealing with the concept of 'structures of expectations' (Tannen & Wallat, 1993: 183) which is doubly represented by the concepts of 'frame' and 'schemes'.

The proper interpretation of an interactive event is subject to the knowledge that comes from experiencing the interactants' world. Thus, meanings negotiated in interaction can only be understood in relation to a model of prior knowledge (Tannen & Wallat, 1993). If two interactants refer to different knowledge schemes, the same interaction will, most likely, be interpreted differently. This is when problems arise in intercultural communication (cf. also Chapters 4 and 6).

Interpretations may be differentiated between subjects who share a basic cultural matrix, but when the subjects come from different cultural matrices, this differentiation will be more pronounced.

However, since the schemes and the frameworks are dynamic, it is possible to interfere and try to ensure more success for the interactions between subjects of different cultural matrices, such as Brazil and China.

Intercultural interactions

One of the concerns of IS is to understand the role of culture (Gumperz, 1982a, 1982b, 2008) in shaping different interactions in a multicultural world. According to Moreira, 'multiculturalism has been used to show the multicultural feature of contemporary societies, an inevitability of the world in our time'[5] (Moreira, 2002: 16).

This concept refers not only to cultural diversity present in each and every society – as groups – but also to the culturally diverse traits of the subjects, shaped by interaction.

By identifying the various groups that constitute the macro-sociocultural level of any given society, we inevitably focus on the disparities with which these social groups are faced. Yet, our main aim with this chapter is to suggest ways that may lead subjects from culturally diverse groups, as is the case of Brazilians and Chinese, to find adequate solutions for the interactional situations in which they take part.

As such, when acknowledging the internal cultural diversity in a society we are not stressing those differences. The aim should be, instead, getting to know and respecting those differences. Getting to know and respecting complement each other: one cannot exist without the other. We intend to contribute to these processes of 'getting to know' and 'respecting' the others' culture, so that interactions may reach maximum success.

Holliday (1999) and Littlewood (1999) discuss the importance of the concept of cultural traits for the L2 context. Holliday distinguishes between the concepts of 'large' and 'small' cultures, defining 'large' cultures as '"ethnic", "national" or "international"', whereas 'small' cultures are defined as 'any cohesive social grouping' (Holliday, 1999: 237–240). Holliday (1999: 239) goes on to stress the importance of the distinction between both concepts, since the concept of 'large' cultures seems to dominate the various approaches of study within the sphere of applied linguistics. For him, 'Small cultures can (...) run between as well as within related large cultures'. In other words, the concept of 'small' cultures is not dependent on the broader concept of 'large' cultures, nor is it 'a matter of size'.

Holliday considers that the concept of 'large cultures', viewed as national identity, has become a mental construction being used as a 'political tool'. He argues, further, that this view is reductionist, in that it identifies national 'culture' with global ethnic identity. This is a process Holliday defines as 'otherisation': '(...) the process whereby the "foreign" is reduced to a simplistic, easily digestible, exotic or degrading stereotype. The "foreign" thus becomes a degraded or exotic "them" or safely categorized "other" (...)' (Holliday, 1999: 245).

It is important to stress that some of our students' statements about teacher and student roles are related to the concept of 'large culture'. Yet, from an interactional perspective, the concept of 'small' culture can be reshaped, independently of the students' perceived idea, which is usually based on certain stereotypes instilled by learning and social contexts.

Diversity raises an inevitable question: is it possible that different cultures are able to interact and communicate?[6]

> Communication between cultures is, at first sight, a problem of language diversity and translation. Contrary to differences in physical appearance and those of language, which are easily perceptible, communication contexts require, not only a set of commonly shared symbols as support, but also some knowledge about the cultural system of the values of each social group. This values system operates partially and invisibly at the communication surface. (Hanke, 2005)[7]

It is important to stress the invisibility of cultural traits responsible for the ways in which we behave. On the one hand, it is easier to deal with the explicit cultural traits, and on the other, those that are imperceptible are those we need to pay more attention to, since imperceptible cultural traits are difficult to manipulate in interaction. Identifying these traits during the interactive process is a way of trying to understand the others and trying to be understood.

Trying to understand others and being understood in interactive processes brings to light an important aspect within intercultural studies: one cannot identify one single cultural pattern to be understood and used as a basis in interaction. After all, culture, as much as cultural identity, is a process, it is dynamic, not an entity. Thus, statements such as: 'Brazilians are ...' or 'Chinese are ...', are inadequate and dangerous. Although we may identify general traits that differentiate cultural groups, the way these traits operate differs from person to person (Gao & Ting-Toomey, 1998). This is so, because diversity is present in every society: men are different from women, peasants from city dwellers and some people have easier access to information than others or interactive contexts that may activate different roles, just as Scollon and Scollon (2001: 169) remind us:

(1) Humans are not all the same.
(2) At least some of the differences among them show culturally or socially predictable patterns.
(3) At least some of those patterns are reflected in patterns of discourse.
(4) Some of those differences in discourse patterns lead directly to unwanted social problems such as intergroup hostility, stereotyping, preferential treatment, and discrimination.

Summing up, it is not possible to generalize. It is for this reason that the methodology we find most appropriate for research in the field of culture is one that investigates face-to-face interactions. In such interactions we have the chance to identify cultural traits microcosmically and analyze them in their dynamics.

As Gumperz (2008: abstract) points out, the aim of IS 'is to show how individuals participating in such exchanges use conversation to achieve their communicative ends in real life situations by concentrating on the meaning making processes and the taken-for-granted background assumptions that underlie the negotiation of shared interpretations'.

Methodology

The subjects of our study are a Brazilian teacher with 12 years' experience teaching Portuguese as a foreign language for mixed groups and only 1 year of teaching Chinese groups, and 20 Chinese students from Beijing Foreign Studies University who are attending the third year of Bachelor in Portuguese studies at the University of Macau, the place of our research.

Our data come from two sets of materials:

- Written texts through which the students indicate their perceptions, beliefs and even desires about teacher and student roles. The data were collected from students' comments on the film *Dead Poets Society*. We gave them the follow questions:

As we could see in the film, different ways of thinking about what education is, leads teachers to adopt different teaching methods. Each culture has different ways of understanding what should be the relationship between teacher and student and which teaching methods are most appropriate. So let us comment on the following questions:

(a) Make a summary of the story, giving your opinion about the events, the characters (teachers, students . . .).
(b) Comment on what you saw of positive and negative in the relationship between teachers and students. So you identify yourself with any of the characters? Why?
(c) What do you think should be the relationship between teachers and students? For you, what is the ideal profile of a teacher? And of a student?
(d) Are teachers in primary and secondary school and university very different? What major differences do you notice?
(e) Comparing Western and Eastern teachers, with which you feel more comfortable? Why?
(f) What would you do (or would not do) if you were a teacher?

• Class videorecording recorded during the first weeks of class in which we can see the Brazilian teacher and the Chinese students in interaction.

To analyze the data, we adopted an ethnographic method (Erickson, 1996).

Understanding the Other: Analysis of the Data

As mentioned, the only way to build successful interactions is trying to know our interactants. Therefore, in this section we are going to analyze the students' views on classroom interaction, and their perceptions, beliefs and expectations about teacher and student roles based on the written texts they produced in class.

From the analysis of the students' texts we identified three major categories that describe the students' views on teacher and student roles and identify the general concept of classroom interaction: (i) responsibility; (ii) the place of interaction; (iii) content/knowledge vs. interaction (Eastern and Western teachers).

What students say about teacher and student roles

From the excerpts, we can access some general ideas that the subjects have about teacher and student roles.

Excerpt 12.1: Responsibility

'Os professores devem ter muito conhecimento sobre a sua disciplina, ser paciente, resolver alguns problemas dos alunos além do estudo, etc. E os alunos devem ser trabalhador, escutar com atenção nas aulas, fazer o trabalho de casa, dar-se bem com os colegas, etc.' Diva – a Chinese student from the 3rd year (Bachelor in Portuguese studies)	'Teachers should have a lot of knowledge about his/her discipline, to be patient, to solve problems the students have in their studies and so on. And students should be hard workers, carefully listen to lectures, do the homework, have a good relationship with colleagues and so on.'
'Acho que na escola primária, os professores tratam os alunos como tratam as crianças, eles fazem tudo para os alunos; na escola secundária, os professores são mais sérios e dêem muitas regras para os alunos observarem, as aulas estão mais chato porque ninguém pode falar e só ouvir o que os professores dizem.' Noémia – a Chinese student from the 3rd year (Bachelor in Portuguese studies)	'In primary school, teachers treat students like children, they do everything for them. In secondary school, teachers are more serious and they give many rules for the students to follow, classes are very boring because no one can talk but only listen to what the teachers say.'

As we can see, the responsibility for the teaching–learning process is a duty of the teachers. Students are not supposed to act, but only react and do what the teacher says (passiveness). The teachers have 'to solve problems the students have in their studies' and the students cannot 'talk but only listen to what the teachers say'.

These statements confirm the general profile of Chinese students from a Western point of view. For us, these statements are related to the concept of 'large' cultures, arising from a generalization based on the cultural classroom experiences of the students.

However, having those ideas does not necessarily mean that the students act upon them. There is a strong difference between what we say and what we do. The cultural environment may have a strong influence on ideologies and beliefs present in our speech. That is why working exclusively on the basis of the subjects' stated beliefs may be a risk. We think that studying interactions we can grasp ideologies and beliefs more effectively.

Excerpt 12.2: The place of the interaction

'Se eu fosse professora, ensinaria os meus alunos com muita paciência. Quando eles tivessem algumas perguntas, explicaria mais claramente depois das aulas. Não lhe daria muitos trabalhos de casa (...)' Lídia – a Chinese student from the 3rd year (Bachelor in Portuguese studies)	'If I were a teacher, I would teach my students patiently. When they had some questions, I would explain more carefully after class. I would not give them a lot of homework (...)'
'Vi que o professor Keating se dava bem com os alunos dele, ele e os estudantes parecia os amigos. Outros professores do colégio só ensinavam os alunos nas aulas, não conversavam com eles nem preocupavam com eles. Na minha vida, também existe este tipo de professor. Quando tinha alguns problemas, não podia falar com aquele professor. Fiquei desesperadíssima. (...)' Diva – a Chinese student from the 3rd year (Bachelor in Portuguese studies)	'I saw that Mr. Keating had a good relationship with his students, he and his students looked like friends. Other teachers in the school only taught the students in class, never talked to them nor even worried about them. In my life, there is also this type of teacher. When I had some problems, I could not talk to that teacher. I really went desperate. (...)'

Taking the above examples into consideration, we see that the classroom is not the place for different kinds of verbal interaction between teachers and students. A student states that if the students 'had some questions, I would explain more carefully after class'. The classroom is not an arena for interaction; for that you have to create another frame outside of the classroom context. Students are not supposed to speak in the classroom; the structure of the interaction between teachers and students is strongly hierarchical. Informal human relations, it seems, are not an aspect of the roles that they can play in the classroom. As a student states: 'When I had some problems, I could not talk to the teacher. I was really desperate.' Therefore, the classroom is a frame where there is no place for sharing experiences, neither as a learning resource, nor as an involvement strategy. The place for more active interaction is outside the classroom.

Excerpt 12.3: Content/knowledge and interaction (Eastern and Western teachers)

(...) professores chineses ensinam mais teorias aos alunos para os entenderem o sistema do sujeito mais rápido, e os professores ocidentais queriam fazer aulas interessantes para atrair atenção dos alunos, (...) (Sílvio – a Chinese student from the 3rd year (Bachelor in Portuguese studies)	(...) Chinese teachers teach more theories to their students in order to make them understand the subject faster, and Western teachers want to teach more interesting lessons in order to attract the students' attention (...)
Os ocidentais têm muitas ideias interessantes, e nas aulas, gostam de discutir tudo com alunos. O ambiente das aulas são muito agradável. Os orientais dão mais atenção no conhecimento dos alunos. Eles esforçam para resolver problemas concretos, isto é sempre sobre os exames. (Irene – a Chinese student from the 3rd year (Bachelor in Portuguese studies)	Westerners have many interesting ideas, and, in class, they like to discuss everything with their students. The atmosphere in class is very pleasant. Asians pay more attention to the knowledge of the students. They make an effort to solve real problems; this means examinations all the time.

The contrastive experiences that the students have with Western and Eastern teachers point out some other aspects of their perceptions about teacher and student roles and the building of knowledge.

In comparison, Western teachers focus on interaction. Chinese teachers focus on the subject, the theories. In the eyes of the students, knowledge and interaction are viewed as almost opposite, as we can see: 'Chinese teachers teach more theories to their students in order to make them understand the subject faster, and Western teachers want to teach more interesting lessons in order to attract the students' attention (…)'. The conjunction 'and' expresses this opposition.

In their experience, knowledge does not come from social and interactional construction. Knowledge is something the teacher has.

From these three groups of examples, we can catch a glimpse of the classroom frame in which the Chinese students develop their beliefs about what it is to be a student and a teacher and about the shape of the interaction inside the classroom.

However, when students are asked to express their opinions about relations in the classroom, the cultural traits that they show are based on stereotypes.

In the next section, we can see that those cultural traits and stereotypes in real interactional situations will be negotiated with the teacher, showing new nuances.

What students do in their student roles

Now we will experience the same Chinese students in interaction with a Brazilian teacher. Many of the traits, values and beliefs raised by the students in their written texts will appear in this excerpt. However, they can be reshaped in each interaction because interactions are locally (Schiffrin, 1996) and culturally (Gumperz, 1982b, 2008) organized and constitute a 'small' culture (Holliday, 1999).

According to Holliday, the classroom context is a good example of 'small culture' dynamics 'where a small culture will form from scratch when the group first comes together, each member using her or his culture-making ability to form rules and meanings in collaboration with others' (Holliday, 1999: 248)

Yet, as Holliday (1999: 248–249) points out, 'small culture[s]' should not be understood in isolation from the nature of other 'small culture[s].' Whenever a new group is formed, its new 'small culture' network informs itself from what Holliday calls 'cultural residues and influences' that each individual brings to the new group, and will help shape its interaction.

Let us look at the next excerpt.

We have here an intercultural interaction in class. And as we stated before, in order to achieve a successful interaction we need to have some cues (Gumperz, 1982a) about the other, we have to get to know our interactants.

In this excerpt, we can see the building of conflict.

Outside the classroom, a student showed some concerns about an oral presentation that the students were to prepare. Therefore, the teacher brought to the classroom a discussion about what to do together. As we could see before, Chinese students seem not to be used to this attitude.

The teacher tries to give the students the opportunity to take part in decisions in class. He is trying to share the responsibility for the organization of the class. We can see this in some linguistic resources:

- Confirmation questions: 'isn't it?', 'are we going to do it as we had previously decided?'
- Modal expressions: 'tentatively', 'would you choose', 'would you like'.
- The person of the pronouns: 'our' presentations.

However the students do not react: silence is the answer. The teacher feels uncomfortable, frustrated: 'Nothing?' He pressures the students, waiting for their answer. A student, also uncomfortable, asks a question 'What do you want us to say?' Actually she is asking for help because she has learned that in the classroom students do not say anything. Teacher and students show different cultural patterns about their roles and this provokes discomfort/conflict in the interaction.

But the teacher does not give up and uses his power to impose his beliefs about student and teacher roles: sharing responsibilities in the classroom.

Although it is an imposition on the part of the teacher (typical of the power teachers have), the aim is to establish a more cooperative interaction. Thus confronted, the students come to abandon a state of physical and verbal immobility to assume a more collaborative attitude within the context of the interaction created in the classroom.

The teacher's insistence forces the students to change their position. If silence was the answer earlier, now, one, two, three, four students are showing their points of view and contributing actively to the interaction:

Student 02:   Seven minutes is so long!
Student 03:   We ourselves choose the theme (the students speak with each other).

Student 04:   I have a suggestion: let us start the presentation next Tuesday.

If the teacher conforms to the Chinese learner stereotype, not perceiving that in each microinteraction identities are rebuilt, in the language class, most likely, active participation of learners may be at stake. Worse still, it may be considered as normal in a language classroom with Chinese students.

As we assumed, in the classroom of foreign languages, the linguistic–cultural identities of interactants with different cultural backgrounds are in the process of negotiation. If the process of teaching–learning is viewed as an interaction, it is possible to create and recreate habits, beliefs and identities in order to build a successful interaction.

As we can see, what the students end up doing can be identified as the opposite of their traditional behavior and traditional beliefs.

The sentence 'I have a suggestion: let us start the presentation next Tuesday' shows us that. The noun 'suggestion' means significant participation. The sentence symbolizes division of responsibilities, such as the teacher seems to pursue.

Thus, under the traditional model, Chinese students would expect the teacher to determine all the proceedings in the classroom. In our excerpt, contrary to what would be expected, the same Chinese students show that they can also participate actively and decide what students should do. The final sentence stresses that, in each interaction, we are constructing 'small' cultures, reconfiguring identities, rebuilding our beliefs and values.

Final Considerations

Like all other roles in society, teacher and student roles are social and cultural constructions. And these roles are built at the moment of the interaction since identities are processes, not entities.

Therefore, it is necessary to undertake microanalysis of the classroom interactions:

- To understand the influence of the cultural patterns in the classroom environment.
- To review beliefs that are actually stereotypes and can immobilize us and our interactants.
- To find an adequate and co-constructed interactional style in intercultural classrooms.
- To stress that the discourse is the place where we build and rebuild worlds and roles.

Considering people as consisting of immutable characteristics is not considering them in their most significant aspect: their humanity. The myths and stereotypes repeated in the discourse of the students and teachers must therefore be thoroughly questioned, discussed and observed not only in terms of ideas or beliefs but, fundamentally, in terms of ideas and beliefs that are in a process of negotiation in classroom interactions.

Notes

1. Stephens mentions a similar experience: 'It is my experience that Chinese students will participate freely and independently where they understand the language that is being used, and where the ground rules for the expression of the ideas are made clear' (Stephens, 1997: 122).
2. Luso-Chinese schools were created by the local Government in order to allow the children of families with less income to be able to study for free. The original concept of this school system provided students with an almost bilingual environment.
3. Second language acquisition.
4. Kelen, regarding the teaching and learning context in Hong Kong, states: 'The naturally social activity of getting the right things done with language, would appear, given the Confucian model of hierarchic flow of authority, as in the three bonds (*san-kang*), to give the teacher, and especially the language teacher, a very clear role to perform: the teacher prescribes the correct words, their correct uses; the teacher corrects the student's errors' (Kelen, 2002: 227).
5. Our translation from Portuguese.
6. We understand interaction as a broader concept, meaning any form of interrelation between people, be it linguistic or nonlinguistic. Communication, in our perspective, refers to the type of interaction in which information is shared and exchanged. Thus, there are interaction situations that involve communication and others that do not.
7. Our translation from Portuguese.

References

Cheng, X. (2000) Asian students' reticence revisited. *System* 28, 435–446.
Cortazzi, M. and Jin, L. (1999) Cultural mirrors: Materials and methods in the EFL classroom. In E. Hinkel (ed.) *Culture in Second Language and Teaching* (pp. 196–220). Cambridge: Cambridge University Press.
Erickson, F. (1996) Ethnographic microanalysis. In S.L. McKay and N.H. Hornberger (eds) *Sociolinguistics and Language Teaching* (pp. 283–306). Cambridge: Cambridge University Press.
Gao, G. and Ting-Toomey, S. (1998) *Communicating Effectively with the Chinese.* Thousand Oaks, CA: Sage.
Goffman, E. (1959) *Presentation of Self in Everyday Life.* New York: Anchor.
Goffman, E. (1967) *Interaction Rituals: Essays on Face-to-Face Behavior.* Garden City: Anchor.

Goffman, E. (1974) *Frame Analysis*. New York: Harper & Row.
Grosso, M.J. (2007) *O Discurso Metodológico do Ensino do Português em Macau a Falantes de Língua Materna Chinesa* [On methodological discourse of teaching of Portuguese at Macau to Chinese L1 speakers]. Macau: Universidade de Macau.
Gumperz, J. (1991) A Sociolingüística interacional no estudo da escolarização. [Interactional Sociolinguistics in the study of schooling.] In J. Cook-Gumperz (ed.) *A construção social da alfabetização [The Social Construction of the Alphabetization]* (pp. 58–82). Porto Alegre: Artes Médicas.
Gumperz, J.J. (1982a) *Discourse Strategies*. Cambridge: Cambridge University Press.
Gumperz, J.J. (1982b) *Language and Social Identity*. Cambridge: Cambridge University Press.
Gumperz, J.J. (2001) Contextualization and ideology in intercultural communication. In A. Di Luzio, S. Günthner and F. Orletti (eds) *Culture in Communication* (pp. 35–53). Amsterdam: John Benjamins.
Gumperz, J. (2008) *Interactional Sociolinguistics: Understanding the Impact of Culture on Interaction*. Abstract presented at the annual meeting of the NCA 94th Annual Convention, TBA, San Diego, CA. 21–24 November. On WWW at http://convention3.allacademic.com/one/nca/nca08/index.php?click_key=1&cmd=Multi+Search+Search+Load+Publication+For+Extra&publication_id=256541&PHPSESSID=18437baf6f0636a0223abf2ac4a3501a. Accessed 1.9.09.
Hanke, M. (2005) Comunicação Intercultural – Uma Perspectiva para as Diferenças entre as Culturas Nórdicas e Latinas. [Intercultural Communication – A Perspective for the Differences between Nordic and Latin Cultures.] *Semiosfera* ano 5, n° 8. ECO, UFRJ. On WWW at http://www.semiosfera.eco.ufrj.br/conteudo_nt_03Hanke.htm. Accessed 1.8.07.
Hinkel, E. (1999) Introduction: Culture in research and second language pedagogy. In E. Hinkel (ed.) *Culture in Second Language and Teaching* (pp. 1–8). Cambridge: Cambridge University Press.
Ho, J. and Crookall, D. (1995) Breaking with Chinese cultural traditions: Learner autonomy in English language teaching. *System* 23, 235–243.
Holliday, A. (1999) Small cultures. *Applied Linguistics* 20, 237–264.
Kelen, C. (2002) Language and learning orthodoxy in the English classroom in China. *Educational Philosophy and Theory* 34, 223–237.
Littlewood, W. (1999) Defining and developing autonomy in East Asian contexts. *Applied Linguistics* 20, 71–94.
Moreira, A.F. (2002) Currículo, diferença cultural e diálogo [Curriculum, cultural difference and dialogue]. *Educação & Sociedade* 23, 15–38.
Nae-Dong, Y. (1999) The relationship between EFL learners' beliefs and learning strategy use. *System* 27, 515–535.
Ribeiro, B. and Garcez, P. (eds) (2002) *Sociolingüística Interacional. [Interactional Sociolinguistics.]* Porto Alegre: AGE editora.
Rodrigues da Silva, R. and Teixeira e Silva, R. (2009) O que é ser bom aluno? Reflexões sobre a construção da identidade de aprendentes chineses em sala de aula de Português Língua Estrangeira. [What does it mean to be a good Student? Considerations about the construction of identity of Chinese learners in the classroom of Portuguese as a Foreign Language.] *Anais do VI Congresso Internacional da ABRALIN* 1.

Schiffrin, D. (1994) *Approaches to Discourse*. Oxford: Blackwell.
Schiffrin, D. (1996) Interactional sociolinguistics. In S.L. McKay and N.H. Hornberger (eds) *Sociolinguistics and Language Teaching* (pp. 307–328). Cambridge: Cambridge University Press.
Scollon, R. and Scollon, S. (2001) *Intercultural Communication*. Oxford: Blackwell.
Scollon, S. (1999) Confucian and Socratic discourse in the tertiary classroom. In E. Hinkel (ed.) *Culture in Second Language Teaching and Learning* (pp. 13–27). Cambridge: Cambridge University Press.
Stephens, K. (1997) Cultural stereotyping and intercultural communication: Working with students from the People's Republic of China in the UK. *Language and Education* 11, 113–124.
Tannen, D. (1984) *Conversational Style: Analyzing Talk among Friends*. Norwood, NJ: Ablex.
Tannen, D. and Wallat, C. (1993) Interactive frames and knowledge schemas in interaction: Examples from a medical examination/interview. In D. Tannen (ed.) *Framing in Discourse* (pp. 57–76). Oxford: Oxford University Press.
Teixeira e Silva, R. (2008) *Luso-Brazilian identities in Interaction in the Classroom of Portuguese as a Foreign Language in Macau, China: Teacher's and Student's Roles*. Paper presented at the CALPIU'08 conference, Roskilde University, Roskilde, Denmark, 15–17 December 2008.
Teixeira e Silva, R. (2009) *Sociolinguística interacional e o português como língua não-materna para crianças e adolescentes. [Interactional Sociolinguistics and the Portuguese as a non-native Language for Children and Adolescents.]* Paper presented at the 2nd Simpósio Mundial de Estudos de Língua Portuguesa (SIMELP), Universidade de Évora, Évora, Portugal, 6–11 October 2009.
Watkins, D. and Biggs, J. (2001) *Teaching the Chinese Learners: Psychological and Pedagogical Perspectives*. Hong Kong: Comparative Education Research Center, University of Hong Kong.